FIRE AND HEARTH: KARLA YOORDA

A study of Aboriginal usage and
European usurpation in south-western Australia

Sylvia J. Hallam

The Charles and Joy Staples
South West Region Publications Fund

University of Western Australia Publishing

First published in 1975 by the Australian Institute of Aboriginal Studies, Canberra, Australia. Permission for facsimile edition with additional material kindly granted by AIATSIS, Australian Institute of Aboriginal and Torres Strait Islander Studies.

This revised edition published in 2014 by UWA Publishing
Crawley, Western Australia 6009
www.uwap.uwa.edu.au
for the Charles and Joy Staples
South West Region Publications Fund

THE UNIVERSITY OF
WESTERN AUSTRALIA

This book is copyright. Apart from any fair dealing for the purpose of private study, research, criticism or review, as permitted under the *Copyright Act 1968*, no part may be reproduced by any process without written permission.
Enquiries should be made to the publisher.

Copyright © Sylvia J. Hallam 2014
The moral right of the author has been asserted.

National Library of Australia Cataloguing-in-Publication data available.

ISBN 978 1 74258 599 4

Cover images courtesy of the National Library of Australia, Canberra.

Lieutenant Robert Dale's magnificent nine-foot panorama, published in 1834, with a "*Descriptive Account of the Panoramic View of King George's Sound and the adjacent country*", runs from westward, through southward to eastward, as seen scanning seaward from Mount Clarence, above the Sound at what is now Albany. It shows a series of many landscape fires, inviting comparison with the "twelve large Smokes" noted by Lockyer in 1827, or the "much burning in different parts" described by Captain Collet Barker as initiated by Nakinah, Coolbun and Mokare in January 1831.

The cover shows the eastward end of this panorama, centred around a campfire in front of Aboriginal huts.

Frontispiece: The South-west of Western Australia, showing places mentioned in the text. Vegetational and geomorphological zones are based on Gardner 1942, 1959; Gentilli [1946]; Mulcahy 1967; etc.

Typeset by Lasertype
Printed by Lightning Source

Also published by UWA Publishing
for the Charles and Joy Staples South West Region Publications Fund

For Their Own Good: Aborigines and Government in the South West of Western Australia 1900–1940
Anna Haebich

The South West from Dawn till Dusk
Rob Olver

Contested Country: A History of the Northcliffe area, Western Australia
Patricia and Ian Crawford

Richard Spencer: Napoleonic War Naval Hero and Australian Pioneer
Gwen Chessell

A Story to Tell
Laurel Nannup

Alexander Collie: Colonial Surgeon, Naturalist and Explorer
Gwen Chessell

Shaking Hands on the Fringe: Negotiating the Aboriginal World at King George's Sound
Tiffany Shellam

"It's Still in my Heart, This is my Country": The Single Noongar Claim History, South West Aboriginal Land and Sea Council, John Host with Chris Owen

Mamang
An old story retold by Kim Scott, Iris Woods and the Wirlomin Noongar Language and Stories Project, with artwork by Jeffrey Farmer, Helen Nelly and Roma Winmar (Yibiyung)

Noongar Mambara Bakitj
An old story retold by Kim Scott, Lomas Roberts and the Wirlomin Noongar Language and Stories Project, with artwork by Geoffrey Woods and Anthony Roberts

Guy Grey-Smith: Life Force
Andrew Gaynor

Dwoort Baal Kaat
An old story retold by Kim Scott, Russell Nelly and the Wirlomin Noongar Language and Stories Project, with artwork by Helen (Ing) Hall

Yira Boornak Nyininy
An old story retold by Kim Scott, Hazel Brown, Roma Winmar and the Wirlomin Noongar Language and Stories Project, with artwork by Anthony (Troy) Roberts

A Boy's Short Life: The story of Warren Braedon/Louis Johnson
Anna Haebich and Steve Mickler

The Charles and Joy Staples South West Region Publications Fund was established in 1984 on the basis of a generous donation to The University of Western Australia by Charles and Joy Staples.

The purpose of the Fund was to make the results of research on the South West region of Western Australia widely available so as to assist the people of the South West region and those in government and private organisations concerned with South West projects to appreciate the needs and possibilities of the region in the widest possible historical perspective.

The Fund is administered by a committee whose aims are to make possible the publication (either by full or part funding), by UWA Publishing, of research in any discipline relevant to the South West region.

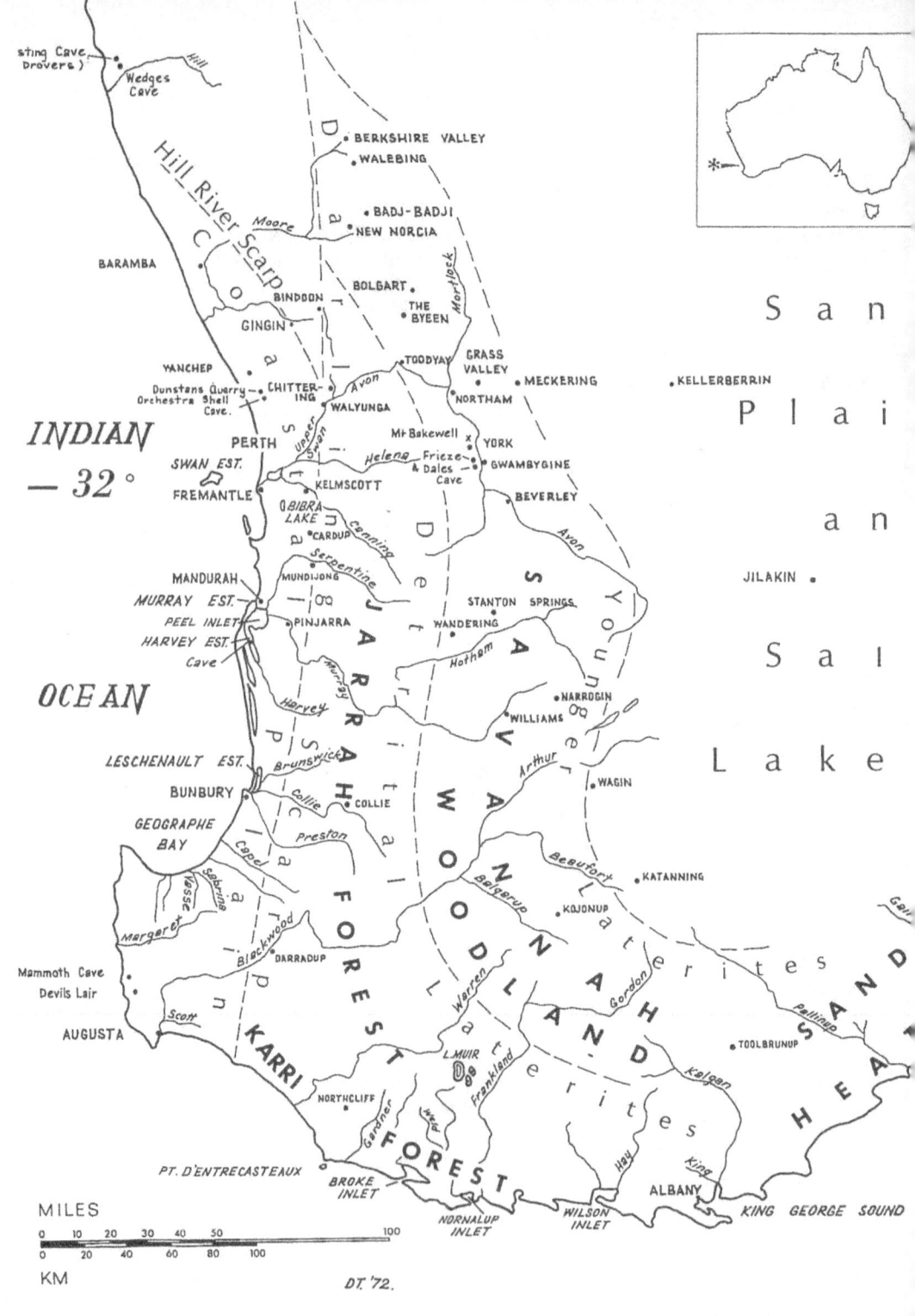

Contents

	Preface to the revised edition by Emeritus Professor John Mulvaney	vii
	Author's introduction to the revised edition	ix
	Preamble	xi
	Preface	xiii
1	Fire in Australian and world prehistory	1
2	Fire and systematic exploitation	9
3	Fire in the South-west of Australia: early historical evidence	16
4	Between the Swan and the Sound	23
5	Regulated burning: the Albany area	29
6	Regulated burning: the Swan River	35
7	Fire and hearth	41
8	Man-made landscapes: the varied background	47
9	Man-made landscapes: some historical data	56
10	Aboriginal and European movement and settlement	66
11	'The place that will be ours'	72
12	Fire in myth and ritual: earth and water	78
13	Fire in myth and ritual: earth to sky	85
14	Fire in myth and ritual: crystals and caves	91
15	The long view: human occupance and firing in the South-west	98
16	The long view: increaisng populations and exploitation	105
	Postscript	112
	Appendix	114
	References	127
	Index	143
	Afterword to the revised edition	159
	References to the Afterword	193

Fire, grass, kangaroos, and human inhabitants, seem all dependent on each other for existence in Australia . . .

                        Sir Thomas Mitchell 1848

Preface to the revised edition
by Emeritus Professor John Mulvaney AO CMG

'The land the English settled was not as God made it. It was as the Aborigines made it'. Such is the challenging claim which opens Sylvia Hallam's majestic pioneer memoir on the interconnections between Aboriginal society, Country and the varied applications of deliberate firing. *Fire and Hearth* (1975) remains one of the most significant publications of the Australian Institute of Aboriginal Studies.

Sylvia Hallam's well documented and closely argued study, represented a breakthrough in its sympathetic presentation of Aboriginal land care and food procurement. This positive approach demonstrated the close links between Dreaming stories and rituals, management of resources and fire.

Republication of this volume is welcome, both for scholars of environment and culture and for Aboriginal communities. Sylvia was stimulated to research the role of fire in Aboriginal Australia by the publication, in 1968, of two original articles which set out a general case for the importance of firing. The authors were Duncan Merrilees, from the Western Australian Museum, and Sydney archaeologist, Rhys Jones. She elaborated in great detail, especially from Western Australian data, that fire, exploited in various ways by Aboriginal communities, had dramatic ecological consequences, while crucially extending food resource availability. She successfully tracked down evidence through an exhaustive survey of historical records.

In its turn, this memoir stimulated others to examine ethnographic and ethnohistoric sources. Fire remains a central topic of research and controversy ever since. Of particular relevance are Marcia Langton's *Burning Questions* (1998) and Bill Gammage's recent magisterial survey, *The Biggest Estate on Earth* (Allen and Unwin, 2011).

Her research provided acceptable explanations for the causes of vegetational change both before and following European colonisation. I illustrate from a personal experience. In 1950 I visited the Glen Isla area, west of Victoria's Grampians (Gariwerd). An old resident pastoralist related that upon his arrival there in the late nineteenth century, trees were so widely spaced that his horse galloped easily through the bush. By recent times the scrub grew so thickly that access proved difficult. He wondered at the cause for change, which I was then unable to explain. Thanks to Sylvia and Gammage, these unwanted transformations may be explained as due to the cessation of regular Aboriginal cleansing of Country through firing.

The opening chapter of *Fire and Hearth* provides a global overview of the earliest evidence for fires lit by humans and its possible ecological effects. It reminds me that when I was a student at the University of Cambridge in 1953, Sylvia was there researching on Roman archaeology in the East Anglican Fenland. I participated in an excavation at Hoxne, also in the same region. Sylvia refers to evidence which resulted from this Hoxne research. The site had been a lake at a remote interglacial period. People had occupied the lakeside and we excavated flint tools which identified their users as Acheulean culture people. The tools are known as Acheulean handaxes, and are a major indicator of human presence in the Old World.

As Sylvia records, microscopic examination of minute pollen and charcoal traces from within the Acheulean strata indicated that firing was practiced. Some marginal deforestation and increased grassland had resulted. Whether these ecological changes were the accidental or deliberate consequences of human firing is unknown. It was an appropriate place at which to commence Sylvia's account, because it was the oldest known association between a human society and fire. And it was so ancient that the first Australians must have brought knowledge of fire with them. As she concludes her memorable study, fire was crucial to 'the shaping of Australian life, legend and land'.

Fire and Hearth:
Author's introduction to the revised edition

Since "*Fire and Hearth*" appeared in 1975 a litany of disastrous bushfires have led people to ask whether preEuropean burning practices and regimes may have been more successful in retaining fire as a reliable servant rather than a capricious master. Interest has arisen from the practical needs of Australian foresters and ecologists in designing fuel reduction regimes to avoid catastrophic fires; but also from debates about such "control burning" among environmentalists, and indeed all those potentially exposed to furious fire. Before the coming of Europeans Australians used burning as a closely controlled management tool. How did they achieve this?

During the decades since 1975 Australians have developed a deeper appreciation of the role of skilled ecological knowledge integrated with deep spiritual commitment in each Aboriginal group's mastery of land. In 2011, historian Bill Gammage, in *The Biggest Estate on Earth*, shows how, by skilled and purposive use of fire, a network of local groups created a unity of managed landscapes across the whole continent.

The original 1975 edition of *Fire and Hearth* examined, for southwest Australia, the then available evidence for Aboriginal burning, its manner and techniques, management patterns, and effects and purposes. In the intervening years more historical sources have been published illuminating each of these topics, important evidence has been gleaned from grasstrees, and debates have arisen over the reliability of evidence. On the question of the space and time context of Australian burning Chapter 1 of *Fire and Hearth* has been long outdated by the advance of global knowledge. All these topics need to be tackled in a new edition.

But so extensive a revision would produce not a new edition but a new book. In deference to those who wish to retain access to the original text,

I have preferred to leave the original text unchanged, and to add a lengthy "Afterword" summarising these new developments and debates. But so much important new work is under way that this will be out-dated before the presses roll.

I thank all those who have stimulated and enlightened me over the years, particularly Ian Abbott, Mike Archer, David Bowman, Neil Burrows, Tim Denham, Charlie Dortch, Joe Dortch, Beth Gott, Chris Haynes, Hank Lewis, John Mulvaney, Roger Underwood, David Ward and Karl Wyrwoll. I remember with gratitude discussions with Rhys Jones and with Duncan Merrilees. My debt to my husband remains immense. The simplicity and precision of his English prose remain for me an unachieved ideal. My thanks are also due to Terri-ann White and UWA Publishing for their care and helpfulness.

Preamble

On 13 March 1827, while his ship *Success* lay at anchor off South Head, Captain James Stirling, with the colonial botanist Charles Fraser and 16 others, exploring the potentialities of the Swan River (see fig. 2) for settlement, camped at 'a spot where the river takes an Eastern direction just above a considerable Creek on the left' (Stirling 1827:559) at the limit of navigation on the Swan. Next day they explored on foot, finding 'several deserted encampments'. Stirling wrote to Governor Darling:

> The Evening was employed by us in making a Garden on the Tongue of Land which intervenes between the River and the Creek; we found there ... rich soil of great depth; *the ground had been cleared by fire* a few weeks before and was *ready to receive seed* ... (*ibid*:560)*

This quotation epitomises the relationship between Aboriginal land-use and European settlement. The land the English settled was not as God made it. It was as the Aborigines made it. I shall look at the evidence for Aboriginal use of fire in the South-west of Western Australia, the place of fire in the pattern of Aboriginal land-use, indeed in the total Aboriginal way of life, and the effect of fire on the vegetation and on European settlement.

---

* My emphasis—SJH.

Preface

This study of the reciprocal impact of Australian populations and Australian terrain is based primarily on ethnohistorical sources. It was initiated by questions which arose in the early stages of what was initially a purely archaeological survey (comprising surface survey and selected excavation) of a transect from coast to inland, centred on the Swan estuary at 32°S on the west coast of Australia.

We needed, for instance, to envisage the Avon valley as it was in the final phase of the excavated levels in Frieze Cave, as Europeans and their sheep moved into pastures which had supported great numbers of kangaroos and thriving Aboriginal communities. Was the park-like landscape we saw from the cave the result of European clearance, or of pre-European usage? The first Europeans to penetrate to these fine pastures, beyond the infertile lateritic gravels and thick jarrah forest east of the Darling Scarp, reported country 'like an English gentleman's park'.

When I began to examine such descriptive material I found it both more abundant and of finer quality than I had thought possible. There is an eighteenth-century breadth of interest amongst these learned and practical gentlemen who were at the same time botanists and classical scholars, linguists and working farmers, explorers and builders. Landor reading his Horace on a remote 'squatting station' on the Hotham, sixty or seventy miles south of York, in 'a broad valley abounding with grass and scattered gum trees', described in meticulous detail the inhabitants and the vegetation of inland and coast. George Fletcher Moore, Advocate-General and farmer, commuting from legal affairs in Perth to agricultural and domestic chores twenty miles further up the Swan, found time to investigate geography and botany, to draw up an extensive and perceptive

Aboriginal vocabulary, and to write voluminous letters and journals. He describes in classical format the peroration of the Aboriginal patriot, Yagan, delivering 'a sort of recitative' on the wrongs of his people, displaced from their pastures and yam grounds, 'leaning familiarly with his left hand on my shoulder, while he gesticulated with his right'; and dutifully dispatches a letter 'instantly' to the nearest magistrate only when the fugitive is safely gone. 'The truth is, everyone wishes him taken, but no-one likes to be the captor. . . There is something in his daring one is forced to admire' (Moore 1884*a*:188). From such depth of empathy, detailed observation, learning and practical sense emerges a clear portrait of the South-west and its people. I have used published sources almost exclusively. A large body of unpublished material remains to be exploited.

To use to the full these descriptive sources I have considered a much wider region than that of the archaeological survey. The most valuable and perceptive descriptions are those of the first settlers (and the explorers who preceded them). These came in 1826 to 1829 to points near the coast between King George Sound on the east, Augusta at the south-west tip, and the Swan on the north, and almost immediately took up an area which was roughly the triangle of land between those three points, but extended rather further inland on its eastern margin. It would thus include the belt of good open pasture east of the jarrah belt, the country from the Avon valley, around York and Northam, south towards Albany and north into the Victoria Plains. This triangle is called the South-west (or south-western Australia) throughout this essay.

The South-west is distinctive not only in its early settlement history, but also in climate, vegetation, and soils. It comprises the moister, largely forested, margin of the continent. To the north-east, towards the centre, one passes into regions which are more arid and carry a more open vegetation, grading from woodland savannah to desert. Climatologists, botanists, soil geomorphologists and settlement historians differ in precisely where they draw the boundary of the South-west. It is not necessary to decide on a particular line. I shall include in this essay the triangle of jarrah and karri forest and savannah woodland beyond it shown on the Frontispiece map, covering the west coastal plain and the detrital and younger laterite belts, and bounded to the east by a line roughly from Albany to New Norcia. Topics or sources will sometimes encroach beyond that approximate boundary.

This essay was first written early in 1971, and revised by June 1972. Minor emendations were made in 1973. Recent changes in the published evidence are noted in footnotes, but no attempt has been made to recast the sections in which they occur. To do so would be to write a different essay. I prefer to let this text go forward as a record of a synthesis which stemmed from the evidence as it stood in 1972. The reader who is familiar with the pace of change in the study of Australian prehistory will take it for granted that a 1974 treatment would have to envisage a 'long perspective' which was longer, perhaps much longer, than that contemplated here, and that the overall lengthening of perspective will have induced a corresponding change (a sort of parallax effect) in our view of the relationship of the most distant to the nearer parts of our picture of man and land.

Acknowledgments

This study was financed by the Australian Institute of Aboriginal Studies as part of an archaeological survey of the Perth region under the auspices of the Anthropology Department of the University of Western Australia. I thank the Council of the Institute for its continued support.

During the writing of this essay I benefited much from discussion with and advice from Miss A. Baird, Dr C. H. Berndt, the late Mrs J. Bolton, Dr M. Brandl, Dr I. Crawford, Dr J. Glover, Professor H. E. Hallam, Dr D. Merrilees, Professor D. J. Mulvaney, Dr G. Seddon, and Professor H. Waring. They saved me from many errors and omissions, but they must not be blamed for my misunderstandings, nor for those errors of omission, commission and emphasis which remain.

I thank Professor Berndt and the University of Western Australia for the opportunity to embark on a study which I have found increasingly fascinating.

I thank my typists and editor for their care and patience in dealing with a difficult script and a difficult author.

Sylvia J. Hallam
May, 1974.

1

Fire in Australian and world prehistory

Humanly initiated fires, whether accidental or purposeful, have long had an effect on global vegetation. From lake deposits at Hoxne in East Anglia, West and McBurney (1954; West 1956) reported a pollen sequence which ran through a full cycle from tundra vegetation at the retreat of the Lowestoft ice sheet (which had deposited the underlying boulder-clays) through warmth-loving interglacial woodland, then coniferous woodland marking climatic deterioration, to park-tundra and solifluction deposits heralding the advance of the next (Gipping) glaciation. During the warm woodland stage (oak, alder, elm and lime) the proportion of tree-pollen dropped suddenly, while that of grass rose, followed by a gradual reversion to the original proportions. The deforestation stage corresponded to the appearance of sparse charcoal and abundant Acheulian implements in the lake-margin deposits. There is also evidence from the Thames gravels at Swanscombe of deforestation accompanying human settlement and traces of fire during the same Hoxnian Interglacial (Ovey 1964; Howell 1960:199). Here a shift in the proportions not of pollen but of fauna, increasing numbers of horses accompanying decreasing numbers of fallow deer (Sutcliffe 1964), indicated that grassland was increasing at the expense of forest, just at a time when Acheulian foragers and hunters were frequenting the valley (Oakley 1952). Charcoal-like material, 'carbonaceous lumps ... subjected to mild heat treatment' was reported (Oakley 1956, 1964) from excavated horizons which also contained broken animal bones, unrolled hand-axes and trimming flakes and reddened flint pebbles (some 'fire-crazed'), but no charred bones and no burnt flint artifacts. This suggests bush fires rather than local camp fires. The molluscan fauna confirmed the dominance of grassland in the upper levels of the Middle

Gravels of the Hundred-foot Terrace, from which the Swanscombe skull came (Castell 1964). Natural bush fires are comparatively rare in cool temperate regions. Hoxne and Swanscombe may therefore imply that, as far back as the Hoxnian Interglacial, human groups initiated fires sufficiently frequent and widespread to affect regional floral and faunal composition, not merely local vegetation.

The increasing effect of increasing populations on world vegetation from the middle into the late Pleistocene has been seen as reaching crisis points in different areas from the final glacial into the early post-glacial by a number of authors (among them Sauer 1956; Stewart 1956; Oakley 1961; Hole and Flannery 1967–68; Binford, L. R. 1968; and Flannery 1969:78). The African savannahs may be the result of periodic burning. Sauer (1971:48–50, 61) links the use of fire drives by late Pleistocene hunters on the North American Plains with the replacement of tree and shrub vegetation by grass and herbs. He sees the hunting of large game as eventually giving way to a greater emphasis on plant products by more localised groups.

Narr (1956:136) suggested that the widespread bush fires on the North German–Netherlands plains at the end of the Alleröd oscillation might have been produced accidentally or deliberately by late Magdalenian hunters. The open Younger Dryas vegetation might be partially a result of these activities. Whether or not final Upper Palaeolithic hunters had such drastic effects on their terrain, Dimbleby (1961) showed that even relatively small-scale foraging could appreciably affect the landscape; the fires of Mesolithic hunters initiated the transformation of the Cleveland Hills of northern Yorkshire from oak forest to open woodland with birch, heather and grasses (which spring up most rapidly after opening up by fire) and finally, through irreversible soil changes, to heath and moor (Dimbleby 1962).

Smith (1970) has recently reviewed the evidence for the influence of Mesolithic groups on British vegetation, in the context of postglacial Europe before the full development of farming, and his conclusions have a wider relevance. The botanical evidence forced him to question the still widely accepted idea that 'primitive Mesolithic man was entirely dependent on nature; he could not interfere with the vegetation' (Iversen, quoted by Smith 1970:81). Even in the Boreal, vegetational changes under way were possibly accelerated by human activity. Charcoal is widespread in the Boreal layers of Scandinavian bogs and the Boreal hazel maximum probably represented a fire climax, encouraged by dry conditions, for the European hazel is fire resistant and springs up readily from burnt stumps. Still more intriguing is the likelihood that in Denmark, France, and possibly Ireland, in late Atlantic times relatively sedentary groups relying largely on fish (as in the Bann valley) were clearing forest to provide pasture for native grazing animals, thus setting up complex interactions between the effects of animals and the effects of humanly initiated fires—a situation similar to that which we shall see in Tasmania and Western Australia. Smith's conclusions for Europe are noteworthy:

> ... before the introduction of agriculture ... man may have tipped the balance where tension existed in vegetation-environment relationship. His activities may have had considerable effects on the physiognomy, floristic constitution and change in the vegetation. (Smith 1970:90)

Proudfoot (1971) sees the main effects of non-agricultural populations upon the landscape as brought about by the clearing of camp sites by cutting and burning; by the use of fire to improve collecting and hunting grounds and for driving game; by the repeated use of plants for food, fuel and construction, and by digging to extract tubers and burrowing animals (particularly near camps, trails, water sources, and through burnt-over zones of easy movement). These activities, particularly the concentration and management of herds of herbivores (in part by the use of fire), will have tended to alter woody vegetation in favour of grassy. Proudfoot sees the use of fire as the first crucial stage in the development of man's changing relationship with the soil.

Flannery has stressed that human utilisation, including firing, must be thought of as part of the overall ecological system of an area, not as extraneous. 'Man was not simply extracting energy from his environment, but participating in it; his use of each genus was part of a system which allowed the latter to survive' (Flannery 1968).

Human populations were essential elements in a dynamic system, which usually maintained a self-regulating equilibrium. But once disequilibrium was initiated by demographic or climatic change, or both, the system moved rapidly through a series of self-perpetuating and accelerating adjustments towards a new working balance. Such changes were widespread over the millennia during the retreat of the last glaciation, between about 15,000 and 5,000 B.C.; and in some (though not in all) regions, formal agriculture and domestication emerged. In Australia at the time of European contact non-agricultural patterns of adjustments of populations and exploitative patterns might be observed, perhaps the optimum adjustments for these climates and soils.

The drastic landscape effects of agriculture and pastoralism are of course well known. Darwin (1859) realised that supposedly virgin heaths were in fact artificially maintained by grazing. He gave a clear account of the fate of saplings springing up within and without a fenced enclosure near Farnham in Surrey, as an illustration of the 'web of complex relations' existing between all the animals and plants of a region. The work of Godwin on the Breckland (1944b) showed that such 'original steppe' had been not only artificially maintained but also artificially initiated. Godwin (1944a, 1956) followed Iversen (1941) in emphasising the role of humanly initiated fires in deforestation. The implications of such transformations have now been extensively explored. It has been shown that not only vegetation but soil was irreversibly changed (see Sauer 1956; Pearson 1956; Dimbleby 1961, 1962); and that the processes which accompanied and followed deforestation could have striking geomorphological consequences also (Jennings 1965; Vita-Finzi 1969). Sauer (1956:61) had presciently realised that even bare rock and sand surfaces may 'record long attrition by man in climatic tension zones'.

It is precisely in such tension zones, particularly round the margins of optimal habitats, that expanding populations are seen to have pressed most heavily on the resources of less advantageous, or deteriorating, environments (Binford 1968; Wright, G. A. 1971; Flannery 1968). Increasingly efficient use of resources by increasing populations must have had marked effects on vegetation and even geomorphology, even without full agriculture. Australian resource exploitation may be seen as stemming from and sharing in such increasingly complex and intensive usage patterns which were developing in all continents from the late Pleistocene and early post-Pleistocene. Everywhere fire had an important place in these developments.

In the upper Nile valley, for instance, there is evidence of a number of differing populations from 15,000 B.C. onward. They are represented by discrete flake, blade, and backed-blade industries. They put differing emphases on large game, on fishing, and on processing plant foods, including wild grain. The plant processing equipment included grindstones (with resultant tooth wear as in Australia). The lustrous sheen on lunates might suggest grain harvesting, but may have been produced by cutting reeds (for fish-weirs and other construction). Burnt layers from several widely-spaced localities imply extensive scrub burning as early as the millennia before 10,000 B.C. (Wendorf *et al.* 1970; Clark 1971). J. Desmond Clark (1971) sees such complex use of plant and animal resources, including the regular use of fire as a tool, as 'pre-adaptation' to domestication. A very similar situation in the Indus valley has been described by Singh (1971). After a windy, arid Pleistocene, there was a phase of slightly higher rainfall, followed by a slight lowering of rainfall from about 7,500 B.C. and an extraordinary rise in carbonised wood fragments indicating the practice of scrub burning by peoples with microlithic traditions.

Clearance and firing in the Indo-Pacific region have, however, no necessary connection with microlithic (backed-blade) industries. We shall see that the first evidence for firing in 'Greater Australia' (including Tasmania and New Guinea) goes back to pre-microlithic traditions which stem from early chopper and flake complexes now seen to be widespread and persistent all around the Pacific. In North America it is the chopper/

scraper traditions of the South-west, associated with gathering economies, rather than the pressure-flaked blade traditions of the hunters of the Plains and the east, which provide the basis for intensified plant utilisation, the 'slow-footed agricultural revolution' of Willey and Phillips (1958:95–106). In South-east and East Asia, edge-ground stone implements and the earliest pottery in the world emerge from a matrix of 'pebble/chopping-tool' cultures which have been thought of as retarded, but which now appear as actively adaptive. Regular firing was part of these developments. For instance, in Taiwan gradually increasing growth of secondary forest and charred fragments of trees from lake deposits provide evidence of persistent disturbance of the primary vegetation, and continuing deforestation, by 10,000 B.C. (Chang 1970:18). Clearance by fire and axe must already have been initiated, and should be seen in the context of early intensive plant utilisation in mainland and island South-east Asia (Chang 1970; Gorman 1969, 1971; Golson 1971*b*; Solheim 1972). The earliest probable plant evidences of 'proto-horticultural' activity are from Thailand and date from somewhere between 15,000 and 10,000 years ago (Gorman 1969, 1971; Solheim 1972; but see Harlan and de Wet for cautions on the validity of this evidence). But the earliest regional evidence for the clearing and burning which must have preceded these developments is dated earlier than 20,000 B.C. and comes from the Greater Australian continent to the south.

Charcoal from the Mammoth Cave in south-west Australia is dated to over 37,000 years ago (Lundelius 1960:143; Merrilees 1968:10) but has no necessary human connection and must be left out of account.*

The earliest unambiguously dated evidence of the human use of fire in the Australian continent (if we except the baked clays from the Arundel Terrace of the Maribyrnong river) attests not bush fire but domestic hearths, with dates from nearly 30,000 to 15,000 B.C., and cremation dated around 24,000 B.C. (Barbetti and Allen 1972; Bowler *et al.* 1972). This evidence comes from dunes around the margin of Lake Mungo and other Pleistocene lakes fed by the Willandra Creek distributary of the Lachlan River in south-western New South Wales. None the less, although the chronology is far from clear, the presence of man and fire in the same general habitat as giant marsupials raises the question of the possible role of fire in their exploitation and extinction (Merrilees 1968; Jones 1968). The association of man, fire, and large Pleistocene herbivores seems established by the presence of charred bone in hearths by Lake Menindee, part of the Darling system and only a hundred miles to the north of the

---

* A long Pleistocene occupation for caves in this south-west corner is now confirmed by the work of Dortch and Merrilees in Devil's Lair. Charcoal from occupation levels gives dates approaching 25,000 years ago, although more than a metre of earlier deposit remains to be examined (Dortch and Merrilees 1973).

Willandra lakes. Certainly also the marsupial megafauna was no longer conspicuous in the lakeside scene of 30,000 B.C., as attested at Mungo by the presence of freshwater fish and shellfish and mammals still found in the region in 1858.

Aboriginal firing, like European clearance, could be expected to have led to increased soil salinity, and therefore vegetational and faunal changes in such semi-arid areas (compare Hole and Flannery 1967 for similar effects of increasing environmental manipulation in Iran). The presence of saltbush in the stomach contents of *Diprotodon* from Lake Callabonna in Victoria (Merrilees 1968:4) emphasises the probable relevance of salinisation in the south-east sector of the annulus of semi-arid land around the always arid centre. Certainly some areas, for example in the south-western semi-arid sector, became saline before European clearance. Irwin writes of newly explored lands east of the jarrah belt: 'In the interior, alternating with the fertile districts, are to be found extensive tracts of inferior land . . . either clayey soils . . . or sandy, or soils impregnated with salt' (Irwin 1835:8).

An Aboriginal legend from Kojonup tells of a time when once-fresh waters became salty (Bignell 1971:12).

The high herbivore biomass on the large areas of shrub steppe, scrub, savannah and savannah woodland around the centre could initially have supported large Aboriginal populations, putting an exceptional stress on large game; and these ecosystems, once impoverished, are likely to have proved unstable (Merrilees 1968) under the impact of anthropogenic change and increasing aridity in the late Pleistocene and thereafter. By the immediate precontact period even the outermost edge of this zone was, in the West, no longer supporting rapid population increase (see p. 106). The wooded margins of the north, south-west, and south-east of the continent, however, will always have encouraged more broadly based ecological systems and have continued to be susceptible of improvement rather than impoverishment by firing; thus the west coastal zone supported steeply increasing usage and populations right up to European contact. Firing will have been of great importance here in establishing clear zones for movement and settlement, and in modifying plant cover and usage. The first *direct* evidence of Australian bush fires comes not from the centre but from the periphery of the continent.

For the time-span between 30,000 and 10,000 B.C. we must envisage a 'Greater Australia' (including New Guinea and Tasmania) stretching from near the equator to nearly 45°S. The spread of intensifying plant utilisation across the equatorial third of that landmass is attested by tools suitable for tackling wooded terrain: 'axe-adzes' and 'waisted blades' from before 24,000 B.C. at Kosipe, 6,000 feet above sea level in the mountains behind Port Moresby, New Guinea (White *et al.* 1970); and *ground* stone axes, some grooved, from a group of Arnhem Land sites, with dates of just after 23,000 B.C. onwards (Carmel White 1967, 1971). Peter White's level 5 at Kosipe contained a concentration of carbon lumps in the levels in which his artifacts were also concentrated. Here is our first likely evidence from Greater Australia of clearing by burning.

The earliest mainland Australian evidence for bush firing, and at the same time for its probable geomorphic effects, comes from the Burrill Lake rock shelter, a coastal site in New South Wales (Lampert 1971*b*:10). Lampert suggests that the rapid deposition of clay, with charred wood scattered evenly throughout, behind a barrier of fallen rock in the mouth of the shelter around 20,000 years ago, may relate to destabilisation of the vegetation on the slopes above the shelter by fire, and consequent slope run-off. This would be particularly interesting at so early a date, when climatic factors would not seem to be in question. Later, post-Pleistocene, examples of humanly initiated changes may be seen as reinforcing climatic effects.

It has yet to be proven conclusively that Aboriginal firing in Australia has had drastic geomorphic repercussions. Burrill Lake provides a probable Pleistocene example. In the semi-humid east of Tasmania, Davies (1967:18–24) has shown the contemporaneity, though not the inevitable causal connection, of human occupation (shown by the presence of worked implements) with the onset of post-glacial aggradation, when changes in the character of vegetation on hill slopes led to accelerated mass movement. He sees a possible link with modification of the vegetation by fire, which would be more effective under drier conditions. Aggradation initiated by about 2500 B.C. (Davies 1967:20) would agree well with Churchill's (1968) dating of about 3000 B.C. onward for increasing aridity and the drying up of the Puntutjarpa soakwell by 2000 B.C. (Gould 1971*b*). Post-glacial dune formation in the sub-humid east of Tasmania also implies diminution of vegetative cover. Gould (1971*a*:21) noted wind denudation of areas of sandy soil where the spinifex had been burnt off in the Western Desert in times of prolonged drought. Tindale (1959) assessed drastic effects in the Canning Desert, where aerial photographs showed dune and swale patterns broken down after vegetation had been fired. West Australian examples of the correlation of occupation and firing to devegetation and dune mobility will be cited later (pp. 103–4). There is no doubt that unimaginative European clearance has heightened the unfortunate effects of aridity and erosion.

Whether 30,000 years of firing has had geomorphic repercussions or not, it certainly has had long-established vegetational effects. Botanical work has long indicated that most of our 'virgin' bush is fire-climax vegetation, and that Aboriginal firing of the bush must have been an important factor in the establishment and maintenance of this vegetation pattern (Gardner 1957, 1959; Davies 1964; Wallace 1966). Lightning may be a lesser factor (see Gould 1971*a*:21) but satellite observation has shown a relatively low frequency of lightning strikes in Australia (Sparrow and Ney 1971).

Firing was brought to the attention of archaeologists as intensely relevant to our understanding of prehistoric Aboriginal ecology by two papers, both published in 1968, presenting similar ideas quite independently of each other. Rhys Jones (1968) considered first the colonisation of Australia and Tasmania in its environmental context, and then the impact of man on his environment. He saw man as the only new (or newly significant) factor available to explain the extinction of giant marsupials in the late Pleistocene, on the analogy of Martin's arguments for North America and Eurasia (Martin 1966, 1967, 1973). Jones discussed separately the effect of fire in changing the environment of the Aborigines, and in creating that which greeted the white settlers. He advanced ethnographic evidence from both Tasmania and the mainland that such fires were not simply accidental but were deliberately kindled, and botanical evidence that the effect of having fired is not simply reversed by ceasing to fire. The suggestion that the Aborigines deliberately, or rather not accidentally, 'extended and maintained an environment suitable to their economy' is an interesting analogy with what agriculturalists were meanwhile doing elsewhere. Merrilees (1968), in an article more closely concerned with the faunal evidence, suggested that the certain effect of the Aborigines on the vegetation, and their probable effect on the fauna, were linked. He mustered more mainland evidence of 'deliberate and frequently repeated firing' and postulated 'profound effects on the mammalian fauna of Australia'. He added the stimulating suggestion that in Africa too the important factor in extinctions was not hunting as such, but fire and its large-scale effect on vegetation.

If we take together Guilday's suggestion (1967) that *large* animals tended to disappear first because environmental balances were most critical for them, and Merrilees's suggestion that 'improved hunting techniques and equipment can be conceived as a response to, rather than the cause of, widespread extinction of species of game animals' (Merrilees 1968:7) we may have a key to a major shift in Australian cultural history, and to the ecological significance of the Australian 'small tool tradition'.*
This succeeded the earlier 'Australian core tool and scraper tradition' as the large marsupials succumbed to an ecological impoverishment which may have been the summated effect of increased evaporation, decreased precipitation, and Aboriginal 'peripatetic pyromania' (Merrilees 1968:5, quoting Meggitt).

---

* Since this was written new work has pushed back the probable chronological position both of Australian megafaunal extinctions, and of the shift towards the use of less heavy, smaller artifacts, some probably hafted, though not microlithic (see, for instance, Dortch and Merrilees 1973; Lampert 1972). The changes may still be linked, but if they correspond to climatic change, this must be at latest interstadial late Pleistocene, rather than post-Pleistocene.

2

Fire and systematic exploitation

It has recently been suggested that the presence of big game resources and the beginnings of agriculture may have been mutually exclusive (Alford 1970 for North America; but see also Martin 1966:342 for Africa). This is one aspect of the wider notion that new patterns of economic exploitation (be they 'broad spectrum' intensive gathering and foraging, or the particular further adjustments we choose to label 'farming') developed or were adopted when ecological disequilibrium superseded a previous balance of exploitation and resources (Hole and Flannery 1967; Flannery 1968, 1969; Ucko and Dimbleby 1969), as in the final Pleistocene of Eurasia (Binford, L. R. 1968). Where game continued to be abundant relative to population there was no imbalance sufficient to set in motion a shift to a radically different pattern.

Harris (1969:8) made the further point that specialised big-game hunters occupy specialised ecosystems, while the more generalised ecosystems within which fisher-hunter-gatherers operate have greater flexibility and adjust more readily. Such generalised systems operated in the late Pleistocene over mainland South-east Asia (which then included Sumatra, Java and Borneo) and extended into island South-east Asia (Flores, Timor, Celebes, etc.) and the north of Greater Australia (including New Guinea). Golson has argued:

> ... the level of correspondence between food uses of the same genera in Malaysia on the one hand and Arnhem Land and Cape York on the other ... may well be due as much to ancient patterns of plant exploitation brought to Australia from the Malaysian region by its early inhabitants as to the properties of the flora itself. (Golson 1971a:207)

In his opinion 'the plant exploitation of Australia's earliest settlers may have been appreciably patterned by traditions established in Malaysia' (*ibid*:209). Within this continuum intensive exploitation, including the use of fire and axes, may have graded into horticulture very early.

In mainland and island South-east Asia there was apparently an early shift to 'modern' fauna, and a correspondingly early intensification in plant usage, producing economies verging on horticulture by the end of the Pleistocene (Gorman 1969, 1971; Solheim 1972; for a contrary opinion, however, see Harlan and de Wet). Did the climatically similar areas on the northern circumference of Greater Australia not share these developing patterns of exploitation? I would suggest that the extent to which they did so has been underestimated.

We can draw on the map of the Indo-Pacific region a line analogous to that which Alford draws on the map of the Americas between the game-bearing grazing of the Plains and the areas of greater plant utilisation (leading to early agriculture) nearer the equator. Such a line would run across Pleistocene Greater Australia dividing its central desert, steppe and savannah from the tropical and monsoon woodland of the north, which shared in the early development of patterns of plant exploitation on both sides of the equator (see p. 6). It would divide areas of high herbivore biomass in an annulus around the centre, from areas with a stress on vegetable foods at the wooded periphery of the continent, with stone axes providing perhaps an index of the latter emphasis (cf. White 1967; Mulvaney and Joyce 1965:169; Mulvaney 1971*a*:374–5, 1971*b*:10). The line curves round to include the eastern, southern, and south-western sectors of the circumference, as well as the north, in a wooded zone where use of plants and small animals balanced a reliance on large game, and where axes were used (cf. Davidson and McCarthy 1957: fig. 7, p. 426; and Ride 1958).

Although Australia in the late Pleistocene had already begun to lose her megafauna, perhaps in part as a result of early firing, the process was gradual and not complete (cf. Bowler *et al.* 1970:55; Merrilees 1968:18), and populations round the less arid margins of the arid centre continued to rely heavily on fauna as well as flora. But certainly post-Pleistocene populations in these increasingly arid central areas could not maintain their high Pleistocene levels (as evidenced by the large number of Pleistocene, and the few late, sites round the lakes of the Willandra Creek system for instance). Even much nearer the periphery of the continent (for example the area just east of York and Toodyay in Western Australia), field survey shows that by the final pre-contact phases numbers had ceased to rise as fast as on the coastal plain (cf. Hallam 1972*a*, 1973*b*). The broadly based ecosystems of the continental periphery proved more resilient in the face of climatic and anthropogenic modification than the more specialised game-focused systems of the centre and circumcentre.

By about 10,000 B.C. Australia was cut off by wider seas from direct participation in further developments in horticulture and agriculture (cf. Golson 1971*b*). The indigenous development of characteristically Australian traditions, for example the hafted adze for woodworking (Gould 1971*b*), appears to stem from the earlier steep-edge scraper traditions common throughout Pleistocene Australia (for the association of a distinctive scraper angle and wear with woodworking see Gould, Koster and Sontz 1971).* It has been suggested, however, that external contacts† across those wider seas contributed not only the dingo but also certain later technical developments within the developing 'smaller tool' traditions, including 'backed blades' which were associated with scrub burning and cereal usage in the Indian subcontinent (Singh 1971; Mulvaney 1969, 1971*a*, 1971*b*; Mulvaney and Soejono 1971; Golson 1971*b*). These developments may be indices of ecological adaptations sufficient to maintain viable population densities (White 1970). Wide-scale fire-management (evident from 5000 B.C. onward) could contribute to more efficient hunting at the margins as well as the centre; while the vegetable component in the diet must have become relatively more important, even in the centre, as game declined. The dichotomy between specialised game economies and generalised gathering and foraging economies gave way to intensified exploitation and regional diversification of technologies throughout the now divided continent. The centre of proliferation of backed-blade traditions, whatever their initial stimulus, lay in the south-east (Pearce 1973 and forthcoming). Other traditions developed elsewhere.

Mulvaney's 'Inventive Phase' (1969 : 106–7) may be the Australian analogue of the new ecological patterns which had crystallised out from 'broad spectrum' utilisation of resources in the classic Eurasian 'hearth' areas by ten to five thousand years ago. Some of these exploitative patterns, as they spread and modified in new environments, we label 'agriculture' and 'domestication'. The full development or adoption of such patterns never occurred in Australia, which before European settlement was barely a starter in the race towards overpopulation. Further pragmatic adjustments may be seen in the regional variants of Mulvaney's 'Adaptive Phase'.

Does the shift in foci of innovation (in language, artifacts, art and ritual) from the annulus around the centre to the margins of the continent parallel a shift in the most advantageous ecological settings? 'Original Australian' early artifact traditions and geometric art forms had Australia-wide distribution, but centred on the now semi-arid annulus with its high

---

* Dortch and Merrilees (1973) now have evidence of the use of hafted tools in Devil's Lair as early as 14,000 years ago, and probably as early as 25,000 years ago.

† Since this was written the likelihood of indigenous, rather than externally stimulated, developments has been reinforced by the work of Dortch and Merrilees (1973) and Pearce (1973 and forthcoming).

late Pleistocene biomass. Backed-blade proliferation had its focus on the lower Murray, nearer the circumference (see Pearce 1973). Peripheral areas like the Kimberleys are prominent in late innovation—linguistic, artifactual, artistic and ritual (see for instance Crawford 1968). What was the role of fire in the successive development (and perhaps exhaustion) of the potential of each zone? We shall examine this question for south-west Australia.

We shall be concerned with the role of fire in enabling the Aborigines of the South-west so to modify and exploit their terrain as to continue to extract sufficient resources for increasing populations. The process of modification is not usually considered sufficiently deliberate, laborious, or drastic to be called farming, though Rhys Jones (1969) uses the phrase 'fire-stick farming'.

Farming as Europeans know it—specialised cereal agriculture—we may see as one narrowly specialised mode among the wide gamut of forms of symbiosis and exploitation between human and other biological communities over a long timespan reaching back at least into the end of the Pleistocene (cf. Higgs and Jarman 1969; Harriss 1971). Original Australians adopted more generalised modes. However they did both exploit and husband their resources systematically, and were careful to maintain continuing supplies. Fire had its part in these schemes of crop and stock management.

Irvine (1970) has discussed the way in which Aboriginal exploitation may verge on cultivation. Stanner (1961:240) sees the Murinbata interpretation of a myth in which the Rainbow Serpent sends his daughters to plant baobab trees as meaning that planting a garden was an old Aboriginal custom. Long (1970:329) cites an amusing example of Aborigines conserving breeding stock, taking dingo pups for the bounty paid on the scalps but leaving the adults to breed next season. A comparable plant example is the Tiwi custom of always leaving a portion of each cluster of edible yams in the hole from which they were dug (Goodale 1970:360; cf. Lawrence 1968:205).

Gathering yams (*Dioscorea*) was anything but a random process, whether in northern Australia or further south; it was certainly not a matter of digging out a root here and there, but of returning regularly to extensively used tracts. Grey, for instance, described in the Murchison–Hutt–Greenough coastal area (Grey 1841:II,12–38) definite '*warran* grounds', as well as swamps producing *Yun-jid* (a species of *Typha*), served by well-established paths and supporting abundant populations in clusters of well-built, clay-plastered and turf-roofed huts; 'these superior huts, well-marked roads, deeply sunk wells and extensive *warran* grounds, all spoke of a large and comparatively speaking resident population' (*ibid*:II,20). Near the Greenough, 'two groups of these houses close together ... would have contained at least a hundred and fifty natives' (*ibid*:II,38). At one point Grey recounts:

> ... for three and a half consecutive miles we traversed a fertile piece of land, literally perforated with the holes the natives had made to dig this root; indeed we could with difficulty walk across it on that account, whilst this tract extended east and west as far as we could see. (*ibid*:II,12)

Grey's summary was that this area was:

> ... the most thickly populated district of Australia that I had observed, and moreover one which must have been inhabited for a long series of years, for more had been done here *to secure a provision from the ground by hard manual labour* than I could have believed it in the power of uncivilised man to accomplish. (*ibid*)*

Grey allowed himself however to be persuaded by his own observations and not all later writers have been able to rid themselves of their preconceptions to the same extent. Certainly such intensive and laborious Aboriginal exploitation of plant products includes one of the notions implicit in our European use of the word 'farming': the notion of hard work. It involves secondly territorial confinement; and thirdly conservation and husbanding, rather than depletion, of a product. If the effect of this were to extend the product outside its original distribution range, as well as rendering it more abundant within that range, Aboriginal exploitation would have included also the fourth element implied by 'farming' or 'cultivation'.

Yam grounds extended farther south than those described by Grey, and we shall find settlers in the Victoria Plains (north of Toodyay) and in the Bindoon–Gingin area north of Perth using them as indicators of fertile soils suitable for European agriculture. Mrs Robin Roe, of Beermullah, near Gingin, has examined 'yam grounds' in the valleys of two small brooks just south of Gingin, where mounds and holes up to five feet across, and said once to have been three or four feet deep, are reported by the present owners to have been 'left by natives digging yams or *Woorine*'.† Early surveys, from the 1840s and 1850s, show such *warran* holes south of Gingin,‡ yet others along the piedmont alluvium of the Swan—just south of the stretch where it flows west after emerging from

---

* My emphasis—SJH.

† Information from Mrs Roe, March 1972. The areas are at c. 39271147 and at c. 39341178, alongside Lennards Brook.

‡ 'Plan of locations No. 113 and 115 ... in the Swan River District as marked on the ground by Philip Chauncy Asst. Surv. June 1850' (Map Swan 4, Battye Library, Perth) shows 'Warrine holes' 300 yards north of Lennards Brook.

the Darling Scarp*—and again on the opposite side of the river after it turns south, just west of the point where it is joined by the Ellen Brook† (see fig. 4).

Another south-west Australian example of conservation verging on cultivation is described by Grey:

> The natives have a ... law that no plant bearing seeds is to be dug up after it has flowered; they can call them (for example) the mother of *Bohn*, the mother of *Mudja*, etc. ... I have never seen a native violate this rule ... (Grey 1841:II,292)

The use of fire will have to be examined in this context of systematic near-cultivation and resource management. Grey interpreted the use of fire to improve root resources as 'a sort of cultivation'. *Yun-tid*, the root of a species of flag (*Typha*) is pounded into a paste, made into cakes, and baked: 'The natives must be admitted to bestow a *sort of cultivation* upon this root as they frequently *burn* the leaves of the plant in dry seasons, in order to improve it' (*ibid*:II,294).‡ These flags were abundant in the swamps of the coastal plain around Perth, as well as further north, and south, and indeed across the continent in South Australia, where also the leaves were burnt off before harvesting the roots (Eyre 1845:II,62).

Another crop which could be so improved was, of course, grass, and most of the rest of this paper will be concerned to establish that the Aborigines were agents of vegetational, and, it may be, geomorphic change (Jennings 1965) in their efforts to improve grazing by firing. George Seddon has drawn my attention to an assessment made by Sir Thomas Mitchell:

> The extensive burning by the natives, a work of considerable labour, and performed in dry warm weather, left tracts in the open forest which had become as green as an emerald with the young *crop* of grass. These plains were thickly imprinted with the feet of kangaroos, and the work is undertaken by the natives to attract these animals to such places. How natural must be the aversion of the natives to the intrusion of another race of men with cattle: people who recognise no right in the aborigines to either the grass they have thus *worked* from infancy, nor to the kangaroos they have hunted with their fathers. (Mitchell 1848:306)‡

I shall cite later West Australian instances of a similarly acute appreciation by the early European settlers of the degree to which they were indebted to the work of their Aboriginal precursors.

---

* Another Chauncy survey (Swan Folio XIX, Battye Library, Perth) shows sets of 'Warran holes' both north and south of the northern boundary of the property of W. Shaw.

† 'Locations on the Right Bank of the Swan River. P. L. Snell Chauncy, Assistant Surveyor, 1843' (Swan Folio No. XIV, Battye Library, Perth).

‡ My emphasis—SJH.

We may thus dismiss as invalid Cleland's argument (1935) that 'Deliberate burning to supply grass in the future would be an example of primitive agriculture, a stage which our natives do not seem to have attained'. They did indeed attain a high efficiency in the management of fauna and flora to the mutual well-being of human and other components in the ecological system. As in America, 'We no longer think of . . . plant collectors as a ragged and scruffy band of nomads; instead they appear as a practised and ingenious team of lay botanists who know how to wring the best out of a . . . bleak environment' (Flannery 1968).

The efficiency of Aborigines as animal as well as plant ecologists is attested by descriptions such as Landor's account of a kangaroo drive 60 miles south of York in Western Australia: 'I stood in the midst of a large plain which they had surrounded on three sides, multitudes of kangaroos—I believe I might say thousands, came rushing past me' (Landor 1847:262).

Eyre quotes a letter which summarises well the relationship of Aboriginal and European land usages and improvement:

> Every tribe has its own district . . . and within that district all the wild animals are considered as much the property of the tribe . . . ranging in its whole extent, as . . . flocks of sheep and herds of cattle . . . the native grass affording subsistence to the kangaroos of the natives, as well as to the wild cattle of the Europeans . . . burning off the grass . . . is done [partly] to provide a new crop of sweeter grass for the rising generation of the forest . . . (Eyre 1845:II,299)

Thus Aboriginal populations did change the vegetational and faunal balance. Fire was a major factor in this pattern of regular exploitation and settlement. I shall examine these achievements in detail for the South-west of Australia, which is particularly fortunate in having abundant and intelligent records.

3

Fire in the South-west of Australia: early historical evidence

I shall restrict my detailed consideration of the early evidence for firing, its methods, aims and results, to the South-west of Australia.

There is plenty of evidence from the earliest voyagers round the western coasts of New Holland for bushfires, as well as campfires, initiated by Aborigines; and for the effects of such fires. In the first years of the seventeenth century the Dutch had sailed along this coast. Pelsart, for instance, observed 'smokes' at a distance in July 1629 near Shark Bay (Flinders 1814:I,iii); Tasman in 1644 saw 'fires and smoke . . . all along the coast' in the north-west (*ibid*:1v). The first detailed published account of the southern part of the west coast is that given by Captain Samuel Volkersen, of the *Waeckende Boey* which sailed from Batavia in January 1658 to search for the *Vergulde Draeck*, wrecked two years before. He described 'a large island . . . in nearly thirty two degrees south latitude . . . about three miles from the continent, with "high mountains" and a good deal of brushwood and many thornbushes, so that it is hard to go over' (Volkersen 1658, in Major (ed.) 1859:66; Collingridge 1895:284; Heeres 1899:79). The mainland was described as 'downs covered with grass' (*ibid*).

Vlamingh, with the *Geelvink*, the *Nijptang*, and the *Weseltje*, also explored Rottnest, first on 30 December 1696, then successively on the 31st, and on 1, 2 and 3 January 1697. On 1 January he saw 'smoke arising' at different points on the mainland, on the 2nd 'smoke arising' again, and on the 3rd after sunset 'great numbers of fires burning the whole length of the coast on the mainland'. On the 5th a visit to the mainland discovered a hut, a fire, fresh water and footsteps, but no men; a trip some 'six or seven leagues' up the Swan on the 10th, 11th and 12th produced more campfires (eight in one place), more huts, more native water supplies, but the men themselves remained elusive (Vlamingh 1696–97, in Major (ed.) 1859:90–4; less complete version in Collingridge 1895:292–3).

The first detailed descriptions of fired countryside in the South-west came at the end of the eighteenth century. Vancouver anchored in King George Sound in 1791, and Archibald Menzies describes in his *Journal* the country the Captain and his Officers explored on foot and by boat:

> [29 September] . . . a small hut . . . *the place had recently been burnt* here and there . . .*
>
> [30 September] . . . There were but *few places* I travelled over this day *but what bore evident marks of having been set on fire* . . .*
>
> 1st of October . . . rich pasture abundantly cropped with excellent grass . . .
>
> 2nd . . . country along the shore thickly covered with brushwood . . . remains of where the natives had recently had a fire.
>
> 4th of October . . . a deserted village scattered about in the skirts of a small wood . . . about six and twenty [huts] . . . Many of the stems of the trees bore evident marks of fire, some were even hollowed out by it . . .
>
> 7th of October . . . [from] Oyster Harbour . . . a large rivulet winded back into a delightful country . . . its banks were here and there bordered with extensive plains and meadows which seemed to *afford easy access* into the country . . . a little way off from the rivulet a thick wood chiefly composed of the *Eucalyptus obliqua* [sic] a beautiful evergreen whose stems were naked and straight for some way up *without any underwood to obstruct our progress* . . . We seldom met with these trees or the other gum plants anywhere about the Sound without observing their stems burnt or scorshed [sic] with fire.*
>
> [By] a small road not far from the shore found another village . . . apparently later occupied. Several places about this village seemed to have been very recently burnt down and destroyed by fire, many of the larger trees had been scorched by it . . . The further we penetrated inland the more favourable the country appeared, diversified with hills and dales, plains and meadows and woodlands *capable of affording excellent range and good feeding* to domestic animals of every description . . .*
>
> The frequent marks of fire and *general burnt state of the country everywhere* round the Sound . . . some attributed . . . to a combustible quality in the earth . . . others entirely to the busy capricious disposition of the natives who are fond of kindling frequent fires round their huts . . . (Menzies 1791:43–74 ff.)*

We can clearly envisage from these descriptions very general but mild and patchy burning, its effect varying with soil, topography and frequency, leaving in some areas (in coastal dunes) thick brushwood and elsewhere open grassland. The interior forests comprised tall, straight, mature trees, all frequently scorched but clear of undergrowth and easy to move through. The pastoral potential was obvious. Islands within swimming distance had shared the burning.

---

* My emphasis—SJH.

Figure 1 'A Deserted Indian Village in King George III. Sound, New Holland'. From 'A Voyage of Discovery to the North Pacific Ocean and Round the World . . . Performed in the Years 1791 [to] 1795 . . .' by Capt. George Vancouver; plate from vol. 1, opposite p. 175.
Note the widely spaced trees, and lack of underwood.

Vancouver himself wrote of:

> . . . *the very extraordinary devastation by fire* which the vegetable productions had suffered *throughout the whole country* we had traversed . . . we did not see a spot . . . which had not visibly felt its effects. Where the country was well wooded the loftiest timbers had their topmost branches burned; yet none seemed totally destroyed . . . (Vancouver 1801:I,177-8)*

The low intensity of the fires must imply a low density of ground litter, and a high frequency of firing. Vancouver describes the forest structure which results from such firing: '. . . in the neighbourhood of Oyster harbour the country is very well wooded; and as the branches of the trees do not approach within several feet of the ground an extensive view is admitted in every direction' (*ibid*:I,170). His woodcut of 'A Deserted Indian Village . . .' (see fig. 1) shows just such a view through widely spaced trees, the shelters set among the trees on ground clear of bushy growth. Vancouver is the first to speculate on the purpose of this firing in the South-west: 'Fire is frequently resorted to by the rude nations either for the purpose of *encouraging a sweeter growth* of herbage in their hunting grounds, or as toils for taking the wild animals' (*ibid*:I,177).*

Later writers (see chapters 6 and 7) echoed this notion of sweet new growth, and it is difficult to know whether they owed their concept of fire as a tool of pasture management to independent observation or to Vancouver. No doubt his speculation was right. The resulting good grazing was to be as attractive to the European pastoralist as to the Aboriginal hunter.

At the beginning of the nineteenth century Matthew Flinders, and at much the same time a French expedition, surveying different sections of the coast, confirmed and extended these accounts. *La Naturaliste*, separated from *Le Géographe* by a storm in Geographe Bay, reached Rottnest Island on 14 June 1801. Freycinet and Fauré landed and found it difficult to penetrate the woods, just as Volkersen had a century and a half earlier: '. . . les bois . . . se trouvant trés touffus . . . *ne nous permettoient d'avancer* qu'avec beaucoup de lenteur et de difficulté' (Peron and Freycinet 1807:I,176).*

They reconnoitred up the Swan River, past the shallows at Heirisson

---

* My emphasis—SJH.

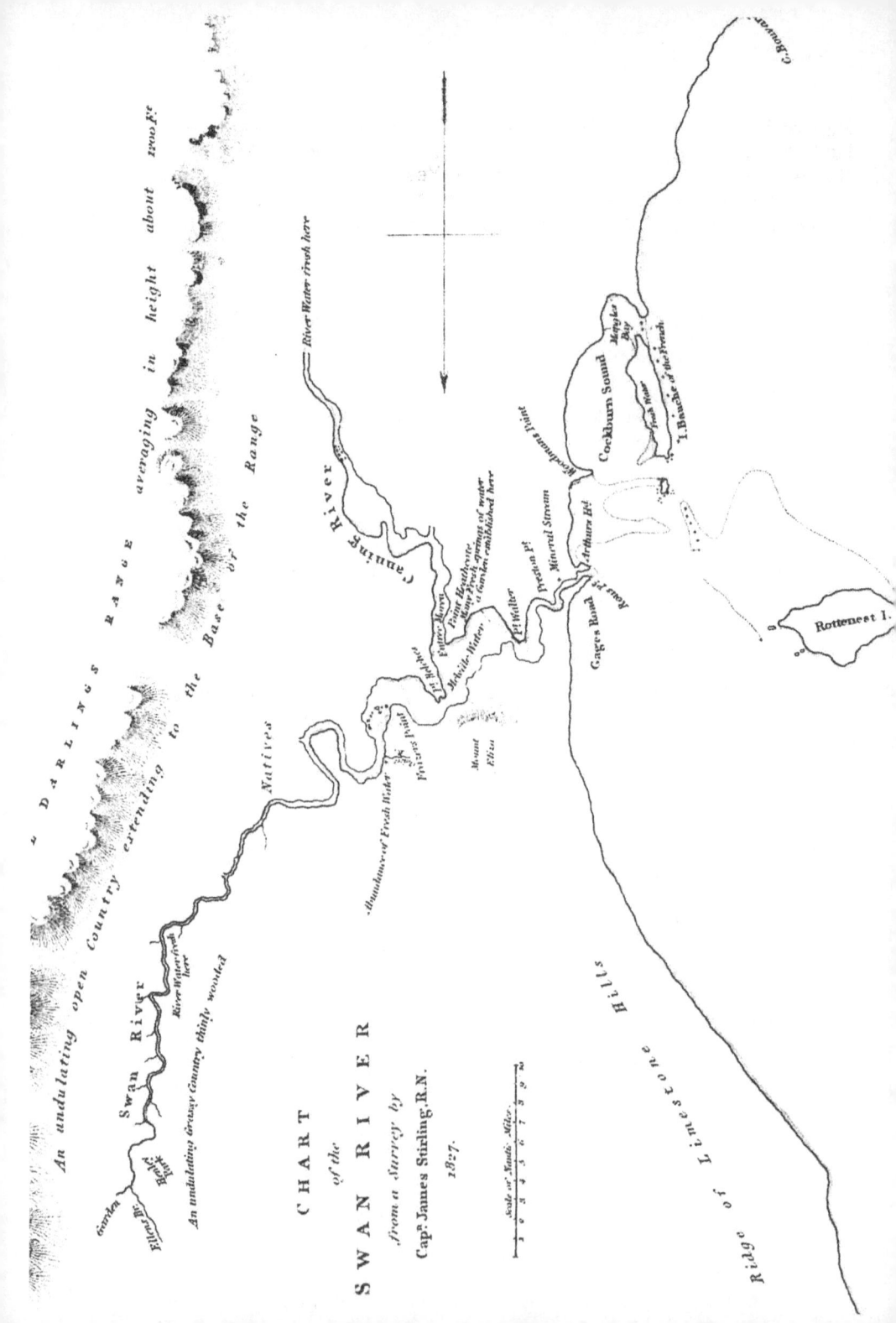

Figure 2 'Chart of the Swan River from a Survey by Capn. James Stirling R.N. 1827'.
Note the 'Garden' at the junction of the Ellen Brook and the Swan River; from Henley Park eastward along the Swan—'An undulating Grassy Country, thinly wooded'; below 'General Darling's Range', 'An undulating open Country extending to the Base of the Range'; and 'Natives' noted east of the River. North is to the left.
Reproduced by permission of the British Library Board.

Islands, but made no similar remarks about the mainland vegetation. The clue perhaps lies in two descriptions of Rottnest: 'Cette île est en général bien boisèe . . . une végétation abondante et vigoureuse' (*ibid*:I,188); and 'Cette île n'est pas habitée' (*ibid*:I,189).

King, exploring the west coast in January 1822, confirmed that 'Rottnest does not appear ever to have been inhabited or even visited by the natives from the main' (King 1827:166). Of Garden Island, 'l'intérieur est parfaitement boisé . . . la végétation est fort active, quoique les terres sont généralement couvertes de sable' (Peron and Freycinet 1807:I,190–1), contrasting with the grassy sand-dunes of the mainland. The mainland contrasted also in its traces of human habitation (for example footprints and wells) and of fire, though it is not always possible to tell whether the explorers were observing campfires, signal fires, or bushfires. Which, for instance, was the big fire which appeared suddenly behind the dunes round Geographe Bay in June 1801 (*ibid*:I,69), or 'ces grands feux auquels nous n'avions rien vu de comparable . . . allumés tout près du bord de la mer' (*ibid*:II,197) around Geographe Bay in May 1803? The great quantity of burnt trees and 'extinguished fires' ('de feux éteints') which Peron encountered inland from Geographe Bay in June 1801 (*ibid*:I,79) were definitely from bush fires, in a district where tracks ('les petits sentiers') along the edge of a river (*ibid*:I,78) attested constant Aboriginal usage and movement.

Matthew Flinders's descriptions apply to the south coast, not the west. His expedition judged the mainland to be inhabited largely on the evidence of 'smokes', though they came closer to the inhabitants when they anchored in King George Sound in December 1801:

> [13 December] Marks of the country being inhabited were found every-where . . . (Flinders 1814:I,57)
> [14 December] Some smokes being observed at the head of the harbour . . . met with several natives . . . (*ibid*)

Gifts were exchanged, and before leaving the party was receiving constant visits from 'our friends the natives' (*ibid*:I,60), and staged for them a parade which was to remain in their folk-memory until Daisy Bates found it transformed into a corroboree: 'When they saw these beautiful red and white men with their bright muskets, drawn up in a line, they absolutely screamed with delight' (*ibid*).

Again the condition of islands where there was no trace of native visitation (*ibid*:I,88) contrasted with the mainland. Near Lucky Bay, for instance, in January 1801 they found native fireplaces ashore, but Mondrain Island '*was covered with brushwood*; some of the party ... set it on fire ... there was a general blaze all over the island' (*ibid*:I,83).*

Captain King anchored at the Sound in January 1818, and found much evidence that the natives frequented Oyster Harbour for its abundant fish:

> Our gentlemen made several excursions ... in the hope of meeting with natives ... they were not however far from us for the smokes of their fires were seen every evening ... (King 1827:I,17)

They looked in vain for traces of the garden crops which Flinders had planted and concluded:

> A lapse of sixteen years will in this country create a complete revolution in vegetation; which is here so luxuriant and rapid that whole woods may have been burnt down by the natives and grown again within that space of time. (*ibid*)

This casual remark illustrates one of the difficulties in looking at early accounts for evidence of native firing and its effects—firing is so common and expected that it is totally unremarkable.

On a later visit the party did establish contact with the natives, and two of their visitors 'each brought a lighted firestick in his hand ... to make a fire, and to pass the night' (*ibid*:II,119).

Thus on distant islands explorers found impenetrable thickets, tinder-dry and ready to blaze; on the mainland grassy dunes by the coast, and inland woods whose 'open forest-like character afforded no impediment to their march' (Stirling 1827:558) along the loamy banks of the Swan above the area that was to become Guildford. Earlier that day (11 March 1827) Stirling's party had viewed (in the area which is now called Belmont) 'the smoke from many fires rising on different Points of view ... a whole Tribe of about thirty Natives [see fig. 2] ... many traces of Natives and of Kangaroos ...' (*ibid*:557–8) and upstream on succeeding days, as we have seen, they encountered 'several deserted encampments ... and ... ground *cleared by fire* a few weeks before ...' (*ibid*:560).*

The natives of the South-west were in general without canoes at the time of European contact (Vancouver 1801:176; Nind 1831:32; Wilson 1835:283; Roth 1902:65; Davidson 1935a:3–4). They could not reach the more distant islands. What effect had they had on mainland vegetation? Early European settlers were soon to give interested accounts.

---

* My emphasis—SJH.

4

Between the Swan and the Sound

Just before and after the foundation of the Swan River Colony in 1829, numerous parties, naval and military, official and unofficial, made short sallies into the country around the Swan, and between the Swan and King George Sound. On the coastal strip and immediately behind it, settlers probed the settlement potentialities of areas first touched on from the sea. Simultaneously, exploration extended beyond the unprofitable jarrah forests on the detrital laterites (Mulcahy 1967) of the Darling Range, east to the more fertile Avon valley, and as early as 1831 Bannister's party got through from the Avon to King George Sound by land. The journals of these little parties give invaluable descriptions of landscapes and Aborigines as they first greeted European intruders.

On the Swan, Stirling early observed an alternation of summer coastal and winter inland haunts and activities. In March 1827 his party had ascended the Swan River as far as it was navigable, to the foot of the Darling Scarp, and explored on foot to north and east finding 'several deserted encampments'. In a letter to Governor Darling, April 1827, he added 'we had afterwards reason to believe that they frequent the high grounds only during winter, and that at this time they were still on the Coast engaged in Fishing' (Stirling 1827:560).

Later he amplified:

> Their numbers are considerable when it is remembered that the sources which supply food are so precarious. For this in Summer they frequent the Sea Coast where their skill in spearing Fish is truly wonderful. In Winter they inhabit the higher grounds, where the Kangaroo, the Opossum, the Land Tortoises, several species of Birds and roots compose their sustenance... (*ibid*:570)

We have already noted his observation of 'ground which had been cleared by fire a few weeks before' (14 March 1827) when he was encamped at the junction of Ellen Brook and the Swan. Late summer, then, was both burning-off and fishing season by the Swan. We shall find the same regular pattern of exploitation by the Sound.

Regular burning occurred not only on the coastal plain, but into the jarrah forest of the Darling Range. In September 1829, Lieutenant Preston with a naval party from H.M.S. *Sulphur* explored the country above where the Canning, a tributary of the Swan, emerged from the Darling Scarp:

> ... siliceous sand and clay in the dales ... large fragments of granite rock and ironstone [ferruginous lateritic concretions] upon the ridges, in many places almost *entirely bare of low vegetation;* the trees, generally of immense size, the largest *hollowed out at the root by fires.* (Preston 1833*a*:10)*

This surely implies frequently repeated firing, such as Vancouver's men had found by King George Sound half a century earlier.

One suspects that a fired countryside was so much the norm that early reporters did not find it noteworthy. 'T.W.H.' returning from the Avon valley, across the Darling Range, near the Helena, encountered 'mahogany [jarrah] trees of extraordinary dimensions ... one which had been burnt down ... 114 feet long' (T.W.H.1833:220). Were it not for the opportunity for measurement, we should have no note of the burning.

Preston again, with Mr Collie and another party, in November 1829 observed from Peel Inlet, near the Murray delta, about 40 miles south of the Swan:

> ... a distant view of several fires among the trees, a circumstance which assists in explaining the *so frequent burnt appearance* of the trees and shrubs in Western Australia; we have no doubt they owed their production to the natives.
> On the previous night our fire rapidly caught the adjoining underwood, and we remarked a considerable space which had similarly suffered between our present and former touching here twelve days previously. (Collie and Preston 1833:49)*

These also were summer burns.

From the sea the same party when further south 'had seen smoke in many places a short way beyond and even close to the beach, between Port Vasse and Port Leschenault, as well as beyond the former in Geographe Bay; and we saw and heard the natives shouting on the beach' (*ibid*:46)—that is from south-west of Busselton north to Bunbury. Northward from the Swan, Preston (1833*b*:78-9) had noted 'Several smokes were observed inland, about latitude 29°'. Neither report makes it clear whether

---

* My emphasis—SJH.

these 'smokes' were campfires or bushfires but Preston obviously regarded the one as relevant to the other.

Burning is repeatedly authenticated for the block of land between Busselton and Augusta. An anonymous correspondent traversing the Margaret River district in mid-March reported: 'This district has been lately burnt'. He passed through 'superior [country] undulating with fine valleys covered with silky grass . . . many excellent situations for farms well cleared of timber' (Anon. 1833*a*:111). Approaching Cape Naturaliste, 'the whole of the country . . . has been burnt' (*ibid*:112).

John Bussell travelled northward from the Blackwood at Augusta along a route further from the coast, and observed by the estuary 'the bush, where unburnt, luxuriant' (Bussell 1833*a*:184). Northward, he came into country which 'for some miles abounded with valuable timber . . . the trees were, many of them, large and fine, many much injured by fire' (*ibid*:185). In yet another account of a journey from the Blackwood to the Vasse, he speaks once more of 'good soil . . . thickly wooded with mahogany [jarrah]' (Bussell 1833*b*:186), and an area 'recently burnt . . . free from woody bush' (*ibid*:187). He proceeded for part of a day's march 'over a country clean burnt . . . land good but rocky often and heavily timbered' (*ibid*:188).

So unremarkable is a burnt countryside that the absence of burning becomes remarkable. At one point Bussell described a flat which 'bore numerous impressions of the feet of natives and kangaroos and where the ground . . . was a vivid green . . . unsullied with burnt sticks and blackened grass trees . . . grass was plentiful' (*ibid*:190–1). He was close to the Vasse, where he was later to settle (Shann 1926; Hasluck, A. 1955) and rhapsodised: 'The country here was so clear that a farmer could hardly grudge the fine spreading trees of red and white gum and peppermint the small proportion of ground they occupied only to ornament' (Bussell 1833*a*:192). Still in the same general area he walked alongside an inlet through 'fields of grass [where] native paths, which traversed these lawns in every direction, gave us easy walking' (*ibid*:194).

John Bussell had written in 1832 from his previous grant on the Blackwood River above Augusta of 'heats unknown to those who have never been in the neighbourhood of a forest blazing with native fires' (Shann 1926:82); but Georgiana Molloy's remark that before she returned to gather eagerly awaited seeds 'a native fire or a hot day had accelerated their ripening and I found the seed scattered' (Hasluck 1955:157), gives a rather different impression of the gentleness of native fires round Augusta.

The country along the south coast, from Augusta to King George Sound, is still very difficult for Europeans to master—a wide coastal strip of sandhills and swamps, with steep granite hills and great karri forests behind. One of the few early accounts (Anon. 1833*b*) came from a party who in 1831 beached their whale-boat near present Northcliffe and, being unable to launch it again in heavy surf, walked to Augusta and from there to the Murray. The coast was well inhabited. On Nornalup Inlet they met Aborigines who 'conducted us to their wells' (*ibid*:115). Near the Gardner River they 'heard the natives and saw their fires about a mile up the river' (*ibid*:116). Even on the south coast it was the absence of firing which was remarkable. On April 21, with the boat beached north-west of Point d'Entrecasteaux:

> ... I and Mitchell ascended the first range of Sand Hills ... the country in the immediate neighbourhood *not having been recently burnt*, I could not get beyond the second range though we were walking upwards of three hours. (*ibid*:118)*

It is unlikely that the whole of the jarrah, and above all the karri, forests were burnt through frequently and consistently in the far south, as were the western and eastern margins of the south-west triangle of forest near the more densely inhabited coastal plain on the one hand and the more open mallee and sandheath country of the drier interior on the other (Gardner 1959). In the latitude of Perth, however, the east and west margins of the forest wedge approach each other and the whole width was penetrated by Aboriginal groups from either side (cf. Hammond 1933:23). Here early reporters (Dale 1833*a–e*; Henty 1830; Irwin 1835; Moore 1884*a*; Ogle 1839) spoke frequently of 'fine open forest' (Erskine 1833:92) and only occasionally of 'thick brushwood'.

Farther south the forest triangle was wider east to west, penetrated less by early European settlers and probably also by Aborigines. It is significant that for a good description of a transect across the forest 80 miles south of Perth, we must turn to a later date. In January 1839 a Mr Elliott set off westward from Williams, a remote pastoral outstation east of the jarrah forest, aiming to reach Leschenault on the coast in three or four days. This involved a journey across the Darling Range 'never before crossed at this point' (Grey 1841:I,310). He became lost, and Grey set out to search for him. From the 'level plain' and 'good feed' of the Bannister–Hotham area, he went south to Williams, then west towards the source of the Harvey into:

> ... an elevated tableland of ironstone and granite [with] little or no herbage; the lower vegetation ... a short prickly scrub, in some places completely destroyed by native fires, but the whole country was thickly clothed with mahogany [jarrah] trees, so that in many parts it might be called a dense forest. These mahogany trees ascended, without a bend or throwing off a branch ... forty to fifty feet ... and the ground was so encumbered by the fallen trunks of these forest trees, that it was sometimes difficult to pick a passage between them ... I have never seen so great a want of animal life ... we had in vain looked for natives. (Grey 1841:I, 321–2)

---

* My emphasis—SJH.

Thus the centre of the jarrah forest belt, around the present milling centre of Hoffman Mill, must when first penetrated by Europeans have been relatively empty of both animal and human populations, burnt only in odd patches—and certainly not frequently—and thus difficult to traverse. It was only as Grey's party approached the point where the Harvey River emerged from the Darling Scarp that they found '... mahogany trees became less frequent ... scrub higher ... beautiful grass ... on the banks of the Harvey ... signs of natives' (*ibid*:I,322) as they reached the coastal plain.

The farther south, the damper and denser the forest. The land around Augusta was described as 'so thickly wooded, as to render its clearing very expensive and discouraging to the settlers' (Irwin 1835:67).

The karri forests behind the south coast were even thicker and less frequented. Bannister in 1831 passed through first jarrah and then karri on an ill-calculated route from the Swan to the Sound. Setting off eastward from Perth in January 1831 he reported that 'the trees are mahogany on the higher and rugged lands [the Darling Range] ... many parts had been recently burnt, probably last year, and this year the herbage was quite green and fresh' (Bannister 1833:101-2). The party then took a southward course which brought them well west of their destination, King George Sound. For the last thirty or so miles to the south coast:

> ... the underwood was so thick ... occasionally we were obliged to make a road with a hatchet. The trees were principally blue gum [karri] ... in height before a branch 140 or 150 [sic] we thought at least ... where the underwood was not remarkably thick grass and herbage grew luxuriantly. (*ibid*:105)

They met no people. It took them nineteen days, subsisting on shellfish, to make their way east along the coast to the Sound. If the karri forests were burnt at all they were burnt only patchily, for example on their western margin, near the Blackwood River, but rarely in the inaccessible interior. Aborigines used these forests only where they could move easily between forest and coast or forest and grass or heath.

The country north of King George Sound, at the inland margin of the jarrah belt, was burnt frequently. Collie (1833*a*), in a week's journey in late April and early May 1831, mentioned successively 'fires with which the natives seem repeatedly to have consumed the vegetable production'; the channel of the Kalgan River 'filled with tall shrubs, now burnt'; an area along the river north-east of the Porongorups with 'sandy or gravelly surface, bearing shrubs, in many parts burnt'; farther north along the Kalgan 'open forest country ... grassy', and returning southward 'a belt of good soil ... Fire had recently gone over its surface'. On another excursion, in February 1832, Collie could not see hills in the vicinity of the Sound from heights above the Kalgan valley, 'the atmosphere not only being very hazy, but thickened with the smoke of native fires' (Collie 1833*b*:171).

When Dale and a party had ascended the Stirlings a fortnight earlier, they had passed through 'patches of good land and grass ... dense forest ... open country' (Dale 1833*f*:162–3) to see from the top of Toolbrunup 'a panoramic view ... Towards the sea coast ... native fires ... materially obstructed our view' (*ibid*:164–5). The *Panoramic View* which Dale (1834) later published showed no fewer than five fires simultaneously, with many additional 'smokes' in the background (see foldout illustration). Dale summarised his impressions as follows:

> ... the country is not thickly inhabited and the forests are extensive ... The fires, which are periodically spread over vast tracts of country for the purpose of driving objects of chase from their fastnesses, must be very destructive of bird life ... The climate of King George's Sound is very fine: extreme heat ... only ... during a few days of the year ... probably increased by the natives having at that season set fire to the country round for many miles ... (Dale 1834:13–14)

Such descriptions make it clear that burning, though the work of a comparatively small population, was impressive in scale, frequency, and undoubtedly in vegetational effects. We must turn to other sources to discern the place and purpose of fire in Aboriginal patterns of social and ecological activity.

5

Regulated burning: the Albany area

Scott Nind, who was medical officer to the small post established on King George Sound in 1827, gave a circumstantial account (Nind 1831) which showed clearly that burning was not an accidental or incidental activity of the Aborigines, but was closely meshed into their pattern of life. He described an 'overall integrated pattern of exploitation', of seasonal movement, sites, territories, resources and activities similar to that envisaged on purely archaeological-ecological grounds for populations in Palestine—'prior to the development of agricultural techniques or more complex economies' (Vita-Finzi and Higgs 1970:16–32).

Nind discussed 'household size' and 'group size', and how the latter fluctuated with the seasons:

> An encampment rarely consists of more than seven or eight huts; for except during the fishing and burning seasons, at which times large parties assemble together, their numbers are generally small, and two or three huts suffice. The numbers of individuals seldom exceed fifty. These encampments consist of near relatives, and deserve the name of families rather than of tribes. (Nind 1831:28)

Nind's account of the socio-demographic pattern in relation to the ecological pattern was masterly:

> At King George's Sound they live upon the productions of nature, varying at different seasons and in different districts ... The population is ... far from numerous ... (*ibid*:35–6)
> As the country does not abound in food, they are seldom stationary, removing according to the time of year to those parts which produce the articles of provision that may be in season ... During the winter and early spring they are very much scattered; but as summer advances they assemble in greater numbers. (*ibid*:28)

Nind's account thus predated by over a century Thomson's picture of 'a regular and orderly annual cycle carried out systematically' and of movements which were not 'merely aimless and random' but 'circumscribed within well-defined limits, even along traditional routes, which, incorporating the experience of centuries, provide at each season the appropriate harvest' (Thomson 1939:211).

The seasonal round might be described most succinctly in the words of Dale: 'The stormy weather of winter is chosen for hunting, and the hot days of summer when the shoals of fish bask upon the shallows, for fishing ... All possess activity, skilfulness and sagacity' (Dale 1834:8-9). Nind's account of these skills and activities, economic and social, is more detailed. 'I believe that during the winter (when the sea coast tribes go into the interior) they are in small parties and much scattered, living upon opossums, bandicoots, kangaroos, etc.' (Nind 1831:36). Individual and small-party methods of kangaroo hunting were employed 'when the rain is pouring heavily or the wind blowing hard, to prevent the noise of their approach from being heard' (*ibid*:29-30); the animals could then be stalked and speared. Thomson (1939:215,217) similarly noted that on the west coast of Cape York large kangaroos could be stalked during the 'wet' 'under the cover of the noise of the great winds'. Emus, rare and much valued, were speared in the winter when they nested (Nind 1831:30). Pitfalls were used to trap kangaroos in the interior (*ibid*).

'In the spring before the burning season commences', a hunting method was employed which required a number of people to break down and tread a cleared path round an area from which game, often 'the small or brush kangaroo' were then driven and 'knocked on the head' (*ibid*). People began to gather into large communities: 'The whole of the males of the tribe are generally present' (*ibid*).

But spring fare consisted mainly of 'the eggs and young of birds, chiefly of the parrot tribe, but also of hawks, swans, ducks, pigeons, etc.' (*ibid*:34). This was still a transition period of reliance mainly on vegetable foods with minor supplements: 'They begin to return to the coast about September or October and at this season they chiefly subsist on roots. In calm weather, however, they procure a few fish. As the season advances, they procure young birds and eggs' (*ibid*:36).

The great burning and fishing assemblages were from full summer to autumn:

> About Christmas they commence firing the country for game, and the families, who through the winter have been dispersed over the country, reassemble. The greatest assemblages, however, are in the autumn ... when fish are to be procured in the greatest abundance. Towards the end of autumn, also, they kill kangaroos, by surrounding them. At the dry seasons of the year large districts are abandoned for want of water. (*ibid*)

> During the summer and autumn months, the natives derive a large proportion of their food from fish. They have no canoes ... neither nets, nor hook and line ... In the mouths of streams or rivers, they take large quantities, by weirs ... but the most common method is pursuing the fish into shoal water, and spearing them ... (*ibid*:32-3)

It was 'in the autumn, when the smaller species of fish approach the shore in large shoals' that fish were most plentiful, and their roasted flesh even stored (*ibid*:33). As on the Swan, fishing and burning seasons coincided. This made large assemblies possible and so had ceremonial implications also (Hassell 1936:698-700).

Thus clustering could be, as Stanner has perceptively noted (1965:5), a response either to plenitude or to scarcity. In the South-west it was both: plenitude of food allowed aggregations, while scarcity of water sources limited scattering. (This is the reverse of the Central Australian situation, where labile groups could form larger congregations only after the rains: Meggitt 1962:49-50.) Any simplistic notion of human 'territories' in terms of the 'exploitative territory' of *a* site (Vita-Finzi and Higgs 1970:25-6) must be modified not only (as they point out) to take account of patterns of movement over time, but also to consider fluctuation in group size. Not only the size and movement, but the very existence of discrete local groups is in question (cf. Hearne 1970).

Archaeological evidence alone cannot tell us whether scattering and reagglomeration took place at random throughout a continuous and unstructured spatial and social network, or whether certain individuals and certain localities may be linked with far greater frequency within rather than without a 'knotted' portion of the network (cf. Spaulding 1960:31,36), thus constituting local community groupings. But we are lucky that our abundant ethnohistorical accounts give us the evidence for such groupings, in individual awareness of belonging to a group and of the 'otherness' of those outside it. In the Perth area such evidence from early explorers and settlers for the contact period may be reinforced by archaeological distribution evidence of site clustering—certainly for late and possibly for earlier periods (Hallam 1972*a*). The maintenance of complex social ties, in part by economic and in part by ritual common participation, must be seen as essential to the regular and continued functioning of a dynamic pattern of movement, dispersion, regrouping and exploitative activity, keyed to variation and fluctuation in resources. Ecological ties to the landscape cannot be considered apart from social and symbolic ties. These are mutually reinforcing mechanisms. Fire had both ecological and symbolic significance in the linking of Aboriginal life and land, in perception by human groups of themselves and their environment, and participation by each in the shaping of the other.

Nind's description of the process of firing is vivid:

> At this season they procure the greatest abundance of game ... by setting fire to the underwood and grass which, being dry, is rapidly burnt ... With a kind of torch made of the dry leaves of the grass tree they set fire to the sides of the cover by which the game is enclosed ... The hunters concealed stand in the paths most frequented by the animals and with facility spear them as they pass by. On these occasions vast numbers of animals are destroyed. The violence of the fire is frequently very great and extends over many miles of country; but this is generally guarded against by their burning it in *consecutive portions*. (Nind 1831:28)*

The careful regulation of this pattern of land use was preserved by a mechanism Nind interpreted as ownership: 'The presence of the owner of the ground is considered necessary when they fire the country for game' (*ibid*).

The notion of a close mesh of usage rights was reiterated by Eyre (1845:II,299) and Dale:

> The natives of the known parts are scattered over the country in their tribes, which differ from each other slightly in appearance and customs, though much in dialect. Each tribe occupies a large and determinate tract which is sub-divided into smaller portions as hunting-grounds for individuals, who jealously watch over and instantly retaliate [*sic*] encroachment upon their shores. (Dale 1834:7)

Burning was not necessarily always on a large scale.

> The women also kindle fires, but only for the purpose of taking bandicoots; they sometimes however, accompany the men at the larger firings for kangaroo or wallaby. As soon as the fire has passed over the ground they walk over the ashes in search of lizards and snakes, which are thus destroyed in great numbers ... (Nind 1831:28)

The differentiation between the small scale firing carried out by the women, and the large scale firing carried out by men, or men and women together, was part of a general differentiation in roles, activities, equipment, and the pattern of each day's doings. Each morning:

> ... the men and the women go out in separate parties in companies of two or three together ... the women to collect roots or crayfish, and the men with their spears to procure fish or game. The women carry a pointed stick, with which they dig up roots ... a bag ... made of a kangaroo's skin, in which they deposit the food they procure: they also carry a firestick. (*ibid*:36)

The fire-stick was partly intended for starting their own cooking fires, but it might also be used for burning off, as part of the day's gathering:

> A portion of the roots, or whatever they may collect, they cook and eat, but reserve part for the children and men, to be eaten on their return to their huts. They also get lizards, snakes and bandicoots, and, in the burning season, set fire to the ground by themselves. (*ibid*:36–7)

---

* My emphasis—SJH.

There was thus also a geographical differentiation between the areas likely to be burnt by the women, and those whose firing was controlled by the men. During their diurnal movements, the women's party 'generally go on the open, downy, or swampy land' (*ibid*:37). Their burning was likely therefore to be mainly of grassland. 'The men also go two or three together . . . They are more frequently found on the shores fishing, or in the woods seeking nests, opossums, bandicoots or kangaroos' (*ibid*). Their burns would therefore be woodland burns and would have to be more carefully regulated.

Besides deliberate firing, one suspects that domestic hearths (for cooking or comfort) and above all fire-sticks must have contributed something to the conflagration potential of the area:

> Every individual of the tribe when travelling or going to a distance from their encampment, carries a fire-stick for the purpose of kindling fires, and in winter they are scarcely ever without one under their cloaks, for the sake of heat. It is generally a cone of *Banksia grandis* which has the property of keeping ignited for a considerable time . . . (*ibid*:26)

One must remember, however, that while the number of potential ignition points was high, frequent periodic burning would have kept the density of combustible material low, and dangerously intense fires, like that which Flinders's men lit on Mondrain Island, would be rare.

Nind's account of controlled 'burning-off' in the Albany area was confirmed and expanded by J. L. Stokes, describing a sally northward from Albany in November 1840, during the voyage of H.M.S. *Beagle*, to:

> . . . a large clear piece of land called the Great Plain, about fifteen miles distant, and a little off the Swan River road. On our way we met a party of natives engaged in burning the bush, which they do *in sections every year*. The dexterity with which they manage so proverbially a dangerous agent as fire is indeed astonishing. Those to whom this duty is especially entrusted, and who guide or stop the running flame, are armed with large green boughs, with which if it moves in a wrong direction, they *beat it out*. Their only object in these periodical conflagrations seems to be the destruction of the various snakes, lizards, and small kangaroos, called wallaby which with shouts and yells they thus force from their cover, to be despatched by the spears or throwing sticks of the hunting division. (Stokes 1846:II,228)*

The 'complete docility' or 'ungovernable fury' of the fires depended on their periodicity, as recent studies by the forestry division of CSIRO have shown. The regulated burning each year of different sections, which is now forestry policy (Gardner 1957; Wallace 1966; Symposium 1971), was just what the Aborigines had been doing.

The total picture given by these accounts is of country-wide burning 'by consecutive portions' as a deliberate, regulated activity, co-ordinated

---

* My emphasis—SJH.

into the patterns of seasonal and diurnal movement and of men's and women's activities; it correlated with the scattering and amalgamation of groups, and the possibilities of contact between wider communities, for both economic and ceremonial purposes.

Firing was one very important component in a 'thorough ... degree of resource utilisation' similar to that envisaged (by Vita-Finzi and Higgs 1970:26) for the Mt Carmel area. Our evidence for tightly organised mosaics of hunting, cropping and firing grounds by the Sound and throughout the South-west confirms the suggestion that 'population pressure would have been felt prior to the development of agricultural techniques or more complex economies', with an 'obvious bearing on the issue of whether technological progress stems from, or promotes, demographic stress' (*ibid*).

Quantitative work, both ethnohistorical and archaeological, on the demography of the South-west is in progress (Hallam 1972*a*, 1973*b*; see below, chapter 16) to determine differential population densities between different areas at European contact, and also the ratios between those densities over time. Results for the Perth area suggest that firing may have been one of the factors affecting rates of population growth, population ceilings, and the time needed to reach those ceilings. Earlier densities were higher, and rates of increase levelled off more rapidly, in the drier interior; here perhaps the initial improvement of grazing would be most effective, and later climatic stress most crucial. Within the west coastal plain, the most seaward zones also had a relatively high early population; perhaps here firing, at a time when the zone was being constricted by encroaching sea levels, took vegetation beyond an optimal adjustment, and initiated devegetation and dune movement. On the other hand, on the coastal plain it was the sites on sandhills adjacent to swamps in the Bassendean Sands zone (McArthur and Bettenay 1960) which showed the greatest and longest continued increase in numbers, so that here there was no doubt still some possibility of intensifying resource usage right up to contact.

Does ethnographic evidence for organised, regular, usage-mosaics exist in the west as in the south? The evidence from the Swan complements that from the Sound.

6

Regulated burning: the Swan River

After the foundation of the Swan River Settlement in 1829, settlers' observations on 'native' fires and their threat to crops and homes were legion. Mary Ann Friend, for instance, chronicles a voyage in her husband's ship taking emigrants to the Swan. On 10 February 1830, after sight-seeing around Perth she 'walked back in the bush ... many parts were burnt by the Natives' (Friend 1931:7). At Fremantle, on 17 February, 'the natives had made a large fire to drive the kangaroos. It spread rapidly owing to the dry state of the grass and reached the encampment of Mr. Watson which was entirely burnt' (*ibid*:8). In November 1834 raging fires almost engulfed Thomas Peel's storehouse at Clarence, south of Fremantle (Hasluck 1965:157).

In Augusta on 22 January 1833, Nancy Ann Elizabeth Turner recorded in her diary: 'The natives burnt the bush at the back of the town. Mrs. Brian's house was in great danger' (McDermott 1928:17).

Lieutenant Bunbury, who travelled from Perth to the Vasse in March 1837, wrote:

> This is the worst season in the year for travelling, being the last month of summer; the rivers and swamps are dry so that water is very scarce and the Natives have burnt with fire much of the country, and the sun burning the grass on the remainder there is no food for horses until the rains in May, when the vegetation springs again and the country assumes a different appearance. Now nothing can be more dismal, the country all black and bare of vegetation, while the blackened and charred trunks of trees look particularly horrid. Whole Districts appear in mourning at this season ... (Bunbury 1930:179)

Nathaniel Ogle, in his 1839 *Manual for Emigrants* confirms that such summer burning was part of a regular seasonal sequence of activities (cf. Grey 1841:II,262), like that described by Nind for the Sound:

> They vary their food according to the season, sometimes frequenting the estuaries for food, at other times eating the flesh of different species of kangaroo ... opossum, bandicoot, dalgert and other small animals ... and sometimes they set on fire the dry grass to capture the snakes and reptiles for immediate sustenance. (Ogle 1839:63)

Besides the firing of grass to capture reptiles (probably the work of women here, as on the Sound) we have already noted Mrs Friend's mention of organised fire drives, certainly the prerogative of the men. Sir George Grey (1841) gives accounts of organised drives using fire to hunt both smaller and larger mammals. His descriptions refer to the area round Perth, where he came to know the Aborigines well in 1838 while waiting to set out for the north-west:

> The smaller species of animal are either caught by surprising them in their seats or by *burning the bush* ... Another very ingenious mode of taking wallaby and the smaller kind of kangaroo, is to select a thick bushy place where there are plenty of these animals; the bushes are broken down ... to form a space of broken scrub about ten feet wide all round a thick bush ... the natives fire the bush and the frightened animals finding their runs stopped up, rush into the fallen branches, [become entangled and] fall an easy prey to their pursuers. (Grey 1841:II,290–1)*

Kangaroo drives involving fire were even more spectacular:

> The animals which are to be killed by a party ... are either surprised in a thick bushy place, where they have retired to lie down in the heat of the day, or else in an open plain; in the former case ... when the blockade is completed they fire the bushes; the frightened animals now fly from the flames ... the bushes are fired in the direction in which they are running, and they are driven back ... until they make a rush through the midst of their enemies, who allow but few of their victims to escape ... (*ibid*:II,270–1)

These confined specific-purpose fires were not the country-wide conflagrations of full summer. I have not come upon a *dated* eye-witness account of a fire drive in the latitude of Perth, but Landor (1847:262) has a description of a hunt in August, in the area south of York and due east of Perth (though with no mention of fire) in which 'multitudes of kangaroos— I believe I might say thousands' were driven. Fire drives would not necessarily be confined to the dry season at this latitude as they were in the wetter south.

Our two most valuable sources for the use of fire in the Perth area are both due to George Fletcher Moore. His journals (1884*a*) are valuable as a continual (though not quite continuous) record from his arrival in

---

* My emphasis—SJH.

November 1830 until his visit to Britain in 1841. From them we can extract information on the topography of native settlements, seasonal movements, contacts, foods in season, etc., and they are all the more valuable because they are raw data, not an attempted synthesis.

In January 1833 Moore reported 'fire on the great plain of Quartania' (Moore 1884a:156).* In February 1834 'the country has been fired by the natives and we have been obliged to use great efforts to save ourselves and our property. The flames are quite terrific and overwhelming' (*ibid*:211). Exploring thirty miles to the north in March he reported that 'the country has been recently burned' (*ibid*:216).

He had quickly acquired some familiarity with the indigenous inhabitants and their language. Aborigines were encamped in March 1834 a mere half-mile from his house in Middle Swan and he visited their bivouac 'close to this place' (*ibid*:215). When there was dissension among them, 'all parties seem to look on me as a friend' (*ibid*:214). He reported now not only their doings but also their purposes. He generalised (May 1834):

> The natives in summer set fire to the grass and dry herbage for the purpose of their hunting ... Over the hills the grants in that locality are less burned, being less frequented by black or white people ... it is surprising how soon all the grass shoots out again when a little moisture comes ... (*ibid*:219)

The best source, however, for information on the role of fire in the activity patterns of the Swan River Aborigines is the *Descriptive Vocabulary* which Moore compiled in collaboration with the second Governor, Hutt, and the official interpreter, Armstrong, 'with such aid as a long residence in the country, and constant communication with the natives, both in a public [he became Advocate-General] and private capacity, enabled me to impart' (Moore 1884b:vi). This was first printed when Moore visited England in 1841, but is most easily available reprinted in 1884 in the same covers as his *Diary* (Moore 1884b).

Language reflects the preoccupations and conceptualisations of its users; more succinctly, 'society creates the environment as a system of meanings' (Mogey 1971). The local nomenclature distinguished between:

> *Bokyt*—A term applied to ground clothed with vegetation which has not yet been burned. (Moore 1884b:12)†

and

> *Kundyl*—Young grass springing after the country has been burned ... (*ibid*:45)

or

> *Balgor*—Young fresh grown trees. (*ibid*:3)

---

* Pagination refers to the 1884 printed version of Moore's journal letters (Moore 1884a).
† Separate pagination of the "Descriptive Vocabulary" (Moore 1884b).

On the one hand there is:

> *Narrik*—Unburned ground, but ready for burning. Land of which the vegetation is abundant and dry, fit to be set on fire, which is done by the natives sometimes accidentally and sometimes on purpose, in order to drive out the animals ... kangaroos, bandicoots, wallobys, snakes ... which they kill ... In Upper Swan dialect, dry; ripe. (*ibid*:60)

On the other hand there is:

> *Nappal*—Burned ground; ground over which fire has passed. Over this ground the natives prefer walking; it is free from all scrub and grass, their progress is not therefore obstructed, and the tracks of animals are readily discerned upon it. (*ibid*)

The vocabulary is rich in such words:

> *Yanbart*—A descriptive term applied to ground where the vegetation has been burnt. (*ibid*:81)

Thomson (1939:212) demonstrated the precision and complexity of Aboriginal ecological concepts from the vocabulary of a Cape York tribe, where a name was given 'to each type of country, to each distinctive botanical or floral association—which is recognised quite as definitely by these people as by botanists and ecologists'. It would be fairer to say of the Swan River Aborigines that they *were* botanists and ecologists, thoroughly conversant with ecological zones, seral succession, and climax vegetation. Chauncy, who was Assistant Surveyor in Western Australia from 1841 to 1853, observed: 'They have names for all the conspicuous stars, for every natural feature of the ground, every hill, swamp, bend of a river' (Chauncy 1878:266).

Their technical vocabulary differentiated shades of meaning which, one suspects, Moore has not always been able to follow. Clark (1970a:108,125) has stressed the importance of a study of how people structure their experience through language to the ecological understanding of non-industrial societies; also the awareness of time shown in naming segments of it. Marshack (1970a, 1970b), investigating the cognitive aspects of European late Pleistocene and post-Pleistocene hunter-gatherer traditions on the basis of evidence from engravings, stressed symbolisation of a variety of habitats and seasonal processes, and conjectured that 'the precision of rendition had a complementary vocabulary for naming and identification' (1970b:62). The Swan River Aborigines had just such a vocabulary with which to take cognition of the complex of environmental interactions with which they had to deal. These were tools as important as any we can retrieve from the sand (cf. Frake 1962; Hallam 1972b).

Like King George Sound, the Swan River area had a regular cycle of seasonal activities:

> *Jilba*—The spring; August and September. *Djubak* is now in season. (Moore 1884b:36)

Compare, however:

>*Djubak*— ... the root of which is the size and shape of a new potato ... eaten by the natives ... in season ... in October. (*ibid*:22)
>
>*Gambarang*—Beginning of summer—October and November. The natives leave off building huts about this time. Young birds begin to be plentiful. (*ibid*:27.) [This is also given as *Kambarang* (*ibid*:10)]
>
>*Birok*—The summer season, December and January ... This is the very height of summer, when iguanas and lizards abound. (*ibid*:10)
>
>*Burnur*, or *Burnuro*—The autumn ... including ... February and March. This is the By-yu or Zamia-fruit season; and mullet, salmon and tailor-fish abound. (*ibid*:16, 10)

The quantities of fish taken must indeed have been prodigious. Irwin reported that near the Aborigines' weirs, 'fish have been found left in heaps by the natives after they had used what they needed' (Irwin 1835:23). Chauncy in the 1840s watched Aborigines 'At Swan River ... drive a shoal of large schnappers into water too shallow for them to swim in, and spear and catch a great number of fish weighing from ten to fifteen pounds each' (Chauncy 1878:248–9).

Grey adds to the products of the full and late summer to early autumn several which would take the Aborigines regularly to the lakes and swamps which occur in lines through the inter-dunal valleys of the aeolian limestone belt, and behind it in the sandplain zone. Freshwater tortoises were in high season in December and January when the lakes had shrunk. Fish abounded. Large flocks of waterfowl were skilfully felled with throwing sticks or spears—Lake Neerabub was 'covered with wildfowl' at this season. Frogs and 'freshwater shellfish' from the size of 'a prawn to a large crayfish' (Grey here intends crustaceans, not molluscs) were most easily taken 'when the swamps are nearly dried up', though the Aborigines would not touch fresh-water mussels (nor oysters) (Grey 1841:I,292–7; II,84,280–7). The frogs and turtles were still being taken in April (*ibid*:II,88–91). By now the swamps were dry enough to be fired, either to improve the flavour of the *yun-jid* (or *yanjidi*) roots which were then being harvested (Moore 1884*b*:81) or as 'a sort of cultivation' (Grey 1841:II,294). In South Australia too the proper season for harvesting flagroots was after the swamps had dried up and the leaves had been burnt off (Eyre 1845:II,62).

Moore describes the importance of these cherished plant products, tended by fire:

>*Yanjidi*—An edible root of a species of flag (*Typha augustifolia*) growing along fresh-water streams and the banks of pools ... The natives dig the roots up, clean them, roast them, and then pound them into a mass ... kneaded and made into a cake ... This root is in season in April and May, when the broad leaves will have been burned by the summer fires, by which the taste, according to native ideas, is improved. (Moore 1884*b*:81)

After *Wan-yarang* or *Geran*, April and May (*ibid*:10), the seasonal round returns to:

> *Maggoro*—The winter of Western Australia, including the months of June and July . . . At this period of the year cobbler-fish abound . . . (*ibid*:47)

We thus have evidence, from both the Swan and the Sound, of regular patterns of occupance, movement, group size fluctuation and exploitative activity with emphasis on inland hunting in relatively small groups in winter. In summer larger groups gathered to exploit swamp and estuarine products—the plant, small animal, and water resources of the coastal plain swamplands and fish from the estuaries and lagoons. These became yet more important in the autumn. Later summer to autumn was the fire season. Similar patterns are attested elsewhere round the margins of the Australian continent, for example on the coast of Victoria (Hope and Coutts 1971).

7

Fire and hearth

To the record of firing for hunting, Moore added the notion of firing to open up the country, to facilitate movement. The Aboriginal vocabulary also noted the fresh new growth of grass which followed burning. Was this part of the aim of firing? Vancouver thought so in 1791 (see p. 19 above).
James Backhouse wrote on 22 January 1838:

> In the cool of the evening we returned to Perth ... Much of the bush on the road had been recently burnt, and one house had been consumed by fire. The natives are now setting fire to the scrub in various places to facilitate their hunting, and to *afford young herbage to the kangaroos*. (Backhouse 1843:341)*

What was implicit in Fletcher Moore's description of new grass growth after burning is explicit here. Country open to travel and affording young herbage to kangaroos will be equally accessible and attractive to the European and his sheep.

Backhouse added that 'the Natives in the Swan River country, as well as at King George's Sound, have their private property, clearly distinguished into hunting grounds, the boundaries of which are definite' (*ibid*:542). On these organised patterns of land use Europeans were increasingly pressing.

Grey also noted that organised battues, which in bushy places involved firing (Grey 1841:II,270), 'are conducted under certain rules. The proprietor of the land must have invited the other natives, and must be present himself' (*ibid*:II,272).

---

* My emphasis—SJH.

The notion of regulated hunting and firing areas is reinforced by his remarks on the gathering of large bodies of people to exploit abundant sources of edible gum (*ibid*:II,260,294,298):

> ... there are even some tracts of land which abound in gum ... which numerous families appear to have an acknowledged right to visit at the period of year when this article is in season, although they are not allowed to come there at any other time. (*ibid*:II,298)

This is just a rather legalistic way of viewing a mosaic of usage rights, or rather a series of overlapping mosaics. A group's range for one resource need not coincide with its range for another, though there will be a core area over which there is the greatest degree of overlap and which is thus most frequented by that particular community. Landor saw some such degree of flexibility: 'Every tribe possesses a certain tract of country. They are not always very particular about trespassing' (Landor 1847:212). A group might go far for a resource rarely available. The 'few places [which] afford sufficient supply [of gum] to support a large assemblage ... are generally the spots at which annual barter meetings are held' (Grey 1841:II,294)—and no doubt ceremonies also (cf. Bunbury 1930:69). The ritual and ecological year had at least a statistical regularity; 'they always regulate the visits to their hunting grounds so as to be at any part which regularly produces a certain sort of food at the time this article is in full season' (*ibid*:297;cf.262). The European settler was thus depriving rightful users of the land of sustenance for some span of the year.

Eyre made the same point as Nind and Backhouse about the rights of usage:

> But particular districts are not merely the property of particular tribes; particular sections ... of these districts ... are recognised ... as the property of individual members and when the owner of such a section ... has determined on burning off the grass [to] enable the natives to take the older animals more easily, and *to provide a new crop of sweeter grass for the rising generation of the forest*, not only all the other individuals of his own tribe, but whole tribes from other districts are invited to the hunting party and the feast and dance or corrobory that ensue ... (Eyre 1845:II,299)*

Eyre may have misinterpreted the question of individual property, but he was undoubtedly right in seeing a close and controlled mesh of usage rights and responsibilities.

Wollaston's journals contained the same ideas. He wrote of bushfires:

> ... caused by the natives, either accidentally or intentionally ... for the purpose of driving the animals and reptiles into one spot, or the margin of some river or swamp where they become an easy prey. The burnt ground, too, sends up in the rainy season a sweeter crop of grass which attracts the kangaroo. (Wollaston 1841-44:13)

---

* My emphasis—SJH.

At Mahogany Creek in November 1848, in the middle of the jarrah forest between the coastal plain and the Avon valley, he 'witnessed at night the magnificence of a bushfire running through the forest burning the dry scrub and preparing the ground for a fresh and greener growth' (Wollaston 1848-56:79).

The essence of usage and firing rights thus lay in the knowledge and familiarity which enabled a group so to work their land as to bring out its maximum potential. The full strength of the link between firing, familiarity and proprietorship is brought out by three entries in Moore's *Vocabulary*:

> *Kalla*—Fire; a fire; (figuratively) an individual's district; a property in land; temporary resting place.
> *Kallabudjor*—Property in land.
> *Kallip*—Denoting a knowledge of localities; familiar acquaintance with a range of country ... also used to express property in land ... (Moore 1884*b*:39)

The linkage between knowledge, usage, fire and rights in land is equally stressed in the reminiscences of Robert Austin about the coastal plain further south (where Bunbury now stands) in 1841-43:

> Each family in the tribe had its own territorial division, its own ka-la or 'fire-place' ... each person knew what there actually was on his own possessions, what birds' nests, etc. ... When anything showed itself in abundance, the neighbours, etc., would be asked to come over and partake. (Roth 1902:55)

Mrs Millett's appraisal (based on Bishop Salvado) saw fire (and water) as the crux of usage rights east of the jarrah belt also:

> ... each family has its own especial tract of land, together with the springs of water thereupon; here he can light his fire and build his hut ... it is his paternal estate ... so that the word 'fire' conveys 'hearth' ... (Millett 1872:77)

Individual hearths are temporary; but *the* hearth, the home, is the land.

Beside hunting and pasture management, Eyre recorded another use for fire which might *result* in bushfires:

> All tribes of natives appear to dread evil spirits ... they fly about at nights ... Fire appears to have a considerable effect in keeping these monsters away, and a native will rarely stir a yard at night ... without carrying a firestick. (Eyre 1845:II,357)

The firestick might, of course, be simply used as a source of light, as in Stirling's observation on the Swan estuary of 'several Natives on the banks fishing by torchlight' (Stirling 1827:561; cf. Irwin 1835:23), or in Grey's account of possum hunting by moonlight: 'the dusky forms of the natives moving about in the gloomy woods, and gazing up into the trees to detect an animal feeding, whilst in the distance natives with firesticks come creeping after them' (Grey 1841:II,287). This source of light might be supplemented by actually firing the bush. 'If they are obliged to move away from the fire after dark . . . they carry a light with them and set fire to dry bushes as they go along' (*ibid*:II,340).

Ritual activities required fire for light, as well as in the ceremony: 'In these dances, called by them *corrobories*, they engage generally at night, near a blazing fire' (Irwin 1835:24).

The use of fire for light could then lead to bushfires near frequented spots. So also might ordinary cooking and campfires, and above all the use of fire for individual warmth. Grey commented on Aborigines' dislike of cold and rain, and love of fire:

> . . . in the height of the rainy season . . . they suffer so severely from the cold and rain, that I have known them remain for two successive days at their huts without quitting the fire; and even when they do quit it, they always carry a firestick with them, which greatly embarrasses their movements. (Grey 1841:II,262)

Among the contents of the women's bags are the means to kindle fire: 'Banksia cones (small ones), or pieces of a dry white species of fungus, to kindle fire with rapidly, and to convey it from place to place' (*ibid*:II,266).

The fungus was presumably to be used as tinder, as at Star Carr, where the bracket fungus was used, and the presence of iron pyrites suggests fire-making by percussion (Clark 1972:25). How was fire kindled in south-western Australia? Percussion is unlikely, but the use of a fire-brand did not signify inability to ignite a fire.

Davidson (1947), on the basis mainly of ethnographic and linguistic material, shows the fire-drill as the only means of kindling fire between the Swan River and King George Sound. Chauncy's description would seem from its context to apply to this area:

> The natives use the stem of the grass-tree to produce fire by friction. This is done by rapidly twirling between the hands one piece of stick in a little hole bitten out of another piece . . . a little dry grass or the dry fuzzy material of the withered seed-head of the grass-tree laid in the hole . . . soon smokes and ignites. (Chauncy 1878:250)

Robert Austin, writing of the Bunbury area in 1841–43, describes in more detail the use of the drill:

> Fire was produced by twirling a stick, held vertically, on to another stick fixed horizontally, the wood so employed being the grass-tree peduncle. The flat surface on the horizontal piece was bitten out with the teeth, upon it the vertical piece was twirled, and as soon as the 'pit' was produced a nick was cut, so as to connect it with the surface edge. Within this same nick was next placed some of the powdered 'fluff' (from the dried-up flowers on the peduncle-top), which acted as a sort of train to the fine dry

shreds of fibre (scraped from the inside of a dead log) lying close below. As soon as the smoke appeared, this 'sawdust' or 'tinder' was fanned into flame by a gentle breath. (Roth 1902:66)

Hammond's description of fire-kindling is similar:

> In making fire the natives use two pieces of wood. One would be a piece of soft wood with a split in it, and the other a stick with a blunt point. The split in the soft piece would be stuffed up with fine dry grass or something similar; the point of the stick would be placed in the split and the stick would be spun around, something like a drill, by rubbing the stick vigorously between the hands to make it spin. In a few minutes the heat caused by the friction would set light to the grass. (Hammond 1936:26–8)

Davidson recognises the use of the fire-saw in addition to the fire-drill in the Murchison and the Esperance areas (see also Hassell 1936:692) immediately to the north and east, but not in the true South-west. Algernon Clifton, however, writing of the Bunbury area in the late 1840s, may indicate the use of a saw rather than a drill: 'their only means of kindling a fire was the very tedious and uncertain one of rubbing two dry black-boy (grass-tree) canes together until the friction created heat enough to set light to the dust caused by the operation' (Johnston 1962:73).

Wollaston refers to 'the firestick generally carried in the bush to save the trouble and delay of obtaining fire by friction' (Wollaston 1841–44:27). The means of applying friction could be either a saw or a drill.

Like Wollaston, Grey implies that it was more usual to carry fire than to light it by friction: 'In general each woman carries a lighted fire stick, or brand, under her cloak and in her hand' (Grey 1841:II,267).

Moore pictures vividly the likely results of such love of warmth:

> *Djanni*—The bark of Banksia and Hakea trees ... In cold weather, every native, male or female, may be seen carrying a piece of lighted bark, which burns like touchwood [sic], under their cloaks ... In the valleys, even in summer, the air is chill before sunrise. The half-clad native starts with the lighted bark; as the day advances the warmth of the sun renders artificial heat unnecessary; the bark is discarded ... A breeze comes ... and the whole country is shortly in a blaze. (Moore 1884b:20–1)

Such accidental firing, mostly at the wettest time of year, would be unlikely to result in really widespread fires, but would be one component in a system in which those areas most frequented were those most often fired. Such frequent firing would be necessary if forest once cleared of undergrowth by firing were to be kept clear. Areas once fired but not frequently refired would have tended to produce thicker rather than thinner forest growth. Indeed European foresters have used fire to encourage thick growth of trees at the expense of grazing (Hutchins 1916:28). The very reverse, grazing at the expense of timber, was the objective of Aboriginal land management. It was not just firing, but frequent firing, which kept the most-used areas of the South-west clear of undergrowth and small timber, and allowed free movement of men and of herbivores.

Moore saw the correlation between population, frequency of usage, burning and clearance: 'Over the hills the grants in that locality are less burned, being less frequented by white or black people' (Moore 1884a:219).

Regular activities produced regular patterns of settlement and movement. Camps and digging grounds were linked by defined paths:

> *Kun-go*—a path; a beaten track. (Moore 1884b:45)
>
> *Gongan*—A sandy district. The easiest road, or usual path. (*ibid*:29)
>
> *Bidi*—A vein; the main path, or track, pursued by the natives in passing from one part of the country to another, and which leads by the best watering-places. (*ibid*:8)

contrasting with:

> *Mundak*—the bush; the wild country; the woods. (*ibid*:57)

Wherever there was a much-used resource—water, fishing, a sandy camping spot—there was clearance, deliberate or incidental.

Landor encountered by a fish-weir on the Harvey estuary 'a clump of trees, a brawling brook... and a patch of excellent grass' (Landor 1847:410). The pattern is recurrent.

In looking for the effects of Aboriginal firing on landscapes in south-western Australia we must not expect to find homogeneity of firing schedules, nor homogeneity of effects, any more than homogeneity of soils or climatic regime. Different areas and sub-areas will have had different resource potentials, and these will have been 'developed' (Whittlesey 1929) in different ways by different Aboriginal groups, with differing preferences and differing patterns and intensities of exploitation. There is room for a multiplicity of detailed local studies. We can look only in the most general way at the evidence, botanical and historical, for the fact of firing, and some of the effects of some patterns of firing on some sorts of landscape and vegetation. Apparent digressions on Aboriginal patterns of occupance, movement and activity are germane to the emphasis on variety.

8

Man-made landscapes: the varied background

We have looked at evidence for the fact of firing by Aborigines, and its role in their economies. In this section we shall look briefly at the variety of landscape and vegetation exposed to that firing, and in the following sections examine the 'contact' evidence for the results of the interaction of human populations and other components in the ecology of these areas, and the effect on European settlement and usage.

The major point that European observers make about Aboriginal firing is that it opened up the countryside. Bunbury gives the most explicit and detailed discussion. He is describing a journey from the Murray to the Vasse and back in 1836:

> It cannot be denied that Western Australia, as far as it is known, is generally of a rather sandy barren nature, partly owing to the constant dryness and clearness of the atmosphere and climate and to the periodical extensive bush fires which, by destroying every two or three years the dead leaves, plants, sticks, fallen timber etc. prevent most effectually the accumulation of any decayed vegetable deposit . . .
>
> By these fires . . . the country is kept comparatively free from under wood and other obstructions, *having the character of an open forest through most parts of which one can ride freely;* otherwise, in all probability, it would soon become impenetrably thick, and . . . the labour and cost of clearing would be so greatly increased as to take away all the profit, and it would change the very nature of the country, depriving it of the grazing and pastoral advantages it now possesses. This has already been proved in the case of Van Dieman's Land, where, in consequence of the transportation of the Natives to Flinders Island, and the consequent absence of extensive periodical fires, the bush has grown up thick to a most inconvenient degree, spoiled the sheep runs and open pastures and afforded harbourage to snakes and other reptiles which are becoming yearly more

numerous. It is true that we might ourselves burn the bush but we could never do it with the same judgement and good effect as the Natives, who keep the fire within due bounds, only burning those parts they wish when the scrub becomes too thick or when they have any other object to gain by it. Upon the burnt ground they can easily track the Opossums, Kangaroo Rats, Bandicoots, Iguanas, snakes etc. which can elude their search in thick scrub—which moreover is very painful to walk through. (Bunbury 1930:105)*

Stokes was similarly explicit, though referring to the Kimberleys, not the Swan: 'The country was more open in character than I had before noticed it, and the numerous traces of native fires . . . seemed readily to account for this' (Stokes 1846:105).

Could firing, joined with grazing and settlement usage, have had such extensive effects? Over what variety of landforms, soils and vegetation might they have operated? Over what timespan and with what results we shall see in more detail in later sections.

Changes on Rottnest Island since its settlement by Europeans may perhaps provide a model of the effects which firing and grazing can have, even over a comparatively short space of time, on the vegetation clothing at least some south-western habitats. Its restricted size enjoins caution in the use of this analogy, though perhaps for an island continent whose populations, both human and animal, have in the last ten thousand years been progressively confined by rising seas to two-thirds of their original area, the parallel is not too strained. Rottnest cannot, of course, provide close parallels to the soil and relief of the South-west outside the immediate coastal belt of dunes and aeolian limestone, but some suggestions may arise about the general manner in which occupation and usage by human populations may effect ecological balances.

The contrast between the mainland and Rottnest lies in habitation and its absence, rather than in soil or climate. This contrast must help to account for the difference between the 'downs covered with grass' which Volkersen observed as characterising the mainland, and the 'brushwood and thorn-bushes' of Rottnest, or the totally wooded nature which the French observers ascribed to the whole island—dunes, inter-dunal valleys and slopes, and limestone ridges alike.

McArthur's (1957) account of the vegetation of Rottnest and Garden Islands, as observed before 1956, noted that the greater part of Garden Island, still relatively unfrequented, was covered with dense low scrub; while on Rottnest, by then long settled and used, 'The relative proportions of species on the island has changed considerably since white man first landed' and that this change 'has been brought about by burning and

---

* My emphasis—SJH.

clearing'. The few thickets of *Acacia rostellifera*, for instance, represented a 'remnant of some former much larger community' (some similar remnants persisted on the mainland); while the '*Stipa-Acanthocarpus* community is spreading at the expense of this association. Where the *Acacia* scrub has been burned or cleared the grass takes over before the *Acacia* can regenerate' (McArthur 1957:56).

The effect of burning and clearing depended, here as elsewhere, on grazing pressures. On Garden Island, *Acacia* regenerated rapidly after a devastating fire in 1956, growing from root suckers, while *Callitris* and *Melaleuca* recovered less rapidly, growing from seed (Baird 1958). On Rottnest Island, also devastated by fire, regeneration of both *Acacia* and *Melaleuca* was effectively prevented by quokka grazing. The small population of Garden Island wallabies put no pressure on the large areas of *Acacia* scrub (*ibid*:107); but the population pressure of quokkas on Rottnest is such that intensity of quokka grazing is the main control on the relative distribution of *Acacia* scrub and the low dense formation of *Acanthocarpus* and tussock grass (*Stipa*). Where these animals are abundant, the *Acacia* is eaten out and replaced by the fire-resistant and quokka-resistant tussock grass. Where quokkas are excluded by fences, *Acacia* thickets expand (Storr 1957; Storr, Green and Churchill 1959).

But what factors controlled the quokkas? The increase in population has occurred since European settlement. Storr (1957) showed that country which had recently been burnt, and had new green growth, offered more forage for quokkas. The opening up of scrub—by felling trees, cultivation, grazing stock, building roads, and settlement—would increase the length of the margin along which scrub met open land, and of bare ground for annuals to colonise. This optimum combination of scrub giving shelter and open ground providing forage for the quokkas would tend to increase the quokka population, increase the grazing pressure, and in turn maintain and extend the cleared areas.

On the mainland, occupation by Aborigines must have had some effects similar to European settlement on Rottnest. They preferred loose sandy soils on which to erect shelters and to sleep, on the margin of bush which would provide material for shelters and sources of fuel and food. Constant movement to and from water, and spots where particular roots abounded; digging and bush burning to collect small animals; firing to drive larger game, to remove obstacles to movement, improve grazing, or simply by accident—all these would deliberately or inadvertently open nodes, and eventually zones, of relative clearance among bush, pushing back the margins of some ecological communities at the expense of others, affecting in various ways different elements in the fauna, and in some situations even soils and soil movement.

The present situation on Rottnest can be of only temporary advantage to the quokkas because it is unbalanced. Food supply in the winter months, derived mainly from introduced annuals, especially grasses, is abundant; but in the almost rainless summer food is scarce. The quokka population is already showing signs of stress affecting its breeding capacity. Perhaps we should envisage similar mechanisms having led to catastrophic fluctuations in numbers among the larger marsupials when Australian environments first began to be intensively affected by human firing, in times of rising sea-levels and increasing aridity.

Human populations thus indirectly affected the ecological balance. The Rottnest situation is analogous to that which Smith (1970) describes for parts of Europe before the spread of full-scale agriculture, when the clearing of forest by men provided increased grazing for indigenous herbivores, which in turn had permanent effects on the vegetation.

The vegetation on Rottnest now resembles the coastal complex on the adjacent mainland more than it did when one was inhabited and the other not; while Garden Island longer retained communities characteristic of uninhabited and unfired islands. Baird (1958:107) remarked on the relatively small number of plant communities capable of regenerating from underground parts on Garden Island (isolated only some seven thousand years), 'whereas in mainland communities only a small percentage of the total species are killed by fire, and the recovery of the bush is in consequence much more rapid'. On the mainland, the vegetation which has survived is that which has been able constantly to recover in this way. The pressures cannot have been decisive before 7,000 years ago, when Rottnest and Garden Islands were cut off from the mainland by rising sea levels (Churchill 1959).

On these offshore islands it has thus been possible to observe, since European settlement, changes in ecological balance similar to those which Aboriginal fire must have wrought on the mainland during the last tens of thousands of years, and particularly over the last few thousand. Tindale (1959) was one of the first to realise man's part in such transformations, for example from rain forest to sclerophyll forest and grassland on the Atherton Tableland and from spinifex grassland to moving sand in the Canning Desert. In Tasmania, certainly, areas on which sclerophyll forest existed under the pressure of Aboriginal firing have been invaded by rain forest now that pressure is removed. Areas of open sedgeland also appear pyrophilic, their boundaries corresponding to natural firebreaks rather than to soil boundaries (Davies 1964:252). On Wilsons Promontory, *Casuarina* woodlands gave way over extensive areas to coastal shrubland around 2000 years ago, probably as a result of burning (Hope and Coutts 1971:112); a further woodland decline followed the advent of Europeans. In Western Australia the mallee and the jarrah forest itself have been seen as communities shaped by, and in the long term dependent on, fire (Gardner 1957; Wallace 1966). The 'savannah woodland' of the eastern margin of the jarrah belt lies in a boundary zone where man-initiated

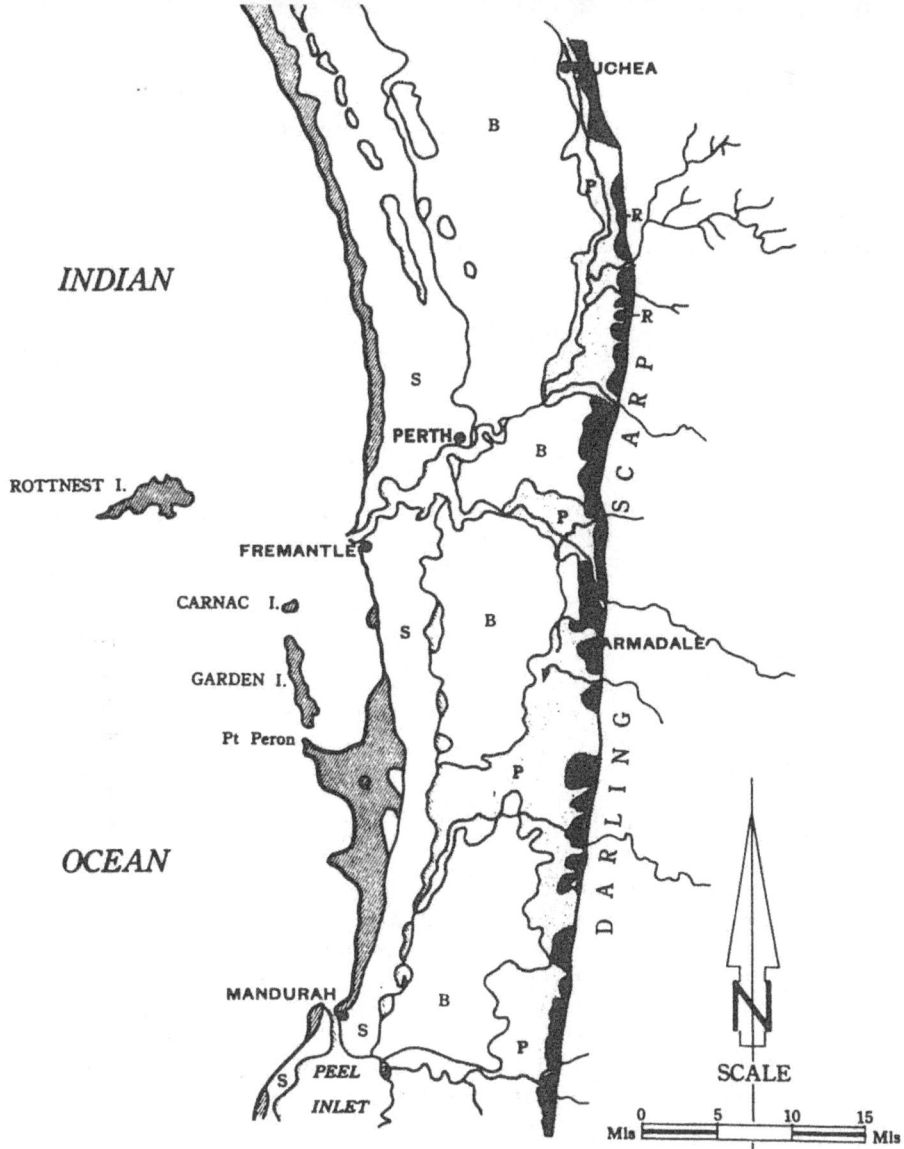

Figure 3 Geomorphic Elements of the Swan Coastal Plain.
Reproduced from 'The development and distribution of the Soils of the Swan Coastal Plain, Western Australia'. CSIRO Soil Publication No. 16, by W. M. McArthur and E. Bettenay, 1960, fig. 2a.
Q = Quindalup Dunes (coastal dunes); S = Spearwood Dunes (aeolian limestone); B = Bassendean Dunes (coastal sandplain); P = Pinjarra Plain (piedmont alluvial plain); R = Ridge Hill Shelf (foothills of Darling Scarp).
Reproduced by courtesy of CSIRO, Canberra.

pressures might change the balance from more wooded to more open country.

A transect from the coast to the interior at 32°S, the latitude of Perth and Rottnest Island, would encounter a variety of north–south zones of landscape and vegetation, first on the coastal plain, then on the ancient plateau east of the Darling Scarp. The mid-nineteenth century descriptions in the next section must be related to this geographical background.

The Swan Coastal Plain divides into four main geomorphic elements (see fig. 3), each a discontinuous belt parallel to the sea and the scarp. The native vegetation of the immediately coastal (Quindalup) dunes (McArthur and Bettenay 1960:14) is characterised by scrub formations comprising mainly *Acacia rostellifera*, *Callitris*, and *Melaleuca*—relatively vulnerable, as Rottnest has shown, to fire and grazing. These formations had not survived everywhere, and indeed in places devegetation had actually set coastal dunes in motion (see p. 103) thousands of years before the advent of Europeans.

The coastal aeolian limestone (Spearwood dunes) system (*ibid*:13) carried distinctive Tuart woodland (Gentilli n.d.:160), with some jarrah, an understorey of *Banksia* and *Casuarina*, and a ground cover of woody perennials. Although Landor (1847:54-5) found that cover so reduced in places that he encountered 'denuded hills of limestone rock' south of the Swan estuary near Fremantle, none the less his descriptions of the rest of that area, and of the thickly wooded country north of the Swan on his route to Perth, accord with the impression that little of this zone was open country in the 1830s. It was unattractive to Europeans, except around the chains of lakes which ran between the dune belts, and its main resources for Aborigines had lain in those lakes and in the estuaries.

The belt east of Perth itself, the coastal sandplain (Bassendean sands) comprises alternating low sandhills and swamps, attractive like those to the west for their resources of fish, fowl, frogs, turtles, gilgies and, above all, water; and in the availability of sandy camping spots. It is still in parts characterised (McArthur and Bettenay 1960:12) by *Banksia* scrub which can develop a very dense understorey of woody perennials, with tea-tree, sedges and rushes round the swamps. When at their driest these were fired to improve the crop of *Typha* roots, and firing might well have been necessary for free movement. From a European viewpoint this zone, like the last, was unattractive. Grey brackets them together as 'the sandy desert country which surrounds, for many miles, the town of Perth' (Grey 1841:II,292).

European farmers were interested only in the piedmont alluvial plain (Pinjarra Plain; McArthur and Bettenay 1960:12) at the foot of the Darling Scarp. Unfortunately for the early development of the colony this belt is very much divided and restricted in extent near the Swan, comprising only areas round Guildford and Middle Swan and along the Canning. It provided, however, land for the gentlemen who had first choice, including Stirling himself, to the chagrin of later arrivals. Wider extensions in the Serpentine and Harvey areas had to await improved communication for successful exploitation, though the widest lateral development of the zone, on the Murray around Pinjarra, and behind Geographe Bay, was appreciated early. This zone provides abundant evidence of Aboriginal occupation (in which the small isolated sandhills blown on to its western margin may be particularly significant) and usage, above all for hunting. Stirling's botanist, Fraser, described his view of it from the Swan as 'an extensive Plain... alluvial... covered with luxuriant grass... hilly promontories of fine red loam... extensive flats... these plains were seen to extend to the foot of the Mountains, interspersed with stripes of good forest land' (Fraser, in Stirling 1827:581).

McArthur and Bettenay interpret remnants as indicating an original vegetation on the alluvial plains of jarrah forest, with some marri, undergrowth of banksia and blackboy, and a woody perennial ground cover. Parts at least had been so modified before contact as to offer good grazing for native herbivores and, for the first settlers, parklike grazing and relatively easy clearance for cultivation (see below, e.g. p. 57).

The actual foothills of the Darling Scarp, and particularly their sandy western margin (McArthur and Bettenay 1960:9) were important in providing sites for Aboriginal occupation in focal positions (e.g. Bullsbrook, Mundijong) for exploiting the resources of several zones—upland, alluvial plain, and swamps beyond.

East of the scarp the picture must be painted with a broader brush (Gentilli 1946:157-65; Gardner 1942, particularly map on pp. xxv–vi; 1959:276-9). It suffices to distinguish the general geomorphic zones of 'Older Laterites' (Mulcahy 1967; see fig. 4), poor soils on secondarily cemented detrital laterites east of the Darling Scarp, bearing jarrah forest, with some marri, and an understorey of banksia and casuarina, blackboy and Zamia, and ground cover of harsh-leafed shrubs; and east of that a broad belt of 'Younger Laterites' interrupted by the better laterite-free soils of the Avon valley itself, the Moore River, the upper Blackwood and so on, corresponding roughly to a savannah parkland zone, where jarrah gives way to wandoo, and forest in the main to open country, with mallet on duricrust remnants, and York gum and jam tree on the better granitic soils. This varied zone is interspersed eastward with patches of sandheath, commoner towards the south coast, covered with scrub rather than woodland when not burnt clear. Farther east, salmon gum dominates more open scrub, and over the sandplain and salt-lake country many eucalypts adopt a mallee form of growth—an adaptation to survive fire by rapid regrowth of multiple shoots from a persisting woody stock (Gardner 1957).

Banksias, which predominate in the coastal limestone and sand, form an important element in the understorey of the jarrah forests and extend into the sandheaths. Banksias are among that remarkable group of species which not merely tolerate fire, but require fire for their propagation (*ibid*). The seeds remain undehisced until after a fire; special mechanisms delay immediate dispersal, so that the seeds fall when the ash is no longer hot.

The predominance of fire resistant and pyrophilous forms in the vegetation has been interpreted as indicating that fire, and fire more frequent than the few caused by lightning (Wallace 1966:40; Sparrow and Ney 1971), had affected the flora of Western Australia 'over a very long period—long enough to have eliminated any species unable to survive fire damage' (Gardner 1957:167) and to have brought to dominance pyrophilous species in the sandplain, the jarrah forest, and east into the mallee.

For economic reasons, most detailed attention has been paid to the effects of burning in forest zones (King, A. R. n.d.; Hutchins 1916; Wallace 1966). The essential points which emerge are that infrequent burning may stimulate close forest growth; more frequent burning, or a combination of burning and fairly intensive grazing, would be required to prevent the secure establishment of new growth after fire, and so maintain wide-spaced forest. If so, contemporary descriptions should provide a clue to the regime, or regimes, of firing which had been maintained up to the advent of Europeans.

Frequent burning would keep the litter on the forest floor to a minimum; burning would thus be mild and present no threat to old-established trees. Wallace (1966:34) described fires which as late as 1930 he had witnessed moving slowly during three summer months, through fifteen miles of such wide-spaced forest of mature trees. It is his opinion that forest would have to be burned every two to four years to maintain this condition. (Recent controlled-burning policies aim at burning each area every five years, and require a work force of three hundred men for that portion of the forest which remains.) This accords well with Bunbury's estimate (1930:105) of Aboriginal burning every two or three years in the 1830s. The practice was probably maintained right into this century by European settlers in parts of the South-west, who would casually set light to a stretch of bush if they thought it was getting too thick.*

The situation was very different after the start of European felling, which when unregulated would leave a residue behind on the forest floor twenty or thirty times as heavy as a year's natural fall of litter. The conflagration which would follow accidental ignition would be correspondingly severe, not merely clearing ground cover, but defoliating and

---

* Information via Glen Roberts from Mervyn Roberts, who farmed at Darradup on the Blackwood River until 1914.

severely damaging mature trees. Young second-growth trees, scrub and weed trees, which followed the opening of the canopy by a severe burn, would compound the fire problem in later years, and make recurrent severe fire more likely. We must dismiss such images when envisaging firing where there had been no felling and where Aboriginal burning had been frequent, as it must have been everywhere around the margins of the forest and across relatively narrow zones of forest (as between Perth and York), though not always across the centre of wider zones (as east of Harvey, where Grey in 1839 encountered considerable accumulations of litter).

Nor was the object of Aboriginal burning the same as that of the systematic European forest management which succeeded early unregulated felling. The European forester would wish to encourage timber at the expense of grazing; native groups had valued grazing, not timber. The forester would use fire to open up the canopy, and then encourage the dense growth of young shoots which developed from seeds falling from opened capsules on to a comparatively weedfree ash bed, by protecting them from further firing for their first few years (Hutching 1916:40). Conversely, refiring within a few years would prevent such dense growth, and under an unbroken canopy ligno-tubers would remain dormant until the collapse of an old tree opened up a light space to allow the development of a dynamic shoot into a young tree. By foresters' standards, the trees in 'virgin' forest were too widely spaced and overmature, massive hundred-foot giants such as 'T.W.H.' had encountered near the Helena in 1833 (in Cross 1833:87-8). Aboriginal firing seems the major factor producing the wide-spaced pattern of trees first encountered, and in places ringbarked, by early settlers (cf. p. 57). Where these initial clearances have been abandoned, regrowth is many times as dense as the forest of old ringbarked trunks, for example at Darradup, on the Blackwood River, where early European settlers followed the Aborigines' occupation of fertile grazing land between spring-line and river.

In summary, jarrah forest is fire-climax vegetation, and witnesses a long adaptation to fires, frequent or infrequent. The particular patterns of growth varied locally with accessibility, and hence frequency and recentness of burning. The karri forest of the wetter south coast had been less exposed and liable to fire, though not unaffected on its coastal margin (see below). The most open growth was on the eastern margin of the jarrah forest, and on the piedmont alluvial plain at the foot of the Darling Scarp; both were areas of relatively good soils and good grazing, where the forest might be most advantageously 'worked' by Aborigines.

Detailed historical descriptions of local variety must be understood against this general ecological background.

9

Man-made landscapes: some historical data

What contemporary descriptions are there of the effect of Aboriginal firing practices on south-western vegetation? What is explicit in Bunbury's account is implicit in many other descriptions from the second quarter of the nineteenth century, from King George Sound, Geographe Bay, the Swan River, inland in the Avon valley, between York and the Sound, and northward onto the Victoria Plains. The early settlers were alive to the variety of geology, from the limestones, sands and loams of the coastal plain to the inhospitable lateritic gravels capping the Darling Scarp and the deeply weathered soils of the Avon region; this diversity is clear in their descriptions. But they give also an overriding impression of openness, in areas which would not necessarily remain open when periodic and frequent burning ceased.

Some of Stirling's party in March 1827 'advanced along the Banks [of the Swan]; its *open forest-like character* afforded no impediment to their march, indeed the lowlands resemble fields of grain, for the high grass* had been turned yellow by the sun' (Letter to Governor Darling, April 1827; Stirling 1827:558).† The botanist Fraser, who accompanied Stirling, described the piedmont portions of the coastal plain and scarp they reconnoitred from the Swan as being 'covered with luxuriant grass ... interspersed with stripes of good forest land ... the summit [of the] Mountains [the Darling hills] is covered with enormous trees ... but with the exception of a few struggling *Hakea* there is no underwood' (*ibid*:581).

---

* Botanically none of the native pasture plants are strictly grasses, that is *Gramineae*.
† My emphasis—SJH.

George Fletcher Moore described the Perth area in March 1831: 'the country has the appearance of being well-wooded, but I should not say it was thickly timbered. In some places there are open plains that resemble well-ordered parks' (Moore 1884*a*:32).

But openness is not universal. As one would expect, the variety of topography and soils (see chapter 8) and the varied degrees and patterns of Aboriginal exploitation on the coastal plain, are reflected in contemporary descriptions. The most detailed descriptions are given by E. W. Landor (1847) for the early 1840s.

Some of the coastal limestone was very poorly vegetated, while the interdunal valleys carried thick bush. On a shooting expedition south from Fremantle, Landor remarked on:

> ... peppermint and wattle trees ... gay with white and yellow blossoms; an infinite variety of flowering shrubs gave to the country the appearance of English grounds about a goodly mansion ... The country presented very little appearance of grass, though abounding with green shrub; and frequently we passed over denuded hills of limestone-rock, from which we beheld the sea on one side, and on the other the vast forest of banksias and eucalypti, that overspreads the entire country. (Landor 1847:54)

Making his way by sand-track towards Perth, 'It was scarcely possible to see more than fifty yards ahead of you, so thickly grew the banksia trees' (*ibid*:64). But on the high land above Melville water, 'The forest through which we passed resembled a wild English park' (*ibid*:65).

However, on the whole, 'with the exception of the rich flats of the Swan and Canning rivers, the vast extent of country between the coast and the Darling hills is a miserable region ... except where occasional swamps appear like oases' (*ibid*:67).

The aeolian limestone and the coastal sandplain remain unattractive to agriculturalists. But the alluvial belt between these swamps and sandhills and the foot of the Darling Scarp, including land along the middle Swan, the Canning, the Serpentine, the Dandelup and the Murray, attracted settlers, including Stirling himself who took his own grant on the 'rich and extensive flats of Woodbridge' (*ibid*:98) by the Swan, near the junction of the Helena River at Guildford. 'The whole country of the middle and upper Swan resembles a vast English park' (*ibid*); only the steep slopes down to the river remained thickly 'wooded ravines'.

Among the waving corn of the settlers' fields 'rose up a number of *scattered, lofty dead trees* which had been purposely killed by ringing the bark' (*ibid*:99).*

These showed the spacing and the size of the forest cover at contact. Even though Irwin's steward was able to build his house at Upper Swan of 'mahogany cut down on the estate' (Irwin 1835:57) we must not imagine

---

* My emphasis—SJH.

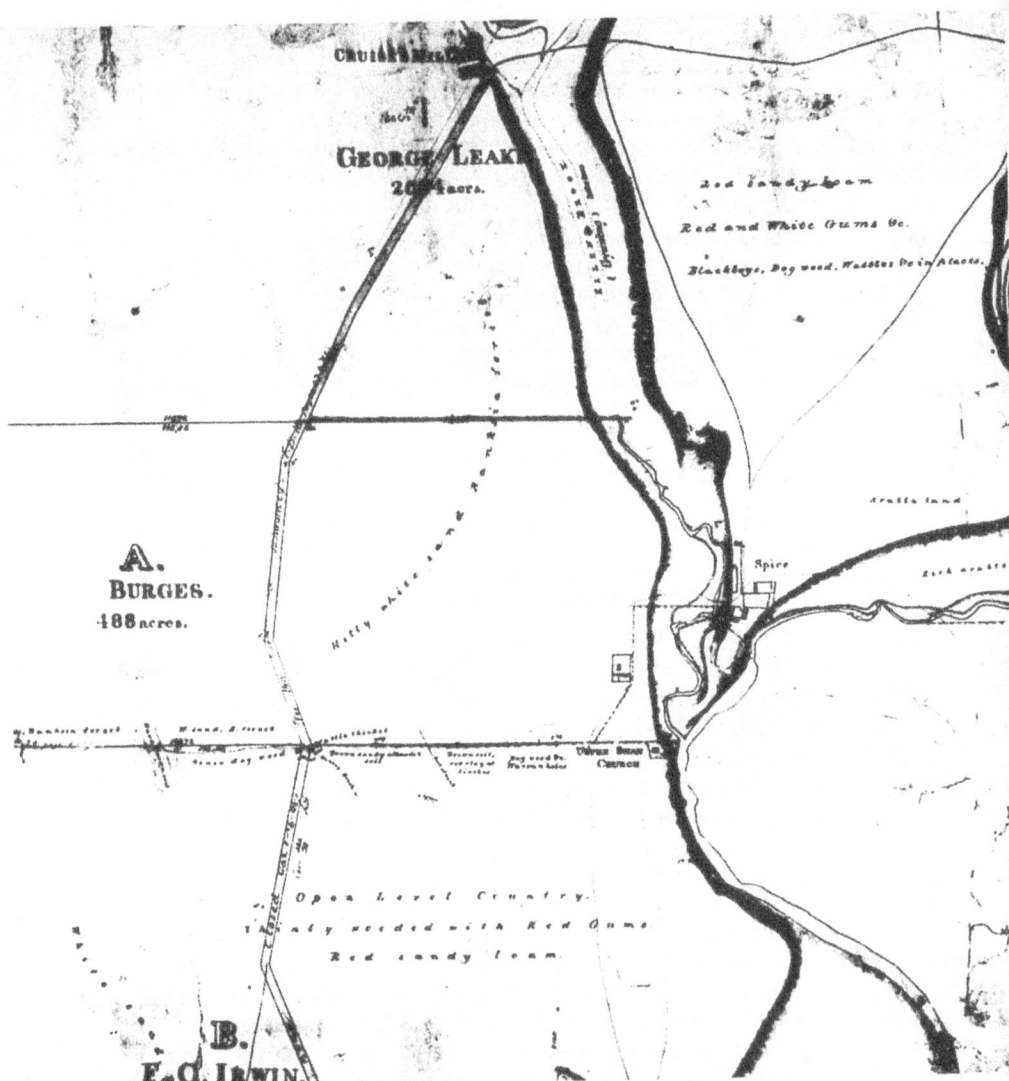

Figure 4 Part of Swan Folio No. XIV (Battye Library, Perth) being a map of 'Locations on the Right Bank of the Swan River. P. L. Snell Chauncy, Assistant Surveyor, 1843'.
Note Upper Swan Church on the west bank of the Swan opposite the junction of Ellen Brook and the Swan River, and F. C. Irwin's property immediately south, described as 'Open Level Country. Thinly wooded with Red Gums [Jarrah]'; 'Warran Holes' are marked immediately west of Upper Swan Church.
Reproduced from the original in the Battye Library, Perth.

that these original settlers on the alluvial plain faced clearance problems like those of the Augusta settlers.

South-east from Perth, Landor set off for the Canning, firstly across the sandplain:

> Passing over two well-built wooden bridges connected by a Causeway, we crossed the river and took the road for the Canning. Thick woods of banksia, wattle and eucalypti closed in the view on every side . . . lacustrine valleys . . . broad swamps choked up with reeds . . . (Landor 1847:153,157)

But when they reached the alluvial soils by the Canning River the picture changed:

> We now had a long canter which brought us to the neighbourhood of the Canning River. The country hereabouts resembles a wild English park. The trees are all of the eucalypti species, *large and dispersed;* the surface of the ground is level, affording a view of the Darling Hills, which appear to be close at hand. Crossing the river by a rustic bridge, we ascended the opposite bank . . . a farmhouse close at hand . . . a wide field of clover . . . (*ibid*:157–8)*

Continuing southward, 'we rode down an extensive plain, covered plentifully with grass, and presenting numerous *clumps* of trees . . . for several miles' (*ibid*:164).* Beyond this the hunting party continued among the rocks, hills and ravines of the Darling Range.

Another expedition on the coastal plain took Landor once more through 'park-like scenery among which the Canning river pursued its lazy course' (*ibid*: 330). He went on through country where:

> A rough coarse scrub, interspersed with small quantities of grass, overspread the sandy soil . . . open prairie . . . thick wood . . . swamp . . . brushwood and thickets . . . plains interspersed with swamps and thickets . . . rambling over plains of coarse grass, penetrating into woods, struggling through swamps . . . (*ibid*:331,335,346)

The swamps and sands of the Bassendean Sands thus contrasted clearly with the fertile alluvial flats along the Canning and the Swan, with their tall dispersed timber and open greenery, as they awaited the settler's plough and stock.

The same open landscape is described by Bunbury in the alluvial zone farther south on the Murray. He settled on a grant near Pinjarra in 1836.

> Behind my hut grew a few large Mahogany trees [jarrah] and Red Gums, while beyond, if I had continued to clear, I should command a view through *fine open country studded* with *groups* of *large trees*, under which grew a green covering to the ground. . . . (Bunbury 1930:168)*

---

* My emphasis—SJH.

Three miles downstream, where 'the Dandelup joins the Murray . . . there is on all sides an extensive tract of rich valuable grassy land richly timbered with magnificent trees' (*ibid*:169). When he chose this grant he spoke of 'the Murray river . . . flowing close under the bank on which my house is to be built . . . on each side of me is a rich grassy flat, which I can either cultivate or *leave in grass*, while behind me is an extensive plain with *scattered* clumps of *very large* straight Gum trees' (*ibid*:65).*

Intensive Aboriginal use of this area is well-attested by accounts of the European settlers' dependence on, and fear of, 'the Murray men' and the punitive massacre at Pinjarra itself (Hasluck 1965:154–7). There were fords across both the Dandalup and the Murray above their junction. European settlers could use these rich soils without further clearance. That had already been done by the natives, as Bunbury explained (see above, p. 47).

Hereabouts, in:

> . . . the last month of summer . . . the natives have burnt with fire much of the country . . . [in] May the vegetation springs again, and the burnt ground assumes a different appearance . . . Whole Districts appear in mourning at this season, and the burnt ground is particularly hot and dusty to travel over . . . (Bunbury 1930:179)

South around Geographe Bay the alluvial zone widens. Bunbury travelled from the Murray to the Vasse in 1836, and described 'good rich country . . . abundance of cattle food . . . Clay plains from the Capel to beyond the Vasse . . . no timber except for a few *scattered* Red Gums . . . swarmed with Kangaroo' (*ibid*:95–6).* We have looked at descriptions of this same countryside in similar terms (see p. 25) in conjunction with many reports of native burning. The settlers had no doubt of the causal connection.

To the north the Moore River, where it flows southward on the coastal plain, also traverses country which was both open and well-frequented by Aborigines. Grey in December 1838 made an excursion northward from Perth, travelling via the interdunal swamps and lakes of the aeolian limestone belt, and on north over sandplain where 'the whole of the country . . . was sandy and bad, being thinly clothed with Banksia trees' (Grey 1841:I,298), to the junction of the Gingin Brook and the Moore River, fifty miles north of Perth, where the much-used alluvial flats along the river contrasted with the wooded limestone and sandhills around. 'The scenery here was very picturesque: high wooded hills were upon each side of us, and the valley was open and rather thinly timbered; but the few trees it contained were of considerable size and beauty' (*ibid*:I,300). No less than sixteen men, plus women and children, eventually gathered to greet Grey (who found himself regarded as one of their kin returned from the dead).

In May 1839, Roe, pushing north to look for the scattered remnants of Grey's shipwrecked party, came at Baramba, twenty miles further upstream,

---

* My emphasis—SJH.

to 'excellent water ... deep pools ... luxuriant pasturage' (*ibid*:II,106). Further north the country becomes dry, sandy and inhospitable to European and Aborigine alike. Abandoned Aboriginal campsites of widely ranging dates are scattered over the present 'Baramba' property and those to the south.*

As on the coastal plain beyond the banksia scrub on limestone and sandplain the open landscape of the piedmont alluvial belt awaited the plough, so east of the Darling Scarp beyond the lateritic gravels of the jarrah belt settlers found fine grazing country on the better soils of the Avon and kindred rivers.

Dale's first excursion to trace the Helena River, in October 1829, penetrated only briefly into forested hills. His second expedition in December of that year had pressed through the hill country without remark on fires or inhabitants for four days and sixty devious miles before his party saw 'eastwards ... a range of mountains' (the far side of the Avon valley) with 'the smoke of numerous fires made by the natives generally close to their base' (Dale 1833*b*). The journal of Lieutenant Erskine (1833) recorded another expedition eastward 'over Darling's Range' in September 1830. They estimated they had travelled between 60 and 70 miles through 'fine open forest' before they came on eight Aboriginal huts, and another fifteen miles through hills and thick brushwood before they had clear views to the east. The country continued thickly wooded until they came down to the river where Aborigines were fishing; they then moved through many miles of 'fine rich pasture land' along its valley where Aborigines were numerous. Swans and wild fowl were abundant. On their return, 40 miles of mainly 'fine open forest' with some patches of thick brushwood were passed before they again met Aborigines at the western 'base of the mountains'.

James Henty, journeying across the Darling Range in October 1830, struggled eastward some 25 to 30 miles from the scarp: 'Iron stone pebble, quartz, and granite rocks were abundant ... the former predominated ... mahogany timber grew abundantly without a vestige of grass [until] a beautiful vale opened suddenly on us, thinly timbered' (Henty 1830).

As they continued eastward 'the soil visibly improved' until they emerged into country 'undulating and more or less grassy ... altogether different from anything I had seen in the colony ...' (*ibid*) and eventually a plain 'covered with grass and about two miles wide' (*ibid*). Several times in describing different views Henty repeated the phrase 'thinly covered with grass and lightly timbered'.

---

* Fieldwork December 1971 to January 1972, following information from Mr W. de Burgh of 'Baramba', Mr F. Edwards of 'Millbank', and Mrs R. Roe of Gingin.

The party encountered Aborigines first near the scarp, an hour's journey up the Helena, but none in the next three days and 40 miles of travelling. In the Avon valley they saw gum trees with patterns cut in their bark, shy Aborigines, and a fire to the southward. Returning westward, they saw no more trace of Aborigines until they reached the edge of the hills and viewed 'the flat coast country between the range and the sea; Rottnest and Garden Islands' (*ibid*), the Swan below them and 'further down the valley on the banks of the river several fires which ... we knew to be those of natives' (*ibid*), probably Walyunga. The pattern of parallel zones—settlement on the coastal plain and into the foothills of the Darling Range, relatively empty lateritic uplands, and settlement in the Avon valley—is reflected in description after description, and persists from the Aboriginal into the European land use picture.

Not only the river flats were grassy. The hills west of the Avon were described by Dale, probing inland in August 1831 [*sic*, but surely 1830] as 'rich and verdant ... clothed in grass to their summit ... moderately wooded with gum trees' (Dale 1833c:57). His party moved eighteen miles along the west side of the river 'over country well clothed with grass ... little underwood ... lightly timbered with a species of gum tree' (*ibid*).

In October and November 1830 Dale continued his explorations south and north from Mount Bakewell (by the site of York) penetrating first 60 miles SSE through 'country of open forest character ... lightly timbered with different varieties of eucalyptus [and] undulating grassy country' (Dale 1833e:157), then northward over 'good pasture country' (*ibid*:159).

By 1831 Moore had heard of 'a vein of good soil ... on the banks of ... the Avon' and that Captain Bannister walking to King George Sound from Perth 'passed over ... ninety miles of luxuriant pasture ground' (Moore 1884a:28) along the east margin of the jarrah forest. Accompanying Dale's party in September 1831, Moore found the Avon Valley soil to be 'a rich loam, producing *patches of grass wherever a tree had been burnt*' (*ibid*:70),* and the whole area 'open level and grassy country' (*ibid*:71). Captain Chidley Irwin described in the York area:

> ... extensive tracts of undulating surface covered with short sweet grass ... ornamented with *clumps* of trees and shrubs ... The situation is cheerful and open. Plains, *resembling park scenery*, and bearing *fine pasture* for sheep, slope down to the Avon ... low hills ... covered with good pasture ... with evergreen shrubs and trees *scattered* over the surface ... (Irwin 1835:64)*

He quotes a letter describing a 30 mile tour around York: 'splendid country ... with an abundance of grass, and a very superior feed for sheep, or that *may be ploughed* almost *without any clearing*' (*ibid*:95).* Exploitation quickly followed exploration.

---

* My emphasis—SJH.

Landor complained:

> The York and Northam districts afford a vast quantity of land suitable for all kinds of grain. The sheep and cattle runs are excellent, but they are now fully stocked and new settlers must direct their steps to the southward. (Landor 1847:249)

Moore finally took up a grant south of York, and said (October 1835) that the pasture on the hills was excellent (1884*a*:287), while southward towards King George Sound (Albany) was more good country—'an undulating country, the hills grassy' (*ibid*:286). Northward, Moore had reached the middle reaches of the river which took his name, reconnoitring from the Swan in April 1836. He reported 'the grass fine, whenever it had not been burned [recently] . . . the soil of the best brown loam' (Erickson 1971:2), and further upstream, approaching what must be now the New Norcia area:

> A hundred acres of ground in our view *might be ploughed without clearing anything* but a wattle here and there. Several miles . . . appeared to be of the same nature . . . I think it fair to presume that a good grazing country continues on the east side of the Darling Range all the way from York to this district . . . very little short of a hundred miles north . . . (*ibid*:3)*

From the York area settlement was to push south towards Albany and north via Toodyay to what became the Victoria Plains (see chapter 10). In May 1837 Moore reported in his journal: 'Settlers are now going to the interior, to the extensive grazing tracts' (Moore 1884*a*:309).

This initially pastoral zone lies roughly within the zone of 'Younger Laterites' distinguished by Mulcahy (1967:216), swinging rather east of south from the Victoria Plains, through the Toodyay–York area, southward towards Williams and Kojonup, north of Albany. Here, 'as we approach the inland margin the forest opens out and gives place to a narrow zone of savannah woodland in which York gum is associated with *Acacia* . . . and the grass flora comparatively well developed' (Gardner 1959:279), a situation likely to result from, and to invite, human exploitation. The Aborigines were already fully exploiting the resources of this area. In doing so they had opened up and improved the land for European exploitation (see p. 73–4): land abounding in kangaroos and grass could be made to abound in sheep and grain. Landor's account of pastoral establishments south of York illuminates landscape and inhabitants:

> Our sheep are generally kept on a squatting station on the Hotham some sixty or seventy miles south of York . . . a broad valley abounding with grass and scattered gum trees . . . We go wandering with our flocks from one patch of good grass to another . . . an immense grassy plain, eight or nine miles wide, without a tree upon it . . . [August] 18th . . . It rained

---

* My emphasis—SJH.

> tremendously ... the natives happened to be hunting in a large party, driving the game before them; and as I stood in the midst of a large plain which they had surrounded on three sides, multitudes of kangaroos—I believe I might say thousands—of all sizes came rushing past me ... in the evening fifty [Aborigines] came about the hut. (Landor 1847:249–59)

Such abundance—of indigenous inhabitants, open land, good grazing and game—was not restricted to one small area.

> It is not until the granite range of the Darling hills is passed over that the principal agricultural districts are found. There are the farm settlements, the flocks and herds of the colony. From the Victoria Plains north of Toodyay, for hundreds of miles to the southward, comprising the fertile districts of Northam, York, Beverley, the Dale and the Hotham, is found a surface of stiff soil, covered over with straggling herbage, and many varieties of trees and shrubs. (*ibid*:67–8)

The pattern of European settlement in Western Australia about 1840 would thus divide into three parallel north–south belts: a scatter of clusters (by the Swan, Canning, Murray, Leschenault, Vasse and Blackwood estuaries) along the western coastal plain; the relatively empty zone of jarrah forest east of the Darling Scarp; and farther east again a belt of intermittent settlement running from the Avon valley (the York–Northam–Toodyay area) down to King George Sound (cf. Hasluck 1942:25).

This third, pastoral, belt ran through the 'savannah woodland' formations (Gardner 1942:xliv–xlviii and Plate X, p.ii) on the eastern margin of the jarrah forest where, as in Tasmania, anthropogenic factors might be expected to affect the balance between forest and open 'parkland' and grassland.

East again are patches of sandheath. But the patchiness of the vegetation which is clear in early descriptions of areas east of a line from Albany to the Avon may be due as much to patchy firing as to soil differences. 'T.W.H.', accompanying Dale eastward from the Avon in October 1830, described the first few miles as 'country ... free from trees ... covered, where it is not burnt up, with a low scrub. This brought to my mind an English common' (T.W.H. 1833:213).

Sandy shrub-heath country, reminding the explorers of English commons, may have had a similar genesis under a combination of firing and grazing pressures, 'open common' alternating with 'thick and almost impenetrable' bush (Dale 1833d:68). They continued to encounter

> ... considerable patches of land ... completely clear of timber ... There are hundreds and thousands of acres of land about this part entirely clear of wood, mostly sand ... open undulating country, very sandy ... a tract of better land with a fair quantity of wood ... two native huts ... the smoke of a native fire ... a view of the native fires ... the native grasses in this part are very good and grow very strong ... (T. W. H. 1833:214–18).

The extent to which 'grassy forestland' may be the product of native burning is suggested by a later journey by Roe, who ranged well eastward into the mallee, but returned westward to the eastern margin of the forest north of Albany. Roe in 1848 travelled south-eastward from Perth towards Esperance. In November he passed over 'tracts of country in which their fires were burning' (Roe 1852:15). He found early in December (*ibid*:27) abreast of Esperance Bay that 'tracks and fires of natives were numerous', and set up bivouac 'amongst burnt sticks and scrub at a brackish pool'. Returning westward he followed at one point 'a beaten track of the natives behind the sea-coast hills' (*ibid*:50). At the east side of the Stirling Range they encamped in 'grassy forestland . . . *extensively fired by natives*'.* On 18 January 1849, they travelled over 'a grassy forest country' and next day found 'the country around . . . extensively burnt by natives' (*ibid*:55). Returning towards Bunbury, he crossed the Blackwood, where 'whitegum became replaced by red . . . better able to withstand periodic bushfires' (*ibid*:55).

Irwin (1835:22) estimated the total Aboriginal population of the settled areas at no more than a thousand; other estimates were higher, Stirling attributing 750 to the Perth area alone (Ogle 1839:62). Moore (1884*b*:84) cited three thousand for the 'located parts of the colony' in 1840.

Whichever the total (see pp. 107–10), these few Aborigines had opened up a landscape in which it was possible for Europeans to move around, to pasture their flocks, to find good soils for agriculture, and water sources for themselves and their stock. The European communities inherited the possibilities of settlement and land-use from the Aboriginal communities. But in so doing, they robbed these communities of the land which had mapped out the patterns of their existence. The dynamic design of the seasons with their appropriate and inevitable economic, territorial, social and ceremonial round was disrupted. Yet each group remained tied to its land.

> Each tribe has its territory and landmarks. If but one is disturbed it experiences a difficulty in falling back, and retiring upon the tribes in its rear, who are similarly situated in their turn. They continue, therefore, to hover about their ancient grounds and depend for their subsistence upon them. (Irwin 1835:107)

The European community thus created the circumstances in which the skilled developers of the land appeared as indolent ne'er-do-wells, who needed encouragement to acquire the means of regular subsistence (*ibid*:70).

---

* My emphasis—SJH.

10

Aboriginal and European movement and settlement

The progress of exploration and settlement had depended and continued to depend on indigenous knowledge, use and development of the country and its resources—'native wells', 'native paths', clearance and vegetation patterns dependent on Aboriginal firing. In Bunbury's opinion (see above, p. 47) the 'grazing and pastoral advantages' of the country depended on their firing.

From the first, Aboriginal informants and signs of Aboriginal use had led the explorers and settlers to water and good land. Vlamingh (in Major 1859:92) on the banks of the Swan found footsteps and several small pools of fresh water, and next day 'a crowd of men' who fled from 'a little pool of fresh water' with footsteps around it. The French explorers, south of Geographe Bay, had observed of the Aborigines that their huts were exclusively along the river and marsh—similarly their saline wells which the explorers themselves had to use (Peron and Freycinet 1807:1,79).

Another party observed several trenches, several feet deep, acting as wells (*ibid*:83). On the Swan, upstream from the shallows at Heirisson Isles, they took water from 'une espèce de petit puits . . . qui ne me parut être l'ouvrage de la nature' (*ibid*:182; 19 June 1801).

Mr Fraser of Stirling's 1827 party, alone by 'a spring of delicious water' (Claise Brook or Walter Brook?) upstream from what is now the Heirisson Island Causeway, was visited by 'three armed natives', and the whole neighbourhood (now East Perth) had 'many traces of its being much frequented' (Stirling 1827:556).

East from this point the traveller bound inland from the coast first encounters the swamps and sandhills of the Bassendean Sands (McArthur and Bettenay 1960). Landor described Perth as having 'a never-failing supply of fresh water from a chain of swamps at the back and wells fed by by them are never dry' (Landor 1847:65). No doubt these were European wells, but they had Aboriginal precursors,* on the evidence of both the French and the English sallies.

The area around Perth city itself (see fig. 4), with the river abounding in fish on one side and freshwater lakes abounding in food on the other, had been, and continued to be, a centre of Aboriginal settlement. James Kennedy, born in 1848, recalled from his boyhood (1927:7–10) 'natives in dozens', spearing cobblers on the waterfront below St George's Terrace and the Esplanade (see also Hammond 1936:185) and camping farther afield by swamps where now are Hyde Park Lake (one mile north of the General Post Office), Monger's Lake (two miles north-west), and Shenton Park Lake (two and a half miles west). Hammond (1933) as a boy in the 1860s frequented the 'native camp' near which his grandfather, William Leeder, had built his house by Monger's Lake. Daisy Bates (1938:69–70) tells of Fanny Balbuk, 'the last Perth woman' who had been born on Heirisson Island (only a mile and half east from Perth's General Post Office) and who followed from there each day the 'straight track' which led to the swamp (now under Perth railway station) where she gathered gilgies, breaking fences and charging through houses where they interrupted her right of way.

Not only in a general sense, by utilising the same tracts of country, but in a very specific sense, by using the same network of nodes (at water sources) linked by tracks, the European pattern of land use was based on (and modified) the Aboriginal pattern. Hammond, reminiscing of life in the sixties, seventies, and eighties, remembers: 'All through the Southwest there were pads of natives, like cattle pads and just as plain' (Hammond 1933:18). The tracks ran from Perth to North Fremantle, across the river, on to Bibra Lake, Rockingham, Mandurah, and alongside the Murray to Pinjarra; another two crossed the river near the Causeway, to Canning, Bibra Lake and south; they led through Kelmscott to the Pinjarra ford and on to Bunbury, Busselton, and the extreme South-west.

Landor's advice to anyone 'travelling in Australia', even on the coastal plain near Perth, was 'Unless, therefore, the ground be well known, it is always advisable to take a native, who can advise you where the pools and springs are situated' (Landor 1847:331). To move through the Southwest, even in the 1880s, Hammond 'had to have the assistance of a native who kept me out of thick timber when travelling across country'

---

* Aboriginal well-digging is a topic which requires separate treatment. Wells were certainly important in summer even on the coastal plain (e.g. Grey 1841:I,324 for a well between the Leschenault estuary and the Harvey), but particularly so on the arid stretch north of the Moore River (*ibid*:II,67,80, 101,114). For other examples see below, pp. 68–9, 71.

(Hammond 1936:112–13). European movement even then depended on Aboriginal tracks, cleared zones, and knowledge.

Similarly in Tasmania, Roth (1899:153,167,171) had reported both specific paths and zones of open country through which Aborigines travelled 'keeping the country burnt for that purpose', contrasting with heavily timbered country 'not occupied by natives'. It was country kept clear, burnt and used by the Aborigines, which attracted early European settlement (Kemp 1963:247). In south-east Australia also, important lines of Aboriginal movement, here largely along river courses with soakages and waterholes, had been inherited by European travellers and graziers (Mabbutt 1971:74). Mrs Erickson (see for example 1969:38; 1971) is one of the few writers who has realised that water supplies dictated that European movement and settlement must follow Aboriginal movement and settlement in Western Australia also. '*Bidi*' and '*Gongan*', zones of easiest and habitual movement between water sources, were as basic to European as to Aboriginal ecology.

Through country they had kept open, Aboriginal groups had moved systematically from camp to country yielding roots, from fishery to grassy hunting ground, from water source to river crossing. 'Native wells' and 'native paths' marked their regular progress through and around their own country. Explorers looking for new pastures reported again and again on wells, grassland and paths.

Lieutenant Dale and George Moore, setting off in September 1831 to explore further the country beyond the Darling Range, had bivouacked east of Guildford, and followed 'a native path leading up the hill' (Moore 1884*a*:67).

From Princess Royal Harbour, Albany, Wilson in December 1829 'proceeded by a native path nearly seven miles nor-northwest' (Wilson 1835:237), and came on 'several flocks of kangaroos ... frequent traces of native dogs ... a native ... on a hunting expedition ... to assist in driving the kangaroo ... *good open forest* land without much timber ... a native reservoir of water' (*ibid*:240–4).* Differential burning is suggested by his notes: 'suddenly re-entered on fine open land; several hundred acres without a tree ... left the good land' (*ibid*:249).

In May 1831 Collie (1833*a*:145), returning from the Porongorups, could not find water except 'far down in narrow deep holes dug by the natives' to which his guide conducted him. In February 1832 he crossed King River at 'the usual wading place of the natives' (Collie 1833*b*) and followed an old path from there 'to the crossing place and huts where boats are stopped at low water on the Kalgan' and continued on along the same path, past an Aboriginal well. Dale (1833*c*) had followed this path for six miles in setting off from Albany for the Stirlings. His journey included 'dense

---

* My emphasis—SJH.

forest', 'patches of good land and grass' and, south of the Porongorups, 'a rich tract of land covered with grass'. The patchiness again suggests firing. Bannister (1833:107) came into Albany from the west by a 'native path'.

The party from a whale boat beached near Northcliffe followed another such path towards Augusta from the east (Anon. 1833b:121). Coming north towards the Vasse they discovered two successive Aboriginal wells, and from the Vasse towards Bunbury set off along a path, which they afterwards abandoned, regretting it when they realised that it would have brought them more quickly to the point at which they must cross the Preston (ibid:127). They were then able to follow a path northward the whole length of the Leschenault estuary (ibid:128).

Such tracks reflected constant movement and usage. Firing was both a deliberate part of such usage and an accidental consequence.

The Leschenault estuary was a veritable Hyde Park Corner of native tracks.

Bunbury, travelling southward from the Murray in December 1836 and January 1837, was escorted by Aboriginal guides along a very tortuous track to their ford across the Harvey, near the weirs at which they took fish and crayfish, by the Miellup lagoons where they took black swans in the breeding season and still 'along native paths' to:

> ... the head of the Leschenault estuary upon which we soon arrived by a *well-beaten* path ... at a small *native well* among the tea trees ... There were several signs of [people] being very numerous in the neighbourhood ... owing to the facility of obtaining fish, a wholesome and plentiful food. *Numerous* and *well-beaten* paths near the banks of estuary indicated the *constant presence* of *considerable numbers* ... many deserted huts ... They would not dare to move at night without a fire-stick ... for fear of the evil spirits ... The numerous lights I saw along the water's edge ... were for attracting fish ... which are speared by this means in great numbers, both in the shoal water on the flats, where the natives wade out to spear Mullet and Cobblers, and also on the banks of the river where *fires on a large scale* are made ... (Bunbury 1930:74–7)*

Was this smoke-drying of fish? Bunbury was followed later in the day by '[no] fewer than one hundred blacks, and often nearer two hundred ... most being elderly or lads' (*ibid*:79), that is all males, so women and children must be added for total numbers. The abundant population gathered around abundant resources—wild fowl (brown ducks, teal, swans); fish (mullet, cobblers, jewfish, tailor and black schnapper); game on good grazing, a 'most rich and luxuriant crop of grass'; and a sweet drink concocted from 'the flower of Banksia from which they extract a

---

* My emphasis—SJH.

sweet dew' (*ibid*:80). Among such plenitude, no wonder they were able to proceed 'along the edge of the Estuary for some miles ... along a native path near the edge' (*ibid*:78) to the crossing of the bar at the mouth of the Collie, two miles below 'a native ford', and to follow into the bush 'a well-beaten path' which would take them to 'a native crossing place' on the Preston (*ibid*:80–2). Bunbury's party had encountered another hundred and fifty Aborigines at the Collie, and 'a large number of native men' (plus women and children) at the Preston, bound for 'a great Corroboree with some. other tribes' (*ibid*:88–95). Another 'good native path' took them onward from the Preston, though from this 'well-beaten path' they became lost in 'an infinity of paths' through thick spearwood swamps before they came into 'an undulating Tooat country of considerable extent, with plenty of grass' (*ibid*:92) and a new guide led them on to a 'well-beaten path' to the Capel and the good rich country of the Vasse.

The whole impression is of a highly articulated patterning of movements and activities, and so of landscape features.

Fire (for light, protection against spirits, fishing, warmth, and large-scale cooking) must have caused frequent bushfires along these zones of frequent summer activity and movement, and so have contributed to keeping them clear and making free movement possible for the many Aborigines and the few Europeans who followed and eventually displaced them.

> A good Native path follows ... the inner side of this line of swamp ... with little interruption ... from the Murray, as far ... as ... nine miles beyond the Vasse. (*ibid*:90)

One route was the precursor of the Old Bunbury Road from Pinjarra, and the direct line of the Old Coast Road up to Mandurah followed another branch from the Leschenault estuary track system.

Where resources were most abundant the country was most clear. The 'belt of open country ... from the Capel to beyond the Vasse ... swarmed with Kangaroo' (Bunbury 1930:95–6). It had 'no timber except a few scattered Red Gums' (*ibid*). Much of this area has now become overgrown with peppermint trees. It proved initially most attractive to European settlers.

Bussell found on the Vasse easy walking along 'native paths which traversed these lawns in every direction' (1833*b*:194). The Bussells, and later other Augusta settlers including the Molloys, eventually abandoned the difficult heavily-wooded karri country of Augusta in the farthest south-west and settled around what is now Busselton. This was the country of 'parklike appearance, with long waving grass, and abounding also in kangaroos' (Georgiana Molloy in letter of January 1833, in Hasluck 1955:103) which John Bussell (1833*a*) had rhapsodised about (see p. 60

above). The Bussells built their house (called 'Cattle Chosen') on the grassland by the Vasse where they found their cow, Yulika, who had been lost in the bush for a year. This incident typifies the way European settlers chose, as good pasture for cattle, land which was also good pasture for kangaroos, and equally valued, frequented, and maintained by its original inhabitants. Captain Molloy in 1839 explained to Governor Hutt why he had moved to the Vasse, it 'being the most frequented part with the greatest number of settlers, the greatest quantity of livestock, and the most numerous native population' (Hasluck 1955:184).

Aborigines were not attracted by European settlement, but vice versa. Aboriginal settlement was heavy throughout this belt of good fired and cleared pasture close to the excellent fishing of the Vasse estuary. John Bussell speaks of 'the natives being so very numerous on the Sabina' (*ibid*:124) which flowed into the same estuary. The French explorers had encountered many fires, paths, and traces of settlement here, around and inland from Geographe Bay, in 1801 to 1803 (see above, p. 21).

John Bussell celebrated in verse the assistance he received from the Aborigines when he moved from Augusta to the Vasse in 1834:

> Welcome as a lover to a maiden's eye
> Passed a wild native to his own wild land,
> His friendly guidance showed the spring hard by
> We filled our pails to cheer the thirsty band.
>
> (Shann 1926:56)

The Aborigines 'shook hands and showed us to the native well' (*ibid*:57). But while the European might take land, 'the natives' must not steal. In September 1835 'Natives stole an axe and were fired upon' (Bessie Bussell's diary in Shann 1926:100).

In July 1836 appears the entry: 'Three women, one man, one boy are known to be dead, but more are supposed to be dying' (*ibid*:107). In August 'a plan was set on foot to go and search after the natives' (*ibid*).

John Bussell, cleric and would-be poet, took a hard-line policy. His home and the lives of his family were at stake.

11

'The place that will be ours'

John Wollaston, another cleric, saw and deplored what must happen when he talked in 1842 to the botanist James Drummond, who had been north into the Victoria Plains country where European settlers were seeking new pastures. He stated explicitly that land good for Aborigines was land good for Europeans:

> *Warrang* (a root which forms a staple diet for the natives) abounds. This root flourishes where the best feed for stock is found. Hence the usurpation of the ground and the secret destruction of the aborigines. (Wollaston 1848–56:144–70)

Thus Bindoon, one of the earliest areas to be settled northward from the Swan–York axis, means a place where yams grow (Glauert 1950). The Brockmans 'heard from natives of beautiful running water and rich land at Gingin' and founded the first farm there (Cowan 1931:49). 'Cheriton' and Gingin thrive. The Aboriginal encampments west of 'Cheriton' are now archaeological sites only.* On two farms just south of the township Aboriginal yam-digging grounds are still discernible as areas of holes and humps.†

Thus, an abundance of resources and population was the cue for Aboriginal displacement. Aboriginal guides led the way for Aboriginal dispossession in the Victoria Plains. The Toodyay area was opened to selection in 1836. Drummond, Anderson and others went to look at the area, taking an old Canning River native to 'see water'. They learnt that:

---

* Information from Mrs R. Roe of Beermullah and field survey 1971.
† Information from Mrs Roe, March 1972. (See above, p. 13).

> *Duidgee* ... was a favourite haunt of the natives ... on account of its natural produce ... the reed mace [which] grows in abundance ... of great importance to the native as furnishing a great portion of the food of their women and children for several months of the year. (Erickson 1969:31)

The Drummonds selected Hawthornden, Yule the 'Byeen'; Scully chose Bolgart and later leased the 'Byeen'. Aborigines who came to the perennial Bolgart springs told Scully of good waters to the north. In February 1841 Drummond, Phillips and Scully explored northward for more pastures, finding 'extensive grassy plains' near the Moore River where Moore had reported them five years earlier. Scully's report runs:

> Country open and grassy ... intervening country open and grassy ... Murra Murra ... fell in with a party of natives, who told us this is the first year this pool has been dry. They then took us to a spring (Badji-Badji) ... the country in every direction was open, undulating and grassy. (Erickson 1971:7)

The Drummonds established a sheep station here, not far from the Moore River, but next year they again joined Scully in looking for more land north of the river, where 'the aborigines told them of good springs for summer water' (*ibid*:8). The country was sufficiently open for them to move by dray.

Wherever there were springs frequented by Aborigines, the area around was clear and grassy. On another such expedition:

> Aug. 23rd ... we reached a permanent spring called Yoolgan where there is excellent grass ... In ten or twelve miles we reached Yeinart, a tea-tree swamp where there is grass and water to be had throughout the year. 25th Badgee-Badgee ... Mouran pool ... ten or twelve miles through splendid grassy country and met with a large tribe of natives [who] offered us some of their favourite root, the *wyrang*, which grows abundantly among these grassy hills ... the most splendid grassy country I have ever seen in Australia ... (Landor 1847:362-9)

When in 1846 Dom Salvado and his companions planned to establish a mission, they set off from the Byeen in Scully's dray with two Aborigines to help pick the site, and shared the waterhole of their first establishment with their precursors.

In 1846 the Lefroy brothers (leasing Bolgart) were looking for more pasture. Gerald's journal unconsciously sums up the relationship between Aboriginal and European usage:

> 30 Nov. 1846. *Went exploring with a native ... found good country and good water. If I remain in this colony I saw today the place that will be ours.* (Gerald Lefroy's diary, in Erickson 1971:16)*

---

* My emphasis—SJH.

In 1847 he was established at Walebing, a hundred miles north of York. Visitors to the substantial early colonial structures erected by his neighbour James Clinch at 'Berkshire Valley' may admire the Aboriginal relics in the mud-block stables.

By the late 1830s and early 1840s settlement had pushed southward from York (see above, p. 63) and linked eventually with exploration north-westward from Albany to exploit the better soils within the belt of 'Younger Laterites' (Mulcahy 1967) along the eastern margin of the jarrah belt. The Kojonup area (Bignell 1971) typifies the repeated conjunction of Aboriginal watering places and 'country ... *extensively burnt by natives*' (Roe 1852:15),* with 'pasturage sufficient to feed the whole of the sheep now in the colony' and many acres 'fit for the plough without a tree to check its progress ... near a pool of water' (Hillman and Roe's 1840 survey reports, quoted in Bignell 1971:30). Repeatedly, it is the Aborigines who direct the Europeans to pools and watering places (*ibid*:1,29,30). There was a numerous Aboriginal population (three hundred once gathered round the Kojonup barracks) and abundant resources—for European as well as for Aborigine. Captain Symer summed up his impressions of the grant he chose: 'the natives call it Balgarrup—fine grass lands, abundant water ... everywhere fertile and beautiful' (Glover 1954:85).

Further exploration continued to depend on indigenous knowledge, and indeed aid. The Gregory brothers in 1846, sallying east and north from the Victoria Plains to find yet further pastures, relied again and again on existing wells and associated good grass (1884:2–12). The following may be quoted: 9 August—'a native well'; 13 August—'native well among flat granite rocks'; 22 August—'excellent grass around a native well'; 27 August—'a native well in a small grassy valley'; 28 August—'a native well and some good grass'; 6 September—'a native well'; 15 September—'a native well in a patch of York gum trees'; 18 September—'country timbered with York and red gum ... the soil a red loam, producing some grass and abundance of everlasting flowers and "Warran" or native yam ... good country' (meaning good for European pastoralists); 20 December—'a large party of natives, some of whom accompanied us for about a mile, pointing out places where we should find water'. On 25 September 1848, A. C. Gregory, leading a settlers' expedition northward from Perth (1884:16–30) looking for new pastoral country '*halted for the night in a patch of good grass, where the thicket had been burned off by native fires*'.* Along the Murchison, he found movement possible only where burning-off had been recent—'an immense plain covered with thickets ... the bush fires which had *burnt some large patches* greatly assisted us'.* On 3 October they were halted by 'thickets of wattle so dense that, although burnt by natives about four years previous they would have been impassable'. As

---

* My emphasis—SJH.

they returned patches of grass around native wells again punctuated the route.

These last quotations strongly suggest that the constant conjunction of grass and water was due to firing. From elsewhere in Australia there are explorers' accounts which not only support this interpretation, but see the firing as deliberate, not accidental:

> The natives seem to have burnt the grass systematically along every watercourse and around every waterhole *in order* to have them surrounded with young grass as soon as the rain sets in ... Their burnings were not connected with camping places where the fire is liable to spread from the fire places and would clear the neighbouring ground. Long strips of lately burnt grass were frequently observed, extending for many miles along the creeks. The banks of small isolated waterholes in the forest were equally attended to ... It is no doubt connected with *the systematic management of their runs*, to attract game to particular spots ... (Leichhardt 1847:354; quoted in part by King n.d.:12)*

Deliberate or accidental, such pasture improvement made possible European movement, and the expansion of European settlement, throughout and beyond the South-west.

It is remarkable that improvement by burning should apply not only to the drier country to the north and east, but also to parts of the dampest areas of the South-west.

Even in the far south, burning made the land more attractive to European settlers. Grahame in 1861 found country west of Broke Inlet 'covered with long coarse grass well adapted for cattle ... We came across a party of natives who were burning the ground' (Stephens 1954:53). The timber country 'consists chiefly of peppermint and tangin with some groves of blue gum [karri]' (*ibid*).

One can understand the conflict which ensued when on such 'grasslands well adapted for cattle' the Aborigines came to complete an essential phase in their economic social and ceremonial year. Grahame's own homestead was near Kojonup. Here in 1862, 'On 15 Dec. my home and all it contained was destroyed by fire ... a native set my run on fire which spread to my house while I was absent' (*ibid*:56). Such conflicts of interest were only ever resolved in one way.

Eastward beyond the Avon valley into what is now the wheat belt, and east again towards the goldfields, the pattern persisted. For instance, the owners of the station at Jilakin Rock, 150 miles inland, obtained from an old sandalwooder the native legend of the isolated grove of jarrah trees there. He, in turn, had got the tale from Aborigines who used to follow a track down from Southern Cross to camp at Jilakin Rock and well (Murray-Gordon 1952). So by the 1860s sandalwood trails followed

---

* My emphasis—SJH.

Aboriginal trails from soak to soak and camp to camp; and settlers, gold-miners, and by the 1890s surveyors, followed the sandalwood trails into the wheatbelt and beyond.

The European usurpation which Drummond had deplored was accepted without question by the Lefroys and most mid-nineteenth century settlers. The assumption of superiority implicit in their every word and action ('the place that will be ours') is perhaps even more shocking than the exaggerated, explicit formulation of the same assumption in the hubristic prose of 'empire builders' like Byrne:

> But as they have been passing from creation they have performed their allotted task; and the fires of the dark child of the forest have cleared the soil, the hills and the valleys of the superabundant scrub and timber that covered the country and presented a bar to its occupation. Now, prepared by the hands of the lowest race in the scale of humanity . . . the soil of these extensive regions is ready to receive the virgin impressions of civilised man . . . (Byrne 1848:II,321)

So in south-western Australia, as elsewhere on the continent, European distributions and lines of communication followed Aboriginal distributions and lines of movement, and both owed much to the opening-up of the landscape by Aboriginal usage and particularly firing—both incidental to camping, gathering and travel and as part of the deliberate management of plant and animal resources. The major differences between the two patterns were firstly that the European settlers would use only a part of the resources and range of the Aboriginal group, though in doing so they would disrupt the systematic exploitation of the entire area; secondly, that the region would therefore support far *fewer* Europeans on its own primary produce than it had Aborigines; thirdly, that certain parts from which Aborigines had been displaced would remain unused (or not used to the full) by the Europeans; and fourthly, in other areas the long-term stresses on the environment would be far greater under the new specialised and concentrated usage than under the old diversified exploitation.

Thérèse Kemp stresses the first of these points for Tasmania.

> The earliest farms were established in the Midlands area . . . from the distribution of localities where implements were found, this was precisely the area of densest Aboriginal population. Settlement disrupted migration patterns, and in particular denied the east coast aboriginal his summer hunting and protein diet. (Kemp 1963:247; cf. Jones 1971: map on p. 276)

Rhys Jones in his discussion of Aboriginal and European populations in Tasmania makes no distinction within the European community between primary agriculturalists and that part of the population depending on minerals, manufactures and secondary services, and bringing in its food from outside the area. He does make it clear however that large parts of

Tasmania have been left unused and unpopulated (Jones 1971:282). If this is true for the moist climate of Tasmania, it is doubly true for the arid interior of the continent. Cleland says of the Western Desert 'the native population . . . are making a much better use of this country than we ever can, and the density of their population is many times that of any possible white one' (Cleland 1935:77).

Preliminary results from a distributional study based on detailed field survey and a review of the ethnographic evidence for an area round Perth (stretching from the Moore River basin to the Murray, and from the coast to the Avon valley) exemplify the dependence of European usage on Aboriginal usage, and the incompleteness of the former compared with the latter (Hallam 1972*a*).

European patterns of occupance resembled Aboriginal in their emphasis on the good soils of the Avon valley and the piedmont alluvium, and the relative emptiness of the jarrah between. The fact that European settlement was densest near the estuaries was partly due to the new element of river transport, partly to the use of Aboriginal 'pad' patterns and crossings in establishing the original track network and its nodes. Concentration was a function of ease of communication, rather than of full use of resources. The European, however, essentially ignored the abundant fish, fowl and plant foods of the sandplain swamps and the interdunal valleys of the aeolian limestone—the 'sandy desert' of the coastal plain around Perth. Grey and his little party staggered back starving in 1838, passing by swamps north of Perth where the natives who succoured them grew fat on frogs, turtles, 'barde' grubs, nuts, fish and fowl (Grey 1841:II,88–93) and roots harvested after the swamps were fired (*ibid*:II,294; Hallam 1974).

In the middle years of the nineteenth century, 'Some of the settlers on the Canning River and in the York district were at times almost dependent on the natives for food, and this during a course of years' (Chauncy 1878:231).

Stokes summed up the European view of the resources of the Swan River Settlement in one memorable phrase: 'You might run it through an hour glass in a day' (Stokes 1846:I,50). The European exploitative system was initially *less* efficient that the Aboriginal, and supported fewer people (about 2300 in 1840—Hasluck 1942:19); though these were far from being supported solely on local resources.

How old-established were the integral patterns of ecological and ritual usage which Europeans thus disrupted, and in which fire had been an essential component?

12

Fire in myth and ritual: earth and water

I have looked at Aboriginal use of fire as it was observed by the first Europeans to explore and exploit the South-west, as it integrated into patterns of Aboriginal ecological activity, and as it affected the terrain Europeans were taking over. The close integration of firing into the Aboriginal cognitive schema has been examined only through vocabulary, and not through other symbolic data—art, myth and ritual. These remain to be examined. At the same time, I shall ask whether it is possible to demonstrate the *past* role of fire in the changing usage and appreciation of territory and resources by earlier Aborigines as they explored and developed the potentialities of the South-west.

The evidence is scattered, diverse and inadequate, but sufficient to establish both the great antiquity and the great importance of fire and firing in past cognitive and ecological patterning, and to show certain related demographic trends.

The data are in part biogeographic and geomorphic; in part archaeological, from excavation and from survey; and in part symbolic, embracing art, myth and ritual. This last category is the most diffcult to use and evaluate in this context. But essays such as those by Frake (1962) among ethnographers, and Marshack (1972*a*, 1972*b*) among archaeologists, using symbolic data to generate cognitive–ecological explanations, show that the attempt can be valuable and must be made. They also show that such analysis of constructs requires a detailed and therefore lengthy treatment to demonstrate its relevance. This will be attempted first, before considering the other categories of evidence, and finally essaying a synthesis relating firing to exploitative and demographic trends.

Ritual and myth, categories of data in which the South-west might well be expected to be deficient, can in fact contribute substantially to emphasising the ancient importance of fire in Aboriginal life patterns.

We have some indications of actual rituals which involved fire. Peron, exploring up the Vasse River south of Geographe Bay in 1801, discovered on the bank a large tree garlanded with greenery, surrounded by grass, then by a semicircle of white sand, patterned with burnt reeds and edged in turn by trampled black sand, that again by a semicircle of turf, comprising some 27 'seats' of greensward; the whole set within a semicircle of a dozen large trees, stripped of their bark. The triangles, lozenges and irregular polygons of the design had been made by standing large numbers of reeds, regularly spaced, in line in the sand, and *burning* them:

> ... l'on avoit planté un grand nombre de joncs, placés tous à une distance égale les uns des autres, et distribués de manière à former une suite de figures ou plutôt de charactères réguliers: tous ces joncs avoient été brules jusqu'au niveau du sol, de manière à présenter autant de points noirs, arrondis, et qui se détachoient fortement du fond de sable blanc ou ils avoient été plantés. (Peron and Freycinet 1807:74–5)

Other evidence of rituals involving fire came from an excavation at Frieze Cave, near York, in the Avon valley 60 miles east of Perth, undertaken by the Department of Anthropology of the University of Western Australia in November 1970, and possibly from the 'Orchestra Shell' cave north of Perth excavated in May 1970. To these we shall return after examining myths to which these rituals may be linked. But first there is another category of rituals involving fire, which emphasise its radical importance in the total Aboriginal conceptualisation of life and death.

The Lake Mungo cremation (Bowler *et al.* 1970,1972) provided dramatic confirmation of the early date which Davidson (1948) and Hiatt (1969) had predicted for cremation in Australia. Fire was used in burials for 15,000 to 20,000 years before Tasmania was separated from the mainland, and continued in use thereafter. Betty Hiatt (1969:111,104) regretted that evidence from the South-west was inadequate to support Davidson's (1948) contention that 'the peripheral appearance of cremation suggests that it is a relatively old custom'. Although true cremation was lacking in the South-west, burial rituals involving fire were widespread, and these reinforce the evidence for both the antiquity and importance of fire in the conceptual as in the economic life. The details varied from area to area.

George Fletcher Moore described a burial at Middle Swan in August 1837, when the dead man's beard was singed and a fire lit in the grave. It is not clear whether this was before or after the body was placed there (Moore 1884*a*:329). In another burial in May 1838 (*ibid*:345–7) and in Moore's general description of burial customs (1884*b*:11), the beard was singed, fire used to strip the nails from the thumb and one finger, brushwood was burnt in the grave, and the ashes brushed out before the body was placed in the grave:

> ... for a long time afterwards a small hut of reeds or boughs may be observed erected over the grave, before which a fire is frequently lighted, that the spirit of the deceased may ... continue still to solace itself as before, in the quiet of the night. (*ibid*:12)

Grey narrated the procedure followed at a burial near Perth itself in June 1839:

> When the grave was completed, they set fire to some dried leaves and twigs, then, throwing them in, they soon had a large blaze on it ... Weeban ... knelt ... to discover in which direction the *boyl-yas*, when drawn out of the earth by the fire, would take flight ... The fire roared for some time loudly in the grave ... (Grey 1841:II,326)

Similarly on the Vasse, by Mr Bussell's account, the diggers threw dry leaves into the grave when it was finished, and set fire to them before placing the corpse in the grave (*ibid*:II,332).

The function of fire *in* the grave before burial was thus thought to be to drive away evil spirits. In an account of the Murray (W.A.) tribe 'as told me by old colonists' William Smart recounted that 'before the body was placed in the grave a fire was burnt in the hole to frighten the devils out of it' (Smart, n.d.). Fire was powerful and destructive, and could avert the malignancy of evil spirits and of the dead, but it was also life-giving and comforting, and could provide solace to the friendly dead. The ambiguity appears in several accounts.

For the Perth area Curr (1886:I,330) implied that 'wood and brush were thrown into the grave, and set fire to, so as just to singe the hair off the body' *after* the body was placed in the grave. These accounts would agree with the small amounts of charcoal found with a burial near the Swan at Claremont (between Perth and Fremantle) excavated by Dr Ian Crawford in January 1970.

Curr's York correspondent associated fires lit for the benefit of the dead with fear of evil spirits by the living:

> The Whajack believe in evil spirits and ghosts ... as widows and mothers fear that the lately dead may visit their camps at night to warm themselves, they make a fire at a little distance from their own for the special use of the departed. This practice is carried on for some months. (*ibid*:339)

A fire *by* the grave was noted for the Kojonup area (*ibid*:348), at King George Sound (Grey 1841:II,334), and further east (Hassell 1936:702). Le Souef (n.d.:399) recorded that after burial 'a fire is kept burning for some weeks'.

Mrs Robin Roe of Beermullah recently recorded the memories of an old man of 82 who recollected a burial place near the junction of the

Gingin Brook and the Moore River (c. 35881268) where the Aborigines 'put a billy on the Christmas tree and sticks for a fire nearby for tea when the corpse came to life after dark'.* Such customs imply an ambivalent attitude both to the dead and to fire. Each is to be treated with friendly propitiation, and with caution.

The use of fire in connection with burial, and to render harmless and propitiate the dead, is one aspect of an antithesis seen between fire and evil spirits, and between fire and a powerful serpent who should be avoided and propitiated. Sir George Grey recounted:

> The natives believe that the *night-mare* is caused by some evil spirit. The way in which they get rid of this evil is by jumping up, seizing a lighted brand from the fire, twirling it around the head, and muttering a variety of imprecations; they then throw the stick away in the direction they conceive the spirit to be in. Some of them have explained this ... by stating that this evil spirit wants a light, and that when he gets it, he will go away ... If they are obliged to move away from the fire after dark ... they carry a light with them, and set fire to dry bushes as they go along. (Grey 1841:II,339-40)

Eyre (1845:II,357) noted the use of fire to keep away evil spirits, particularly at night.

Stokes visited the Swan River settlement during the voyage of H.M.S. *Beagle*. In a fine romantic passage he spoke of:

> ... an evil spirit haunting dark caverns, wells and places of mystery and gloom, and called *Jinga* ... Miago had never seen this object of his fears, but upon the authority of the elders of his tribe he described its visible presence as that of a huge many-folded serpent; in the night when the tall forest trees moaned and creaked in the fitful wind, he would shrink terrified by the solemn and mysterious sounds and tell how, at such a time, his countrymen kindle a fire to avert the actual presence of the evil spirit, and wait around it ... chanting their ... rhythmical incantations ... for the coming dawn. (Stokes 1846:I,58)

Roth, relying mainly on Robert Austin's account of the Bunbury district in 1841-43, recounted similar beliefs:

> ... at night time the earth was permeated with evil spirits whom they feared. Such spirits could be checked or repelled by means of fire ... something supernatural lying in ambush in every deep water, or in any fairly-sized permanent waterhole—some ... snake, or iguana inhabiting it. (Roth 1902:52-3)

Moore's *Vocabulary* contains the following entry:

---

* Information from Dick Jones of Gingin, given to Mrs Roe 26 October 1971.

> *Waugal*—An imaginary aquatic monster, residing in deep dark waters, and endowed with supernatural powers, which enable it to overpower and consume the natives... Its supposed shape is that of a huge winged serpent... (Moore 1884b:75)

He echoes here Sir George Grey's account (1841:II,339).

The antipathy of serpent and fire, and the connection of the serpent with water and also with dark caverns, are themes seen as recurring within and without the South-west of Australia. I will set out some elements in these serpent and fire tales, then examine their occurrence.

Paradoxically the serpent was among the original bringers of fire, a rôle he, a creature of water, shares with the birds, creatures of air, and women, diggers of earth, whose digging sticks sprout fire and who hide fire in their vulvae. Fire springs from earth into air; the rainbow and lightning, both associated with snakes, link fire and water, air and earth. Thus in the north the essence and the antithesis of fire and water are both symbolised through the medium of a waterdwelling serpent, ambivalent, powerful and dangerous. In a Murinbata (Northern Territory) myth, this *Kunmanggur* took all the fire, meaning to extinguish it in water, from which it was retrieved for human use by the Kestrel, who then fired the countryside (Maddock 1970a:186). Kenneth Maddock (1970a) has studied Australian myths concerned with the acquisition of fire, firstly in Arnhem Land, where he ordered a number of myths as segments within a supermyth; then elsewhere in the north and east, where already-recognised themes recur, some quite specific and detailed. He interprets these shared features as indicating 'an ancient fire mythology [over] an indefinite area of south-east Australia'. Some of these common elements are recorded in Tasmanian stories (Maddock 1970a:195), suggesting part at least of this corpus had developed before the separation of Tasmania 12,000 years ago, confirming the importance of fire in the life of the Aborigines from at least the late Pleistocene. If the use of fire in the 'Western Third' of Australia shared a similar antiquity, we might expect to find some elements of these fire (and serpent) myths in the South-west.

The serpent is of course widespread, but one might not expect much evidence of his importance or his association with water and fire to survive in the South-west. In fact serpent beliefs had a very long life in this region. At the eastern border of Western Australia, the Eucla people regarded the treeless limestone Nullarbor Plain as 'the haunt of an immense serpent which had devoured all the animals, grass and trees which are supposed, ages back to have grown on the now barren waste' (Curr 1886:I,401).* Daisy Bates (1938:132) associated this 'mighty magic snake

---

* Does this story hold some echo of a wide and fertile coastal plain devoured by the sea (cf. Wright 1971a, 1971b)? Or of the joint effects of the consequent increased population pressures, and perhaps increased firing with increasing aridity on the vegetation of an arid, limestone area?

called *Gumba*' with the blowholes which lead into underground caverns, often with lakes, like Koonalda 'the gates through which *Gumba* passes to his sea home'. The Yirda Meening (Curr 1886:I,402) believed that thunder was made by the black snake, and had tales of monster birds, and men and women who ascended to the Milky Way (*ibid*:I,402–3); these recur as elements in fire myths further west.

Daisy Bates saw the *woggal* themes permeating the folklore of the Bibulmun of the South-west. Deborah Buller-Murphy (1958:7–10) retold Aboriginal stories from the extreme south-west, including a Rainbow myth, in which *Wagal*, a sea-spirit, and *Gilgie*, a land-spirit, both figure, and the story of an evil giant snake who infested a pool near the Scott River (*ibid*:32).

For the area around Perth Landor recounts tales of two spirits, one associated specifically with the pools and limestone caverns of the Yanchep area.

> Beside *Chingi*, the evil spirit who haunts the woods, there is another in the shape of an immense serpent, called *Waugal*, that inhabits solitary pools ... One day, whilst bivouacking in a lonely and romantic spot, in a valley of rocks, situated some forty miles north of Perth, called *Doodamya*, or Abode of Dogs, I desired a native to lead my horse to a pool, and let him drink. The man, however, declined with terror, refusing to go near the pool, which was inhabited by the *Waugal*. I therefore had to take my horse myself to the spot, while the native stood aloof, fully expecting that the *Waugal* would seize him by the nose and pull him under water. (Landor 1847:210–11)

A description of this same Yanchep valley by Sir George Grey, travelling south in December 1838, makes clear why its pools might be expected to contain an inhabitant of deep, dark, underground waters.

> I left the main party with two natives, and travelled up a swampy valley, running nearly in the same line as the chain of lakes we had followed in going [north]. The natives insisted on it, that these lakes were all one and the same water; and when, to prove to the contrary, I pointed to a hill running across the valley, they took me to a spot in it, called Yun-de-lup, where there was a limestone cave, on entering which I saw, about ten feet below the level of the bottom of the valley, a stream of water running strong from S. to N. in a channel worn through the limestone. There were several other remarkable caves about here, one of which was called Doorda Mya, or the Dog's house. (Grey 1841:I,308–9)

Another cave in this same aeolian limestone belt, the 'Orchestra Shell' cave half-way between Yanchep and Perth, has on its roof slope straight grooves, a single splayed and many meandering snake-like markings (probably made with a handheld claw) and evidence of fire from about 4,500 B.C. to 200 A.D. (Hallam 1971). The joint occurrence of undulating multiple-line markings, and the use of fire in a context unlikely to be domestic, echoes Koonalda (Wright 1971a, 1971b). Serpent legends are associated with both the Nullarbor limestone caves and the Perth aeolian limestone.*

Recently yet another similarly marked cave was discovered in the coastal limestone just west of the Harvey estuary, 60 miles south of Perth (Hallam 1972a), with fresh water available at the deepest level (as it may have been in the 'Orchestra Shell' cave, if the level of Lake Neerabup was accessible before collapse and slumping occurred). These various remains and stories from the coastal limestone caves suggest a body of ritual–symbolic traditions concerning a serpent associated with water and with dark caves, approachable only with due ceremonies, with fire as an essential element in both the myth and the ritual aspects of the tradition.

Similar traditions extend eastward into the wheat belt. From the station 'Stanton Springs', a prolific source of water in the open pasture country south of York, Mr Bostock reported around the turn of the century:

> The natives have a strong superstition concerning [the spring]. The old ones who believe in the *woggle* (snake) are scared of the spring, and they flatly refuse to get into it and clean it out and are definitely frightened when anyone else does so. (Auld 1954:40)

Mrs Erickson (1969:118) has gathered similar tales of the great snake *Moulack*, and of sacred snakes in every permanent waterhole, from the country eastward from York towards Kellerberrin.

Radcliffe-Brown summarised the nineteenth-century accounts of a serpent who lives in water, antithetic to fire:

> I have been able to trace the belief in the rainbow-serpent living in deep permanent waterholes through all the tribes from the extreme south-west at least as far north as the Ninety Mile Beach and eastward into the desert. In the tribes round Perth ... certain waterholes are pointed out as being each the abode of a *wogal* ... (Radcliffe-Brown 1926:22)

In addition to the main serpent–fire theme, are there any subsidiary elements in this body of mythology which may be common to the north and east and to the South-west, and so emphasise the ancient and essential bond between the ritual and the ecological aspects of the use of fire? The next two chapters examine this question.

---

* It remains to be seen whether the Perth basin caves may once, like Koonalda, have given access to supplies of silicified Eocene limestone, or whether the abundant fossiliferous chert artifacts of the coastal plain were obtained by trade westward from distant sources along the south coast, or from sources now offshore (Glover and Cockbain, 1971).

13

Fire in myth and ritual: earth to sky

Outside the South-west, the snake myths of the Kimberleys are well-known (Crawford 1968:103–13) and are connected with water, the rainbow and the sky as in Arnhem Land (Maddock 1970b:452–4, 461). At least one Kimberley legend links a snake and the moon (Crawford 1968:106–9). The serpent coiled round the moon (*ibid*:fig. 93) reminds us that round Exmouth Gulf the Rainbow Serpent was equated with the moon's halo (Radcliffe-Brown 1926:22). Rows of parallel dashes decorate the bodies of some Kimberley snakes (Crawford 1968:figs.90,93,97), particularly the Gibb River python and her young (*ibid*:fig.94).* Once more, snake and fire appear antithetic (*ibid*:113).

Are any of these specific mythic, artistic and ritual elements associated with fire and serpents in the iconography of the South-west? The moon appears in association with Dale's Cave, Gwambygine, containing negative hand stencils and a painted red disc overlaid by a white mesh (Serventy 1952). In Frieze Cave, half a mile away, the parallel-dash motif is painted in snake-like form on the roof; fire-using rituals were probably employed. They are linked, by the art and myths of this cave and its neighbour, to stories of the heavenly bodies, movement between earth and sky, and fire. I shall look at Dale's Cave and its stories first, then at analogous fire stories, and return to the Frieze Cave evidence.

---

* The parallel dashes might perhaps be looked at as a special variety of splash spots. Splash spots are regarded by the Aborigines as signifying especially the Rainbow Serpent. They could be speculatively interpreted as symbolising rain spots (Maddock 1970b:462). Notice that repainting Wandjinas may bring rain and lightning (Crawford 1968:50) and that some Wandjinas also have rows of parallel dashes decorating their bodies (*ibid*:pl.19,36).

Dale's Cave was discovered and described by Ensign Dale during an expedition 'to the eastward of the Darling Mountains; in August 183[0]' (Dale 1833c:57). It is 'in the face of a granite cliff overhanging the valley of the Avon River' (Chauncy 1878:222), about five miles south of York, and half a mile west of the river.

George Fletcher Moore, visiting the cave the following year, doubted that it was a place of worship because 'the natives do not appear to have any object of veneration, nor is there any indication of a path leading to it' (Moore 1884a:73). Later he associated it with the moon. 'The natives can give no rational account of this. They tell some fables of the moon having visited the cave and executed the work' (Moore 1884b:25). Sir George Grey collected legends about the cave, but unfortunately he cautiously avoided detail:

> I had been told that the natives had some very curious traditions current amongst them with regard to this last cave, and after having visited it ... I set about collecting some of the native stories that related to it. These legends all agreed on one point, that originally the moon, who was a man, had lived there ... beyond this there was nothing in common to them all ... and the amount of marvels and wonders [each narrator] unfolded ... were exactly proportioned to the quantity of food which I promised to give him. I once or twice charged them with trying to impose on my credulity, and ... they only laughed, and said 'that was a very good thing which they told me, and the ... (white men) liked it very much'. (Grey 1841:I,261)

James Drummond, the botanist, journeying south in 1840 from Toodyay towards the newly opened areas of Williams and Kojonup, was taken to inspect this cave:

> A most curious cave called by the natives the Moon's House ... remarkable for having imprinted in the living rock a circular figure eighteen inches in diameter together with several mysterious prints of the human hand. The tradition of the natives is that the moon made these marks when he existed here in the shape of a black. (Wollaston 1841–44:100–1; Erickson 1969:55)

Chauncy in 1849 visited and described this cave. Those from whom he enquired feigned nonchalance, but eventually he obtained a story 'that the moon once dwelt in that cave, but becoming tired of the confinement, he ran up the roof of the cave, leaving his imprint at the top as he jumped into the sky, where he has been wandering around ever since' (Chauncy 1878:222).

What connection has a myth of a heavenly body moving between earth and sky with fire tales? At Gwambygine, in the moon stories from Dale's Cave and the snake-like line of parallel dashes in Frieze Cave, we may suspect some echo of the moon–snake linkage in Kimberley legend. We may go further afield, and connect these Western Australian tales and sites with general notions and specific details recurring throughout the north and east of the Greater Australian continent, including Tasmania (Maddock 1970a); in these beliefs fire is linked with movement between earth and sky, the heavenly bodies, birds and a snake.

A Tasmanian legend (Smyth 1878:I,461–2; Maddock 1970a:195) tells of two men who are now Castor and Pollux who from the summit of a hill threw fire among the black men, who fled frightened, but returned and made a fire with wood; the two men also used fire to revive two women killed by a stingray; all became stars. The stingray has here the role of the serpent, antithetic to fire. In a River Yarra story (Smyth 1878:I,459) a woman, now the Pleiades, kept fire in the end of her yamstick. The crow made snakes, put them under an ant-hill, and invited her to dig for eggs; she turned up snakes, and he ran off with the fire which fell out of her yamstick when she struck the snakes. The crow scattered the fire among men and started a grass fire. Other Victorian variants (Howitt 1904:430; Maddock 1970a:193) portray varying roles for women and men, involve birds versus snakes, hiding places within the earth and high on mountains, sky-spirits, and people who become heavenly bodies—usually stars or a planet.

Occasionally the sun or the moon figures in a similar myth. From Maryborough, Queensland, Howitt (1904:432) recorded the getting of fire by men who travelled far and found that the sun came out of a hole in the morning and went into another at night; rushing after the sun, they knocked a piece of it off and thus obtained fire (Howitt 1904:432; Maddock 1970a:190). Once more, fire origins are connected with movement between earth and sky; at the lower end of that movement, fire (the sun) has a hiding-place in a hole. Mountford reports a Tiwi tale of an eagle and a kestrel who make fire, from which torches are lit, the larger carried by a woman who becomes the sun, the smaller by a man who becomes the moon (Mountford 1958:25–6; Maddock 1970a:185).

Several early descriptions of Dale's Cave interpret the circular painting within it as the sun (for example, Dale 1833c:57) although Chauncy (1878:222) by implication equates it with the 'imprint' of the moon, who 'jumped' into the sky. The red circular patch is now overlaid by a mesh of white lines, suggesting a net. This need not necessarily controvert a sun or moon interpretation, for fire is caught or kept in a bag in several of the stories brought together by Maddock (for example 1970a:191). Possibly Dale's (1833c:57) 'rudely carved image of the sun' and Chauncy's moon imprint are both echoes of a story in which moon *and* sun have male and female roles: compare the Wuradjeri myth (Berndt and Berndt 1964:413) in which, to reach the sky, spirits must pass through a fissure guarded by a Moon-Man with coiled serpentine penis, and a Sun-Woman with fire hidden in her womb. Here the waning and waxing Moon presides over death, as over conception; his 'supposed powers over a woman's functions

... made him a creator god' in north Queensland (McConnel 1931) and probably elsewhere. The lighting of fires in graves in the South-west accords well with such a notion of fire as life in the womb of the Sun-Mother, while the antithetical Moon-Serpent is yet essential to renewal, springing skyward like flame.

The Gwambygine myths recounting movement of heavenly bodies between earth and sky may well be part of a fire-myth cycle. Dale's Cave is a shelter high in a scarp, ready for a heavenward leap; yet it is approachable by a hole in the roof, which from above is a hole into the earth (as in the Maryborough story). Frieze Cave is approachable by not one but several deep and narrow shafts between the great granite boulders of a high hill, leading through dark and difficult crevices into the rear of the shelter (compare ten Raa 1971 for similar settings in Africa). These are suitable settings for earth–sky myths and for fire rituals.

The probable fire-connection of stories of movement between earth and heaven is underlined by a south-western fire-story of a great tree at Kellerberrin, 60 miles east of Gwambygine. The story is found in Hammond's reminiscences, edited in 1933 by Hasluck. Hammond was born in 1856. When a child living in the house of his grandfather, William Leeder, he used to play with the original inhabitants camped by Lake Monger (Leederville); he later travelled extensively with Aborigines throughout the South-west for many years and knew their language well. Hammond recounts:

> In the early nineties I went with several others out eastward from Northam for some hundred miles or so on a kangarooing expedition. We took an old Eastward native with us. He was born at Kellerberrin, was about 65 years of age, and had learned to speak good English. Sitting at the camp fire one night, this old native told us a story about a very large tree to which the eagles used to come and build their nests. Sometimes, he said, these big eagles got the little picaninnies and took them to their nests to feed the young eagles. The blackfellow could not throw a spear or a 'koilee' up to the nests or climb the tree, so they made up their minds that the tree had to be burnt down. All the natives from far and near had to come to help burn this tree down. This took many moons (months) to do, and wood for the fire was carried from all the country within a radius of half a mile of the place.
>
> The old native said that he could take us and show the mark of the tree on the ground where it had been burnt up. We went on about ten miles from where we had camped that night, and he showed us a place where there was an outline on the ground that seemed to suggest that a huge tree had been burnt up there. According to the outline, its length on the ground would have been something over 500 feet, its trunk something over 17 feet in diameter and the width across its branches over 70 feet. Inside the burnt outline not a vestige of herbage or shrub was growing, and the old black said that grass and bushes would never grow in that place again, and that no blackfellow trod on the cleared spot for fear that the '*jingee*'

might come. He said that no one could tell when it was done. The outline was plain and completely bare, though many years had apparently passed; and another strange feature was that this was not a district where any large timber was growing. (Hammond 1933:64–5)

The *jingee* or serpent figures in this fire story. Note also the role of the birds; the fire made with wood as in the Tasmanian legend; and the tree tall enough to be at least a partial bridge between earth and heaven, like the Roper River tree (see below) or the hill in the Tasmanian 'Castor and Pollux' story.

The Kellerberrin story is not alone in Western Australia. Calvert (1894:38) tells, without precise location, of an evil spirit, *Mullion*, who 'lives in a high tree and seizes blackfellows to devour in a higher abode, for he lives in the Milky Way'. Here again there is an evil spirit; a tall tree acts as a jumping-off point towards heaven; in this version not only children, but people in general ascend; and they are taken not merely up the tree, but right up to the Milky Way. Tales of movement between earth and heaven via a tall tree are widespread (for example, Howitt 1904:433 for South Australia) and in one such story the climber becomes the moon (*ibid*:428). In a myth recently recorded near Balranald (Hercus 1971) Eaglehawk put a small child high up in a tall tree, from which it was rescued by the Brown Tree-creeper, who in so doing dropped his fire-stick into a hollow within the tree, which burned down and fell, forming a ridge dividing Yunga Lake. Like the Kellerberrin tree, this tree–fire–eagle–earth–heaven story linked with an observable natural feature.

The Kellerberrin story also resembles a Northern Territory (Roper River) myth (Spencer and Gillen 1904:628–9; Maddock 1970*a*:187) of a great pine tree, by which men, women and children used to climb up to and down from the sky; in a dispute between hawks the country was set on fire and the pine tree burnt down, so that the people have had to remain in the sky. Crystals implanted in their heads, knees and joints flash as stars. There are several points here which parallel south-western tales. Firstly, birds (at Kellerberrin, eagles; in the Northern Territory story, hawks; at Balranald, eagle-hawks) have a recurrent connection with fire throughout Australia. From the Fraser Ranges Mrs Bates recounts a women's song of how the *karrgain* or blue pigeon brought fire to men (article in *The West Australian*, n.d.). Secondly, a country-wide fire is a common feature but it is rather different from the great Kellerberrin fire for which the wood had been deliberately gathered. Thirdly, the people stayed in the sky. The Kellerberrin and Balranald trees were so tall that when children were taken up by eagles they could not be reached. Movement between earth and heaven is represented in the Kellerberrin story, in Calvert's tale, and in the Gwambygine moon story, for which there are northern, eastern, and Tasmanian analogies. Fourthly, this northern fire myth—like others, for example in Tasmania—involves stars, which are present also in the 'Mullion' tale, but not at Kellerberrin. Lastly, the linkage of stars and crystals, explicit in northern myths, may be implicit in the south-western evidence also.

Crystals, the sky, heavenly bodies, fire and power against (and of) evil spirits form a set of linked themes for which we can find south-western instances, and which will bring us back to serpents and fire rituals.

14

Fire in myth and ritual: crystals and caves

Crystals, embodying the properties and powers of fire, formed a component in ritual complexes which included blood-letting, the cutting of decorative scars, and decoration of rock surfaces with engraved or blood-red slashes.

In Frieze Cave, Gwambygine, two perfect crystals and an industry of minute backed blades in crystal quartz were found in excavations late in 1970. Many early accounts of Swan River Aboriginal beliefs mention sorcerers and crystals. Sir George Grey discussed:

> *Boyl-yas*, or native sorcerers ... [who] can transport themselves through the air at pleasure ... If they ... dislike ... a native, they can kill him by stealing on him at night ... They enter him like pieces of quartz ... Another boyl-ya has, however, the power of drawing them out ... in the form of pieces of quartz. (Grey 1841:II,337)

A terrified Aborigine told him: 'The *boyl-yas* eat up a great many natives, they eat them up as fire would ... They come moving along in the sky' (*ibid*:II,339). Once more the properties of fire and of movement through air were equated, and the fire might be embodied in quartz. Moore also quoted the supposed power of the Aboriginal magician to transport himself through the air (1884*b*:13). Scott Nind described the sorcerers'

> power of driving away wind or rain, as well as bringing down lightning or disease upon any object of their or others' hatred. In attempting to drive away storm or rain they stand out in the open air, tossing their arms ... to remove disease ... they are less noisy, and make use of friction, sometimes with green twigs perviously warmed at the fire. (Nind 1831:41)

Lightning thus shared fire–air properties; crystals also had star-like, fiery, ethereal components. Grey added 'the natives of South-western Australia likewise pay a respect, amounting almost to veneration, to shining stones or pieces of crystal ... None but their sorcerers are allowed to touch these' (Grey 1841:II,340).

Crystals were used on sacred occasions involving men only, and were not to be looked at by women. Some of the old men would carry such objects (ochre, gum, crystalline quartz, hair) in a dilly-bag hanging in the left armpit (Roth 1902:62).*

> All natives believe in sorcery ... They have many sacred implements ... carefully kept concealed ... especially from the women, such as pieces of rock crystal ... blood letting is practised occasionally ... by opening a vein in the arm with a piece of rock crystal. (Eyre 1845:II,359,361)

Quartz had of course uses other than sorcery. Some of these uses were sacred or semi-sacred, others purely secular. Chauncy specified that 'Western Australians use small splinters of quartz for making the long deep cuts which may be seen on every native—both men and women—across the breast and arms' (Chauncy 1878:250), and gave three additional uses for quartz splinters when hafted: as cutters for trimming kangaroo skins, as teeth in a saw-knife, and as barbs in a spear (*ibid*:280–1). Millett (1872:365) mentioned the use of quartz for spear-barbs and for cutting decorative cicatrices. The secular uses for quartz spicules are not our concern here. But we should note that special virtue resided in those pieces, unhafted it would seem (Eyre, *loc. cit.*), which were made from crystal quartz, and that these were ritually essential in ceremonies which involved opening a vein. The physically essential attributes of such a ceremonial-surgical instrument would be a sharp point, and a blunt back on which pressure could be exerted. Small pointed blades in crystal quartz dominate the archaeological content of the Frieze Cave deposits, backed occasionally by using a facet of the crystal, but more usually by steep blunting retouch. The radiocarbon dates from the cave show this presumably ritual usage of backed blades to have persisted right up to contact times (Hallam 1972a).† Crystal blades might also be required for cicatrix-cutting, for which again neither Chauncy nor Millett specified that the splinters used were hafted.

---

* Ethnographic examples have been described over a long time-span. See Etheridge 1890:370–1;1891:39–40,pl.VIII,4; Radcliffe-Brown 1926:19,22; 1930:342; Elkin 1930:349.

† This does not necessarily, or even probably, imply late use of backed blades for ordinary domestic and economic purposes. Late surface assemblages are dominated by fabricators and small amorphous quartz chips, presumably used as spear and knife components. Assemblages on domestic sites which span a presumably earlier phase include a backed-blade component. (Studies by Mr R. Pearce, Department of Anthropology, University of W.A., are in progress.)

Analogies from outside the South-west may suggest the possible ceremonial contexts which may be envisaged.

Davidson (1935b:157–9) found lumps of calcite cached in a niche in a cave in Wardaman territory (Northern Territory) and described the way such stones were ceremonially used to make rain. He found none in archaeological excavations in Wardaman caves, including the rain increase site at Delamere. Arndt (1962:170) found the Wardaman still recognised calcite and quartz crystals as rainstones. His informant, Kulumput, said that 'the old fashion way for making rain was to cut the Old Man Rain to make him bleed' and showed 'rain cuts' or parallel grooves adjacent to animal, snake and serpent paintings on the east face of the rock, on whose opposite face the Lightning Brothers had recently (within the last half century) been painted. Though Arndt dismissed Davidson's idea that the rock-cut grooves resemble cicatrix patterns on the bodies of Wardaman adults, he none the less cited Curr's (1886) description of rain-making rites in Central Australia in which the old men of the tribe were actually slashed with stone knives.

The Delamere incisions are reminiscent of those at Willeroo (Mountford and Brandl 1968), at Nackara Springs (Edwards 1965) and Morowie (Tindale and Mountford 1926) in South Australia, and at Devon Downs on the Lower Murray*; the considerable antiquity of the latter incisions is proved by their having been buried under archaeological deposits containing microliths (Hale and Tindale 1930). On the Murray sites the arrangement is in rows. McBryde has described (1964) an even more regular arrangement of engraved parallel grooves in multiple friezes (very like the multiple *painted* friezes in Frieze Cave), on sites from the Clarence valley in northern New South Wales (Nobby's Creek, Seelands, Whitman Creek and Upper Copmanhurst). She suggests a functional analogy with the 'rain cuts' at Delamere. At Delamere, and in Arnhem Land in general, the context is an extensive body of legends and paintings concerned with the production of rain, thunder and lightning, in which the source of the lightning is either a stone axe or a serpent. The red of blood and the red of fire link incisions or red parallel dashes, in ritual caves as on ritual participants, with quartz blades and crystals and the fire-virtue they hold.

Probable evidence of fire rituals in south-western Australia comes from an excavation undertaken at the end of 1970, with the kind permission of Mr Merton Clifton, as part of the Archaeological Survey Project of the Department of Anthropology of the University of Western Australia,

---

* Wider analogies might draw in the whole body of Australian linear markings, including Kintore, Cutta-Cutta and Koonalda; and glance towards recent work on 'scratchings' in the upper Palaeolithic and Mesolithic of Europe (for example Marshack 1970a, 1972a). This fascinating topic cannot be pursued here.

under the sponsorship of the Australian Institute of Aboriginal Studies. The site was Frieze Cave, five miles south of York. Charcoal was sparsely scattered throughout the deposit in and around a gully running from back to front of a deep shelter in an enormous granite boulder, one of a hill of great boulders half a mile west of the granite scarp which edges the west side of the Avon valley. A small amount of moisture was seeping into the gully from the rock-face behind, and probably from between and under the boulders. The roof of the shelter was decorated serpent-fashion with rows of parallel dashes similar to those which adorn the snakes of the Kimberleys (see above), or for which in engraved form McBryde (1964) sees a rain increase function.

Ensign Dale and his men sheltered in August 1830:

> ... under a shelving rock ... of considerable size, having the shape and appearance of a thatched roof of a cottage. In the neighbourhood of our bivouac, and for some distance around, were large masses of granite: in one of these we discovered a cavern. On one side was ... a representation of the sun [and] the impression of an arm and several hands. This spot appeared to us to be used by the natives as a place of worship. (Dale 1833c:57)

The description of the first shelter coincides with the appearance of Frieze Cave. The second, Dale's Cave, is well known, and its paintings have been described many times (for example, Serventy 1952). The Frieze Cave paintings remained undescribed, though visitors engraved their names, for example Wall and Massingham in November 1848.

Dale's party did not mention that Frieze Cave was painted. The inconspicuous painting—a row of parallel dashes, in places multiple, in an undulating frieze from end to end of the 40 foot shelter has been repainted in parts several times, and there are a few additional motifs (radiating lines, a stencilled hand) in deep red, all later than the original simple design in orange ochre and earlier than the final retouchings, after roof-flaking, in a poor yellow ochre. Swallows' nests in the roof lie over part of the frieze.

In this cave and its neighbour are drawn together many elements in the sky-sun-moon-stars-crystals-fire-birds-tree-earth-cave-womb-blood-red-firestick-serpent-water-fertility complex of ideas. Other areas may help us to envisage the sort of rituals which may have occurred, although these must not be interpreted as detailed analogies. Gould (1969:121–8) recounts ceremonies at Pukara, a sacred waterhole south of the Bell Rock Range about a thousand miles east of Perth. After lighting fires and sprinkling penis blood over rock piles about a mile away, four men of the Two Watersnakes cult-lodge had burnt off the bush round the waterhole. The eldest had painted his chest with parallel lines in red ochre to represent the chest scars of the Two Watersnakes. The blood-sprinkling was 'just like rain' to maintain supplies of *wama* (sugar) from the *Grevillea* flower. Next day they cleaned out the waterhole, finding in it pieces of water-logged wood and smooth natural rocks, which belonged to the Watersnakes. They painted the rim of the pool with red ochre, and inscribed serpentine designs with their fingers on mud which they spread over an adjacent embankment. In western Arnhem Land ceremonies performed at full moon were reported (Berndt and Berndt 1964,1970) to have included dancing through flames. In other rituals, initiates crouched in a trench representing the womb of the Mother, sometimes equated with the Rainbow Snake, and so both female and male, protective and punitive. The grave-womb could in some cases also represent a sacred waterhole; snake designs were incised on its walls; dances were performed, firesticks thrown, and the participants were painted with blood on a base of red ochre mixed with termite mound (Berndt and Berndt 1964:242;1970:129,139). In Frieze Cave there were stones and waterlogged wood within the now-choked gully. Charcoal throughout the deposits provided evidence of recurrent burning. Tiny pointed backed blades in crystal quartz were almost the sole component of an industry suitable for blood-letting or scarification. Parallel lines in ochre decorated the cave roof instead of (or perhaps as well as) men's chests. In each case we may have linkages between fire rituals, blood-letting, parallel ochre lines connected with a snake motif, probably the notion of rain and increase, a hole sacred to a snake, and votive deposits of rounded stones and sticks.

Neighbouring Dale's Cave adds evidence of ideas concerned with the themes of sun–moon–stars, movement between earth and heaven, and so perhaps links to the sky–lightning–rainbow–snake–water–fire complex of ideas which occurs in the Kimberleys.

The radiocarbon dates from Frieze Cave range from 3000 B.P. to modern.* Ochre occurs in the lowest levels, so that the artistic exemplification of these traditions had used red colouring for at least three millennia. One quartz crystal came from the bottom levels of the gully, another near the top. Charcoal and backed blades of crystal quartz occurred throughout. The ritual activities indicated must span the entire time-range.

The 'Orchestra Shell' cave in the aeolian limestone north of Perth (see pp. 83–4 and Hallam 1971, 1974), with undulating snake-like, and a few straight line, markings on the once-soft limestone of the roof, has evidence of recurrent fire over a time span ranging from about 6,500 to about 1,700

---

* The details are:
ANU830 Trench I, square 0, depth 36–38 in. 3090 ± 240 B.P.(c. 1140 B.C.)
ANU828 Trench I, square 3, depth 12–15 in. 1150 ± 70 B.P. (c. 800 A.D.)
ANU829 Trench II, square 5, depth 8–9 in. 1100 ± 70 B.P. (c. 850 A.D.)
ANU827 Trench I, square 0, depth 5–6 in. 110 ± 70 B.P. (modern)

years ago.* The discovery of yet another similarly marked cave from the Swan coastal plain limestone establishes the likelihood of a definite regional ritual tradition, which may link with Nullarbor traditions, where again serpent legends persisted to the near present. (A tradition of working Eocene limestone may form another link with the Nullarbor.) Here in Koonalda a much greater, late Pleistocene, age of at least 20,000 years was established for non-representational markings, and for quarrying. The wall markings are mainly multiple meanders (Edwards and Maynard 1967; Wright 1971a, 1971b), but partly rectilinear geometric (cf. the serpentine association of such designs in, for example, Marshack 1972a:fig.117).

One might suggest from the dated evidence that ritual traditions involving the joint potencies of snake and fire persisted through the south and south-west of the continent from the Pleistocene to the present, though the particular artistic and ritualistic forms in which these traditions were expressed changed over time.

Perhaps we can go further, and see fire as linked with fertility; earth-apertures with the uterus of a Fertility Mother; blood, water and snakes with male potency, at once antithetical and essential to earth–fertility: so that the opposition and fusion of the two concepts, earth–fire–fertility and snake–water–potency, incorporate power and fruition in all their maleness and femaleness. The Moon-Man, Sun-Woman, or fire in a dilly-bag motif in Dale's Cave suggests a yet wider distribution for the Fertility-Mother concepts which, with the Lightning-Snake and Rainbow-Snake concepts, appear to have had such wide currency in Aboriginal Australia (Radcliffe-Brown 1926, 1930; Berndt and Berndt 1964:209–41; Maddock 1970b:461).

At Frieze Cave we may envisage rituals involving tribal elders, with imputed powers of driving away or summoning wind, rain and lightning, engaged in rites involving sacred crystals, in which 'cuts' the colour of blood, in serpent form, were renewed on the roof, and fires lit on the floor on either side of a gully through which there was probably some flow of water during rain. The tiny geometric microliths and backed blades in crystal quartz which dominate the artifact content of the deposit are all suitable for blood-letting or scar-cutting, which, like the painted 'cuts' in the stone, might well be used to promote rain towards the end of a dry summer, or, more generally, to ensure increase. Here, in a shelter on top

---

*ANU621 Squares 4–5, depth 5–9 in. 6470 ± 120 B.P. (c. 4520 B.C.)
ANU622   Square 1, depth 8 in. 1730 ± 850 B.P. (c. 220 A.D.)
ANU623   Square 5, depth 27 in. 3310 ± 150 B.P. (c. 1360 B.C.)
ANU624   Square 5–6, depth 27–30 in. 3820 ± 100 B.P. (c. 1870 B.C.)

The charcoal occurred as abundant flecks and pieces in dark earth filling the spaces between blocks at the foot of a rockfall sloping steeply down from the mouth of the cave. The date inversion suggests material was funnelling down between blocks into the voids at greater depths, leaving some older material perched above rockfall at a higher level.

of a hill as near the sky as possible, yet with crevices going back into the hillside which emphasise ideas of earth, and which could provide hiding-places for sacred paraphernalia, we have a suitable setting for rites linking through fire and blood a serpent which dwelt in water and in caverns, with his skyward manifestations and properties in rainbow and lightning and rain, and with the fiery power of sun and moon and stars; their potency could be captured and stored in powerful crystals, like the two complete quartz crystals found in the gully, or the crystals from which the tiny but beautifully worked bladelets had been shaped. Elsewhere, birds had provided a medium for the transmission of fire between serpent and men, or had themselves discovered fire. Swallows nest under the roof of Frieze Cave, and in Dale's Cave. Fire was both propitiatory and protective, an offering to the powers of darkness and a defence against them: ambiguous in its sacred as in its secular functions.

If these elements in south-western ritual and myth—death, life; serpent, fire; earth, water, sky; birds, moon, stars, crystals; burnt trees and burnt countryside; movement between earth and heaven—do indeed belong together we have here a constellation of ideas, antitheses, fusions and ambiguities which must have proliferated into its great variety of formulations from the very early days of settlement in the Australian continent, certainly prior to 10,000 B.C. and probably prior to 20,000 B.C. Like the structure of Australian pyrophilous plant communities, the structure of Australian mythology has fire, *bush* fire, as an essential component, and thus bespeaks a high antiquity for man-made fire in Australia.

The importance and antiquity of fire in the ritual, as in the extractive, schema emphasises that here we have not two systems but one, in which symbolic activity is meshed inextricably into the knotted design of total activity. *Through* myth and ritual and art Aboriginal groups apprehended the land of which they were part, in which they partook. Unchanging in their adherence to tradition, they were able to adapt the specific content of their ecological and symbolic lore to change and circumstance throughout the tens of millennia during which their occupance transformed the continent and was itself transformed.

15

The long view: human occupance and firing in the South-west

We have concentrated our attention primarily on the more recent aspects of Australian prehistory—that growth zone which receives such hybrid designations as ethnohistory and ethnoarchaeology. Can we attempt to triangulate from this baseline of the contact situation back into the 'still receding and already far distant past' (Megaw 1967)?

We had until recently relatively little published evidence for the Pleistocene settlement of Western Australia, but this is a measure only of the lack so far of sufficient personnel to explore one third of the continent, and is rapidly being righted by the work of Dortch and Merrilees (1971; Dortch 1972; and Dortch and Merrilees 1973). On general grounds, one likely route for the Pleistocene peopling of Australia in periods of low sea level would be via the Indonesian islands and the shelf of what is now shallow sea north-west of the Kimberleys: this involves shorter 'hops' than a route which would cross Weber's Line further east, to reach the New Guinea–Cape York area (Keast 1959; Mulvaney 1964; Mulvaney and Soejono 1971; Golson 1971*b*). Evidence is accumulating from the West for cultural traditions which have their roots in that early stage before rising sea levels cut Tasmania off from the Australian mainland, and Australia from New Guinea (Jennings 1971). The use of fire in Western burial rites links with Pleistocene evidence for cremation (Bowler *et al.* 1970; Bowler *et al.* 1972) and its persistence in Tasmania (Hiatt 1969). Surviving fire myths from Western Australia and Tasmania suggest bodies of myth as well as ritual linked by common elements; while simple non-figurative art, and stone industries emphasising steep scrapers (cf. Hallam 1972*a*), appear to be variants of early common Australian traditions. Ride (1958) reported from the South-west ground stone axeheads which are, in the main, relatively unstandardised implements. Ride (*ibid*:176) speaks of 'great diversity of types' and 'experiments in edge-grinding [which] had not yet had time to settle down to a definite pattern' and suggests early associations. The south-western axes may prove to belong to an early tradition, later functionally replaced by the peculiar 'kodja' axe-hammer (Davidson and McCarthy 1957).

Charcoal dated to more than 35,000 B.C. from Mammoth Cave in the south-west tip of Western Australia may have had a human connection (Lundelius 1960:143; Merrilees 1968:10). Davies (1968) described a human tooth from Devil's Lair (Nannup Cave) in the same aeolian limestone area, between levels from which Lundelius had obtained charcoal with dates of about 10,000 B.C. and about 6500 B.C. (Lundelius 1960:144). Part of a baler shell and stone artifacts were reported from these same levels (Merrilees 1968:12). The deposit has been re-excavated by Dr Merrilees and Mr Charles Dortch, and further evidence of Pleistocene human presence was obtained (Dortch and Merrilees 1971).*

From a group of sites in the valleys of several creeks in the Avon River system, some 80 miles east from Perth and within 20 miles of Northam, comes an industry† in which steep-edge scrapers predominate. Some are massive. Among them are examples with scraping surfaces in more than one plane, often on thick flakes with a high striking angle rather than on cores; others of classic 'horsehoof' type; and keeled variants. There are also flatter scrapers on flakes, still with the same steep or undercut edge angle, some with alternating convex and concave margins; and various heavy unifacially trimmed blocks and pebbles. Odd examples of such steep scrapers and choppers occur along the edge of the Darling Scarp (for example at Gingin, in the Chittering valley, and at Walyunga) between the relatively unattractive uplands capped by lateritic gravel, and the swampy and sandy coastal plain.‡ This steep-edge scraper material is reminiscent of that from sites elsewhere in Australia which have been shown to be early.

Sites in this 'steep-edge' tradition include Lake Mungo, with hearth dates going back to 32,000 years ago (Bowler *et al.* 1970; Bowler 1971; Barbetti and Allen 1972; Bowler *et al.* 1972); Burrill Lake (Lampert 1971*b*:fig.5) with radiocarbon dates ranging back about 20,000 years; Kenniff Cave,

---

* The occupation dates now go back almost 25,000 years, and the bottom of the deposit has not yet been reached (Dortch and Merrilees 1973).
† Some examples donated by Messrs Jessup and Meiklem are in the Western Australian Museum; surface collections were made as part of the Archaeological Survey Project of the Department of Anthropology of the University of Western Australia, under a grant from the Australian Institute of Aboriginal Studies (Hallam 1972*a*).
‡ Butler 1958; information from Mrs Roe, Mrs Collins, Charles Dortch, and fieldwork—SJH.

dated from at least 19,000 up to 5,000 years ago (Mulvaney and Joyce 1965:figs.17–19; Mulvaney 1969:fig.31; Mulvaney: personal communication); Ingaladdi with ages of 7,000 to 5,000 years (Mulvaney 1969:figs.36, 37); Green Gully, with some material older than 9,000 years (Mulvaney 1969:figs.32,35; National Museum of Victoria 1970; particularly Bowler 1970, and Mulvaney 1970:figs.3d,e,6b,d); and Puntutjarpa, with dates of a similar order of magnitude, and with unhafted tools in use alongside hafted right through to the present (Gould 1968:fig.9). The 'steep-edge' assemblages from these sites may be seen as components in those 'Australian core tool and scraper traditions' which flourished throughout late Pleistocene Australia, including Tasmania (Jones 1968; Mulvaney 1969:150–165; Lampert 1971a:126–7,fig.10) and persisted in modified form after Tasmania was cut off from the Australian mainland between 15,000 and 10,000 years ago. Such industries in Western Australia, then, are likely to have originated well before 10,000 years ago, though they no doubt persisted later.*

I have argued elsewhere that an early element among the coastal plain sites is represented by an industry whose distinctive lithology (Glover and Cockbain 1971) demands either very long distance trade round the south-west coastal margin or derivation from sources† inaccessible since the sea level rose in the millennia through to 3000 B.C. Artifacts of this Eocene fossiliferous chert do not occur east of the Darling Scarp on the direct line towards the nearest presently known surface outcrops; such deposits are found from Albany eastward into the Nullarbor. Typologically this industry has its main emphasis on a very unstandardised variety of steep-edge scraper and adze forms, and those assemblages which comprise artifacts of fossiliferous chert are entirely or almost entirely devoid of blades. Those sites then are likely to precede the establishment of backed-blade industries in the west, again indicating an age of probably more than 5,000 years.

In the continent as a whole the earliest dates for assemblages containing definite backed blades would now appear to be around 3500 B.C. (McBryde 1968:84–5; Mulvaney 1969:151 *et passim*; Lampert 1971b:65; Pearce 1973, n.d.), while in the western third of the continent there are as yet no dates for assemblages with a backed-blade component before 2000 B.C. at Puntutjarpa in the Western Desert, though other 'small tools', possibly hafted, were part of these asemblages for many earlier millennia (Gould

---

* Views on the complexity, development and time-span of such industries have changed rapidly since this section was written (for example, Lampert 1972). The Avon material is large and heavy, and likely to represent a very early phase, with an antiquity possibly greater than the ages cited.

† Either offshore, or deep in caves; cf. Jennings 1961 for the penetration of the deep Nullarbor caves, through the Miocene Nullarbor Limestone, into the underlying Eocene Wilson Bluff Limestone, from which was quarried a silicified limestone very similar to the fossiliferous chert of the Perth Basin.

1971b:158-9; for a much greater antiquity see now Dortch and Merrilees, 1973). The Frieze Cave dates show 'small tools' (here principally very small backed blades with a specialised ritual function) fully established by 1000 B.C. Unfortunately, there was no earlier deposit in this cave, so that it offers no evidence of the length of time by which the transition preceded this date. Dr McBryde's New England evidence would lead one to expect to discover sites of the fully established 'small tool' phase more frequently than those belonging to its first inception (McBryde 1966:291). It would be surprising if the western developments towards a backed-blade tradition did not parallel those in the Western Desert prior to 2000 B.C. The Puntutjarpa evidence makes it clear that the emergence of the final standardised assemblages with backed blades was the culmination of internal shifts and changes with a long prior development within a continuing industrial tradition, in which the adze components showed the greatest potential for innovation (see also now Dortch and Merrilees 1973, for the Devil's Lair evidence of the very early indigenous development of hafted tool traditions). The west coast assemblages which show a preponderance of fossiliferous chert, and of adze/steep scraper forms, are thus likely to belong to a phase mainly before 3000 B.C. on both typological and lithological (and some also on geomorphological) grounds.

It is likely on *a priori* grounds that human groups used and valued fire throughout their tenure of the continent. The best confirmatory evidence comes from the fire myths which are discussed in the last section. In summary, common elements recurring in myths throughout mainland Australia, including the South-west and Tasmania, confirm the possession of fire and a fire mythology as part of the 'common stock' of traditions current throughout 'Greater Australia' before it was split up by rising sea levels, that is, from the Pleistocene onwards.

Thus a number of lines of evidence make the presence of man and manmade fire in the South-west of Australia for at least the last 10,000 years virtually certain, and for 15,000 to 30,000 or more years very likely.* Throughout that span the West Australian vegetation and landscape will have been exposed to the effects of increasingly frequent firing.

We turn now to the question of what more direct evidence there is of early humanly initiated firing in the South-west.

Fire certainly has been a factor, and, one would expect, an increasingly important factor in the West Australian landscape over many thousands of years. The caves of the South-west provide some hints of this, the swamps more certain evidence.

Radiocarbon dates for faunal sequences from caves in the coastal limestone came often from charcoal mixed with soil material washed in from

---

* Now confirmed by the work of Dortch and Merrilees (1973) in Devil's Lair.

outside. Lundelius (1960:143) considered this charcoal was 'probably derived from bush fires' and does not discuss possible human occupation. If bushfires *are* indicated, were they humanly initiated? Looked at on a world scale, lightning strikes in Australia are relatively rare (Sparrow and Ney 1971), and were perhaps less likely to cause widespread fire in the humid late Pleistocene than in the increasingly dry post-Pleistocene. What is the origin of charcoal older than 37,000 years from Mammoth Cave (Lundelius 1960:143; Merrilees 1968:11) near the most south-westerly tip of Western Australia? Devil's Lair yielded charcoal dateable to around 10,000 B.C. (12,175 ± 275 B.P.—Lundelius 1960:144).* The relatively greater number of dates from about 7,000 B.C. onward might correlate with more bushfires: Drover's Cave (Hastings Cave) 7850 ± 170 B.P. (Lundelius 1960); 'Orchestra Shell' cave 6470 ± 120 B.P. to 1730 ± 85 B.P. (ANU621–4; Hallam 1971, n.d.); Wedge's Cave 3750 ± 240 B.P. (Lundelius 1960).

Churchill's bores in swamps in the South-west show increasingly frequent burning over recent millennia. In the Scott River Swamp, just east of Augusta, a severe fire nearly destroyed the original peat (with pollen indicating *Melaleuca* scrub, with *Banksia* around) in about 7340 B.C. (Churchill 1968:142), suggesting the onset of firing at a date comparable to the cave charcoal dates. In Weld Swamp, halfway between Augusta and Albany, Churchill (*ibid*:140–1) found a high proportion of *Banksia* and low proportions of *Eucalyptus* in peaty sands with 'a great deal of charcoal [which] indicates that fires were prevalent at that time', at the onset of peat formation at a depth of 290–200 cm (and a date of around 4000 B.C. by extrapolation). Around the 175cm levels with radiocarbon dates of 2750 B.C., a rapid increase in *E. marginata* (jarrah) pollen, with a corresponding decrease in *Banksia*, is taken to indicate that conditions were becoming drier. At 120 to 150cm (probably around 1400 B.C.) there occurred a sandy horizon with abundant charcoal, providing evidence of 'at least one fire of sufficient magnitude to burn the peat and severely truncate the bog'. Thus early fires were in this area relatively infrequent and intense. Churchill's bore diagram (*ibid*:fig.7) shows later periodic fires as increasingly frequent, and none are noted as particularly intense. The early, less frequent, but more severe fires might indicate lightning or merely human presence and activity, rather than a deliberate firing régime. More frequent but less intense fires should indicate developing patterns of human exploitation, affecting even this least attractive and least used part of the South-west, in the last millennium B.C. and onward.

Although Churchill concluded that 'there appears to be no change in the pollen spectrum after any fire', the marked increase in the proportion of

---

* And now dates of around 25,000 years ago are reported well above the base of the deposit and in definite occupation levels (Dortch and Merrilees 1973).

jarrah does follow early levels in which 'fires were prevalent' (Churchill 1968). Similarly at Scott River the original vegetation was open *Banksia* scrub, and eucalypts appeared some time after the initial severe firing, *E. marginata* (jarrah) becoming dominant in the first millennium A.D.

Falls in the ratio of *E. diversicolor* (karri), which Churchill takes to indicate decreasing dampness, occur about 3000 B.C. (Weld River Swamp, Boggy Lake) and again about 1400–1200 B.C. (also Weld River Swamp) and about 500 A.D. (Weld River Swamp, Flinders Bay Swamp, and Boggy Lake). Corresponding increases in *E. marginata*, or in *E. calophylla*, taken as indicators of drier conditions, occur from 3000 B.C. (Weld Swamp), around 1400 B.C. (Boggy Lake), and most strikingly between A.D. 500 and 1400 (Boggy Lake, Scott River Swamp). This seems to be the time at which firing and devegetation were having most widespread impact on coastal dunes and dune movement (see below). Overall, Churchill's graphs indicate that karri has been losing ground to jarrah, which is more closely adjusted to fire, throughout the last 5000 years or more, though more rapidly during some phases which are therefore taken to be drier, and most rapidly in the last two millennia, reaching perhaps its nadir rather more than 500 years ago.

Coastal dunes are now producing evidence which agrees with the general picture from south-west Australian caves and swamps. On the south coast near William Bay, only 30 miles south-east of the Weld Swamp area, charcoal from burnt-over karri forest engulfed by sand (and since calcified) had yielded dates of about 4700 to 4000 B.C. (V-93—7610 ± 165 B.P. and V-98—6940 ± 110 B.P.; Bermingham, Packham and Vines 1971), and raises the question of whether the onset of peat formation at Weld Swamp might possibly relate to fire clearance, in the way that recent flooding in the South-west relates to European clearance. A later phase of burning, devegetation and sand movement gave dates around 600 years ago, closely comparable with similar dates for the slow engulfing of vegetation by mobile dunes a hundred miles further east (Butler and Merrilees 1971), where the process is still continuing.

Near the mouth of the Moore River mobile dune sands moving over an old ground surface, apparently burnt, have engulfed remnant vegetation, including a dead tree rooted under some feet of sand. In the immediate neighbourhood wind erosion had removed not only mobile white sands but the underlying yellow sand, leaving exposed in the hollows (perhaps derived from the old ground surface) concentrations of artifacts of a very distinctive lithology. More than 90 per cent of the pieces are made from a very unusual fossiliferous chert, recently investigated by Glover and Cockbain (1971), who showed that from presently known sources this material would have had to travel five hundred miles to reach its west coast distribution. Its abundance on coastal plain sites in general, and its almost exclusive occurrence on a few typologically early sites, strongly suggest that less distant sources were once available, before the advent of backed blades, and probably before the rise of the sea level to near its present levels by four to three thousand B.C. (Churchill 1959) obliterated probable offshore, deep channel, or possibly deep cave sources nearer at hand. The occupation of the Moore River site-group, the devegetation of the area around it, and the beginning of sand movement, should not be far removed in time from a date when the shore approached its present position. The presence of two or three backed blades on one site in the group suggests the occupation lasted just up to the advent of backed blades in the Southwest, at some date before the first dated occurrence of the fully fledged tradition at Frieze Cave around 1000 B.C. (ANU380—3090 ± 240 B.P.) and perhaps before 2000 B.C. when backed blades are first dated within the hafted-adze tradition of the Western Desert site of Puntutjarpa (Gould 1971b:159).

Thus William Bay and Moore River both suggest intensifying effects of human exploitation, including firing, not only on vegetation but also on geomorphology, from the millennia from 4000–3000 B.C. onward, when a narrowing coastal plain (Churchill 1959), the onset of drier conditions* (Churchill 1968), and the advent of more efficient extractive equipment and techniques successively converged to disturb previous ecological balances.

Taking the peat and dune evidence together we should perhaps envisage a periodicity in the stresses on vegetation and geomorphology, produced by fluctuations in the rate of increase of aridity, increasing exploitation (implying increasing population) and increasing firing. The periods when these stresses were felt most centre around four to three thousand B.C., coinciding with the final stages of rise of sea level and with the various developments within Australian artifact traditions (Gould 1971b:157–63) out of which were to emerge the backed-blade and other distinctive industries of Mulvaney's 'Inventive Phase' (1969:107,151); and around 1200–1400 A.D., which may have seen further technological, and presumably, ecological, *ad hoc* adjustments, leading into Mulvaney's 'Adaptive Phase' (*ibid*:91). Whether increases in rates of cultural change imply increased rates of change in demographic and exploitative patterns, and what may be the connections with rates of vegetational and apparently climatic change, are questions which the evidence poses but does not enable us to answer.

---

* Compare the increasing desiccation in the Western Desert which led to the silting and abandonment of the soakwell at Puntutjarpa by about 2000 B.C. A 3840 B.P. hearth post-dated the filling of the pit (Gould 1971b:168).

16

The long view: increasing populations and exploitation

The increasing, and increasingly regulated, use of fire was part of an overall pattern of increasing exploitation and population. The Weld Swamp and William Bay evidence show that one of the wettest and least productive areas of the South-west felt considerable effects from humanly initiated firing over some six thousand and more years, increasing right up to European contact, with probably some periods of accelerated change, particularly in the last millennium. Areas of greater potential for grazing and for plant, swamp and estuarine products (for example on the eastern margin of the jarrah belt, and on the west coastal plain) are likely to have been affected earlier and more intensively by increased exploitative and demographic pressures. Initial relatively random firing with severe effects would lead to more regular firing of vegetation increasingly adapted to increasingly frequent and regular burning. Drastic vegetational and even geomorphic repercussions would be first seen in the most vulnerable areas—the drier interior, and the coastal limestone dunes—but eventually even in the damper forest areas; while the swamps and estuaries of the coastal plain would continue to absorb a longer and a later intensification of exploitation and population density.

An archaeological survey of the area round Perth (Hallam 1972a, 1973b) allows preliminary quantification of these statements. Differentiation of sites into wide time brackets on the basis of certain recurrent patterns of characteristics in their artifact assemblages does appear possible, even though distinctions must also be made on the basis of relative permanence (long span to ephereral); type of group (few people to many); function (multiple to single specialised activity); and role in the economic pattern (utilising swamp products, estuarine resources, etc.). Briefly, a few sites, with predominantly scraper and steep scraper/unstandardised adze assemblages, appear on typological (and sometimes lithological) grounds to be entirely early; some others, with a high proportion of quartz and quartz chips, relatively amorphous, with a stress on fabricators, can be characterised as late; while in a few 'final' assemblages crude techniques combine with worked glass, claypipes, etc. to attest post-contact usage. Assemblages rich in backed blades suggest an intermediate middle phase, though most sites occupied during this phase also span through the early or late phases, or cover all three phases. A more thorough analysis of these data would require consideration not only of numbers of sites, but of quantities of material on each.

To translate ratios between numbers of sites or quantities of artifacts of different phases into changes in population densities over time would require two further sets of data: the time-spans of each phase, and density figures at the end of the late phase, upon European contact. The range of possibilities for contact densities are discussed below; even if fairly arbitrary figures are used for time-spans this will not affect contrasts between trends in adjacent regions.

The archaeological evidence thus allows comparisons of densities for the same area during different phases (assuming the chances of sampling do not vary from phase to phase); and makes possible general comparisons of trends between areas.*

Preliminary examination of the ratios between early (pre-blade), middle (backed-blade) and late occupation on sites on a sample transect from the coast (centred on the Swan estuary, and stretching to the Moore River and the Murray) inland to the Avon valley, suggests—particularly if one takes account of the large *quantity* of material in each early Avon site—that the ratio of early population to late was greater for the interior than for the coastal plain. On the other hand, the final population increase was not so rapid in the interior. On the coastal plain numbers rose twice as sharply to a higher ceiling.

Within the coastal plain, utilisation ratios changed over time between the coastal limestone, with a higher proportion of early sites, and the sand-plain and swamps, where rise in usage, as indicated by site numbers, was most marked in the late period. The piedmont alluvium has not so far been sufficiently investigated.

---

* The method is essentially that followed by Schwarz (1956) for north-west Arizona. He divided his material into six geographical areas, and assumed that 'relative increase or decrease in habitation units bears a direct relationship to rise and fall of population, without the necessity [to take] into consideration the exact numbers of people'. The time-spans involved were, however, much narrower. Compare also Hallam (1970) for a study of population change, and changing distribution over time, from archaeological data; and Stockton (1970) for a phase-distribution study of an Australian area.

Paralleling these demographic trends, we must see the resources of coast and estuary, swamp and grazing, as increasingly 'worked' over recent millennia and centuries, giving tighter adaptive patterns, and a closer mosaic of usage rights and extractive techniques, including firing. The regulated patterns of exploitation observed in the early nineteenth century can be seen as stemming from, and promoting, demographic and environmental stresses building up over millennia, and affecting different areas in different ways, at different stages and at different rates.

The type of régime we have seen clearly portrayed in nineteenth century sources and implied back to the seventeenth century had developed over a span, not of two, but of more than two hundred centuries. There is no need to envisage a highly regulated, seasonal, sequential firing within defined territories as spanning the entire time range. Such a close framework of responsibilities need have developed only as population densities became relatively high, number of groups per unit area high, and group range correspondingly restricted.

Where such highly regulated patterns existed within areas which now have little to offer, as on the less arid margins of the most arid—and it always has been arid (Jennings 1967)—interior, this may imply that demographic optima were approached relatively early, when the carrying capacity of these areas was high; and that there was later deterioration under the stress of increasing aridity, and possibly also of increasing salinity under the impact of firing (cf. p. 6 above). On the other hand some areas, for instance the heavily wooded heart of the forest triangle in the South-west, and particularly the karri areas in the far south, never supported a high biomass, nor really intensive human activity and population.

The end products of these varying patterns of development were the varying demographic–exploitative patterns witnessed at contact. We have discussed the space-scheduling and time-scheduling of usage, including firing (see chapters 5 and 6). How far does the evidence allow us to clarify the related demographic patterns which determined and were determined by the *intensity* of usage, including firing, and its effects?

Eyre sagely remarked that:

> There is scarcely any point connected with the Aborigines of New Holland ... upon which it is more difficult to form an opinion even approximating to the truth, than that of the aggregate population of the continent or the average number of persons to be found in any given space. (Eyre 1845:II,368)

There are however some figures for the South-west which, though varying in detail, suggest that by contact times densities were at the high rather than the low end of the continental range, nearer those for Arnhem Land than those for the Western Desert.

Irwin estimated the total Aboriginal population of the settled areas at a rather low figure: 'The Tribes who frequent the districts in the vicinity of the Swan, Port Augusta and King George's Sound ... do not exceed perhaps a thousand souls' (Irwin 1835:22).

Moore, on the other hand, cited three thousand for the 'located parts of the colony' in 1841 (Moore 1884*b*:84), and this estimate would apply to much the same triangle, with some extension east and north in the York–Victoria Plains area. This official figure from the statistical returns is quoted also by Chauncy, who added the obvious rider that 'the white population was much smaller' (Chauncy 1878:221)—it was officially 2311 in 1840 (Hasluck 1942:19). With such conflicting estimates, we can expect to do no more than define the range of possibilities.

In calculating density figures the answer estimated will differ according to the extent of the area taken. A high figure for a small area round the Swan estuary would be modified by taking into account, as one should, a corresponding slice of the forested hinterland. The average for the coastal plain and its hinterland will differ from that for the interior margin of the forest; and either again from an overall average which takes into account the even emptier southern forests.

The estimate given by Western Australia's first governor, Stirling, for the Perth area was surprisingly high:

> The numbers of Aborigines ... can only be guessed at. Sir James Stirling conceives there is probably one native to two square miles. Seven hundred and fifty were known to have visited Perth from the district surrounding it, about forty miles each way. (Ogle 1839:62)

This is, however, by no means an impossible figure for the favoured and much frequented area centred on the Swan estuary. The range indicated by Ogle would include a strip of the twenty-mile wide coastal plain stretching north halfway towards the next centre of population in the Moore River–Gingin district, and south halfway towards the concentration around the Serpentine–Murray–Harvey estuaries. It would command not only estuarine resources, but those of the interdunal and sandplain lakes and swamps, the rich grazing of the Swan–Canning piedmont zone, and scarp-foot localities commanding the valleys of the Darling Range. Eastward it would stop short of the separate groups in the York–Toodyay area. One wonders, however, whether the aggregation Stirling described did not include the Murray men, the Gingin folk, or even the York people, for these are certainly mentioned from time to time as visiting Perth, or having kin there.

A high density is even more probable for the folk who centred on the inlets south of the Murray—the Leschenault, and those behind Geographe Bay. Bunbury, travelling south alongside the Leschenault estuary in December 1836 to January 1837 encountered successively 'no fewer than one hundred blacks . . . and often nearer two hundred' (Bunbury 1930:79), all male, 'many deserted huts' indicating 'the constant presence of considerable numbers' fishing in the shoals and at weirs, by which were 'fires on a large scale'; beyond the Collie River 'about 150 natives . . . belonging to another tribe'; and again beyond the Preston another 'large party of natives'. He then proceeded southwards 'in company with a large number of native men, the women and children remaining on the right bank . . . going to a great Corroboree with some other tribes' (*ibid*:89). The total gathering must have been three or four hundred men, plus their women and children, in an area even richer than that around the Swan. As soon as he 'ascended the first range' inland from the Preston, Bunbury found himself, however, among 'a hill tribe' unknown to his coastal friends from the Vasse and the Murray (*ibid*:162).

Stirling's figures and Bunbury's together indicate that for the southern portion of the west coastal plain and its immediate hinterland densities were indeed very high, though absolute precision is impossible. The coastal strip from the Moore River to Cape Naturaliste is roughly 200 miles long, and at the very maximum the inland range of its people may be as much as forty miles to the north of Perth, though level with the Leschenault inlet the quite separate hill people were encountered only twenty miles inland. Bunbury's encounters must represent at least eight hundred individuals, and possibly twice as many, in the southern half of this strip. Stirling's imply again seven or eight hundred for possibly the Swan alone, or, if we interpret him differently, possibly the men from the Murray, the Swan and Moore Rivers. The range of possible areas, and possible totals, give densities which *must* be at least twenty, and *may* be as much as fifty, persons per 100 square miles.

Lower densities in the Avon valley area would be given by the documentary evidence cited by Rica Erickson (1969:38) for some twenty families around Toodyay, in an area 25 or 30 miles across, and including a fair proportion of poorer land: something like ten to fifteen persons per 100 square miles, if a 'family' averaged about four people. Moore (1884*a*:219) also saw the land 'over the hills' as carrying a lower population—'less burned, being less frequented'.

Stirling's and Bunbury's figures render very unlikely Irwin's estimate of only one thousand for the whole of the triangle between the Swan, Augusta and the Sound, which implies only one person to every 15 or 20 square miles, about five to seven per 100 square miles. Breton's account, however, of groups of thirty to fifty men, women and children whose grounds usually include a square of twenty to thirty miles within which 'they change their boundaries as the season may answer' (Breton 1833: 188-9), would give densities which accord more nearly with Irwin's estimate. Moore's figure (1884*b*:84) of three thousand for the 'populated area' by 1840 seems of the right order of magnitude, and gives overall density figures of the order of one person in 5 to 7 square miles, or about eighteen to twenty persons per 100 square miles. Besides the densely settled west coast and its hinterland, this estimate covers the inland area of moderately populated country from north of York down to Albany, but also the triangle of poor lateritic gravels carrying jarrah forest (which at least from Harvey southward was relatively little used except where penetrated by major rivers like the Blackwood) and the karri forests of the deep south.

Thus overall estimates for the entire South-west, including estuarine concentrations and 'empty' forests, lie somewhere between 5 and 20 square miles per person (between twenty and five persons per 100 square miles), and, most probably, between 7 and 10. These figures are comparable with densities of one person to 6 or 7 square miles for the Kimberleys (Meggitt 1962:32) and Tasmania (Jones 1971:201), rather than with one person per 35 square miles (about three people per 100 square miles) for parts of Central Australia (Meggitt 1962). Localised coastal plain concentrations would give figures well above these—certainly no more than 5, and perhaps no more than 2, square miles per person (twenty to fifty people per 100 square miles) between the Moore River and Geographe Bay.

This agrees well with Stanner's (1965) suggestion of a gradient in density of population and compactness of territory between the arid centre and the well-watered margins of the continent; though the gradient may have been less steep, or even have run in the reverse direction, under earlier and different conditions. The difference in the densities of the Avon valley and the coastal plain at contact, a dozen persons to 100 square miles in the first, as against twenty to fifty in the other region, also accords with Stanner's hypothesis. Conversely, the lesser difference which we have seen implied at an earlier date may imply a lesser difference in environmental conditions. Coastal populations continued to increase steeply when increasing climatic-exploitative stress had slowed down demographic expansion nearer the interior. The final levels reached on the coastal plain were very high indeed, by the standards of the continent as a whole, and imply heavy, effective and highly organised usage, including firing, with corresponding effects on the vegetation. Here, on the damper continental margin, intensifying occupance would open up and improve, rather than deplete, regional resources.

A long time-span for the processes of modification and remodification of plant communities (with no doubt a reciprocal feedback modifying and remodifying the economic and demographic patterns of Aboriginal communities) is required and allowed by the botanical evidence. Gardner (1957) envisaged the humanly initiated fire factor as affecting the flora over a long enough period to have changed the structure of plant communities by eliminating any species unable to survive fire damage. Within the South-west of Western Australia much of the flora is pyrophilous and fire-climax. Some species, for instance many banksias which are so conspicuous in the vegetation of the sandy coastal plain, do not merely tolerate fire: they require it for their propagation. The mutual dependence of plant and human communities must have required a considerable period to reach its nineteenth century balance.

Whilst firing may initially have been important in developing the grazing potential of the annular zone of shrub and savannah around the centre, it may also have contributed (perhaps like European clearance through increasing soil salinity), at a time of increasing aridity, to stresses in the system, resulting in decreased biomass, both marsupial and human. Nearer the circumference, the savannah woodland would remain longer susceptible of improvement by repeated firing, though usage and population may have approached a ceiling by contact times. Certainly increasing human and animal pressures on the margins of the south-west forest triangle will have tended both to increase non-wooded habitats at the expense of wooded, and increasingly to modify their plant communities. Meanwhile the economies of Aboriginal groups will have become concomitantly adapted to the exploitation of these changed environments: on the coastal plain, to an intensified exploitation of the available fish, fowl, plant and grazing resources of estuary, lake, swamp and open piedmont woodland.

It is usual to consider the Aborigines too 'primitive' to have become farmers. But cereal farming as practised by European communities is but one highly specialised mode of ecological modification. Aboriginal groups *did* modify the structure and distribution of floral and faunal communities. For the more generalised but highly skilled and tightly regulated Aboriginal usages, Rhys Jones' phrase 'fire-stick farming' is exactly apposite. The Aborigines had indeed 'worked' for their crop of grass and their stock of herbivores. Their effects on the landscape may have been more crucial than we can yet fully demonstrate.

Postscript

> The natives have a tradition that Rottnest, Carnac, and Garden Island, once formed part of the mainland, and that the intervening ground was thickly covered with trees; which took fire in some unaccountable way, and burned with such intensity that the ground split asunder with a great noise, and the sea rushed in between, cutting off these islands from the mainland. (Moore 1884b:8)

This Swan River legend recounted by Moore seems to contain some echo of the rising sea levels which, by around 5000 years ago, flooded the interdunal lake that became Cockburn Sound, and cut off Rottnest Island (Churchill 1959). It suggests also that some tectonic disturbance* may have coincided with the final phases of sea-level rise.

This story epitomises the ancient and changing role of fire in Aboriginal life. 'Wild' fire figures appropriately in the early Swan legend, for although Aborigines had used fire throughout their tenure of the continent, it is only from the times of final rise of sea level that the evidence of caves, dunes and swamps shows humanly initiated fire beginning to make any real impact on the South-west coastal plain. The increasing impact of more frequent, regular, and deliberate firing on the terrain of the wider Southwest, felt most strongly initially in the interior, may in turn be mirrored by the legend of the burning of the great tree at Kellerberrin. Fire usage culminated in the last two millennia in the systematic regulation, the 'burning by consecutive portions', found throughout the South-west at contact. *Kalla*, a fire, equated in Aboriginal speech with property in land.

---

* From the extreme South-west, the Aboriginal tales of the Great Shaking and the Big Water, recounted by Deborah Buller-Murphy, also suggest tectonic movements.

The Aboriginal exercise of such usage rights shaped the countryside Europeans would use.

Fire was integral to long-established ritual and mythic as well as ecological patterns in the South-west. Detailed parallels, not only with mainland Australia but also with Tasmania, point back to a time when similar constructs prevailed over an undivided continent. Fire remained an important element in burial rites, as it did in Tasmania also, and as it had been in the Murray basin 25,000 years earlier. The archaeological and ethnographic evidence together underline the deep-meshed importance and antiquity of fire in the symbolic and ecological patterning of land and life, in 'the shaping of the environment as the people themselves construe it' (Frake 1962).

Just as surely as swidden-agriculturalists—with whose world Australia had close links (Golson 1971*a*)—marsupial-graziers, root-gatherers, and fire-farmers round the margins of the Australian continent had to 'establish a controlled biotic community of sun-loving annuals and perennials in a climatic region whose natural climax community [was] radically different ... periodically putting the forest through its successional paces' (Frake 1962). At the same time, 'This niche-carving activity of man not only remolds existing biotic communities, but also has a shaping effect on the tools—that is on man's cultural knowledge and equipment—themselves' (*ibid*).

As well as the archaeological evidence of a continuous time-trajectory for the interactions of terrain and people, ecology, technology and symbol, Australia offers a cross section of these processes at the time they come into European view.

Such opportunities become increasingly attractive as archaeologists recognise that they have tended too narrowly to visualise cultures in terms of their tool traditions; that tool traditions stem from cognitive traditions; and that the basic fabric of the hunter-gatherer's culture was the 'highly developed skills of observation and recognition in the diverse realms of his environment ... knowledge of seasonal periodicities ... [and] symbol making that is "art" ... ritual and ceremony' as vehicles for the retention, enrichment and modification of this basic lore (Marshack 1970*b*:59,62). Valiant and valuable attempts have been made to extract evidence of such cognitive patterns from the cumulative and sequential use of images and symbols in the hunters' art of late glacial Europe (Marshack 1970*a*,1970*b*). Australia offers the possibility of studying not only artistic, but mythic and ceremonial, evidence of symbolic constructs; not only archaeological evidence of changes in distribution and density, but ethnographic evidence of the patterns of territorial attachment and seasonal exploitation, movement and ceremony, grouping and regrouping, technology and demography, which reflect ecological and ritual lore, and by which cognitive traditions impinge on landscape.

Fire had an ancient and crucial role in this antique reciprocity, in the shaping of Australian life, legend and land. We are ineluctably its heirs.

Appendix

References to fire and firing in the South-west.

These references are derived in the main from easily available published sources only, and no systematic search has been made of ephemera and unpublished journals.

References to *domestic* and *symbolic* use of *fire* are not exhaustive, but may be included when they may be confused with, or relevant to, the production of *bushfire*. These items are indicated by an asterisk. Entries are in approximately chronological order.

Observer	Year	Area	Date or Season	Extent, intensity etc.	Purpose and/or possible effect	Source
Willem de Vlamingh	1697	Swan River, coast opposite Rottnest	1 Jan.	'smoke arising at different points'	—	Major (ed.) 1859:91
			2 Jan.	'smoke arising'	—	*ibid*
			3 Jan.	'great numbers of fires ... the whole length of the coast'	—	*ibid*
Archibald Menzies (with Vancouver)	1791	King George Sound, hinterland	29 Sept.	'recently burnt ... here and there'	—	Menzies 1791:f.44
			30 Sept.	'few places ... but bore marks of fire'	—	*ibid*:f.46
			2 Oct.	'natives had recently had a fire'	—	*ibid*:f.50
			4 Oct.	'interior lately burnt ... trees bore ... marks of fire' trees hollowed by fire	'skirts of it ... covered with a luxuriant crop of grass'	*ibid*:f.52–3
			7 Oct.	'seldom met ... trees ... [not] burnt or scorshd' [*sic*]	'without any underwood to obstruct our progress'	*ibid*:f.55

Observer	Year	Location	Date	Observation	Comment	Reference
Capt. George Vancouver	1791		7 Oct. (*cont.*)	'several places about ... village ... very recently burnt down', larger trees scorched	—	*ibid*:f.57
			Sept.–Oct.	'general conflagration of the country'	'excellent range and good feeding' seen as due to 'busy, capricious disposition of natives'	*ibid*:f.61
			Sept.–Oct.	'general burnt state of the country'		*ibid*:f.62
		King George Sound, hinterland	Sept.–Oct.	'very extraordinary devastation by fire ... throughout the whole country'	'encouraging a sweeter growth of herbage' and 'taking wild animals'	Vancouver 1801:I,177–8
La Naturaliste and *Le Géographe* under Baudin	1801	Geographe Bay, coast	1 June	great fire behind the dunes	—	Peron and Freycinet 1807:I,68
		Geographe Bay, hinterland	4 June	everywhere a great quantity of burnt trees, extinguished fires	—	*ibid*:I,79
Matthew Flinders	1801	Point Hillier, W of King George Sound	8 Dec.	'smokes' on coast	—	Flinders 1814:I,79
		King George Sound	14 Dec.	'smokes'	—	*ibid*:I,57
Nicolas Baudin	1801	Geographe Bay	2 June	'three large fires ... too big and spreading for the inhabitants to be near them ... very likely lit by them'	—	Baudin 1800–3:171
			4 June	'many traces of fire'	mobile dunes, plains 'scattered ... full grown trees'	

Observer	Year	Location	Date	Description	'paths well-worn... much frequented'	Reference
			4 June (cont.)			ibid:174
La Naturaliste and Le Géographe	1803	Geographe Bay, coast	10 May	enormous and extensive fires all along the shore ... great fires to which they had seen nothing comparable since their last stay	—	Peron and Freycinet 1807:II,197
Capt. Philip King	1818	King George Sound	*21–31 Jan.	'smokes of their fires every evening'	—	King 1827:I,17
			,,	'whole woods may have been burnt down and grown again' within 16 years	—	ibid
			*24 Dec.	two natives 'each brought a lighted firestick'	'to make a fire and pass the night'	ibid:II,124
	1822	N of Swan River, coast	16 Jan.	'No native fires between [Jurien Bay] and Rottnest' cf. 'large smokes' further N	—	ibid:II,166
Scott Nind	1827–9	King George Sound, hinterland	summer	'fishing and burning season'	—	Nind 1831:28
			,,	'fire the country'	'for game'	ibid
			,,	'setting fire to the underwood and grass'	—	ibid
			,,	'violence ... frequently very great ... over many miles; ... generally burning by consecutive portions'	'for kangaroos or wallaby'	ibid

			"		'women also kindle fires'	ibid
			spring	'before the burning season commences'	—	ibid:29
			Christmas	'commence firing the country'	'for game'	ibid:36
			"	'women . . . carry a firestick . . . in the burning season set fire to the ground'	'get lizards, snakes and bandicoots'	ibid:36–7
			*?	burial—fire 'in front' of grave	—	ibid:46; Grey 1841:II,334
			*?	friction using twigs warmed at fire	to dispel disease	Nind 1831:41
Capt. James Stirling	1827	Swan River, Belmont	11 Mar.	'the smoke of many fires . . . different points'	—	Stirling 1827:557
		Swan River, Upper Swan	13 Mar.	'ground cleared by fire a few weeks before'	'cleared'	ibid:560
		*Swan River, estuary	16 Mar.	'fishing by torch-light'	light, etc.	ibid:561
		*Geographe Bay, the Vasse	24 Mar.	'fire'	'to warm themselves during the rain'	ibid:564
Capt. Charles H. Fremantle	1829	Swan estuary, near junction of Canning	3 May	'the trees were burnt and the bark stripped from them . . . the soil about this part was very black in many places occasioned by burning the trees and country.'	'there were many open places where the natives appeared to have been recently dwelling'	Fremantle 1928:38

Lt. William Preston	1829	Canning River E of Darling Scarp	Sept.	'trees... hollowed out by fire'	—	Preston 1833a:10
T. W. Wilson, Surgeon	1829	King George Sound, hinterland	*Dec. *Dec.	'[at] dark a large fire was kindled' 'at noon the natives kindle a fire'	large assembly, dancing 'to obtain knowledge of each other's situation'	Wilson 1835:274 ibid:282
Preston and Collie	1829	Geographe Bay to Leschenault estuary Peel Inlet, Murray delta	25 Nov. 29 Nov.	'smoke in many places' behind beach 'several fires' among the trees, 'so frequent burnt appearance', area burnt in last 12 days	— —	Collie and Preston 1833:46 ibid:49
Richard Dale	1829	Avon valley	10 Dec.	'the smoke of numerous fires' at base of hills eastward	—	Dale 1833b:33

Mary Ann Friend	1830	Swan River, Fremantle
		Swan River, Perth
		Swan River, Fremantle
			7 Feb.
			10 Feb.
			17 Feb.
				'numerous fires'
				'many parts [of bush] burnt'
				'large fire' burnt settler's encampment
					'made heat intense'
					—
					'to drive kangaroos'
						Friend 1931:6
						ibid:7
						ibid:18

Dewar and Smith	1830?	Augusta Augusta to Cape Naturaliste	15 Mar. 15–21 March	'district lately burnt' 'whole country... has been burnt'	— —	Anon.1833a:110 ibid:112
Richard Dale	1830	E of Avon valley	1 Nov.	'sheet of water... around which were seven native fires'	'extensive downs'	Dale 1833d:67

Observer	Year	Location	Date			Reference
'T. W. H.'	1830	E of Avon valley	28 Oct.	'where *not* burnt ... low scrub'	—	T. W. H. 1833:213
			30 Oct.	'the smoke of a native fire ten miles [E]'	'native grasses grew very strong'	*ibid*:215
			1 Nov.	'a view of the native fires'	—	*ibid*:216
		Jarrah forest, E of Darling Scarp	6 Nov.	114 foot tree 'burnt down'	—	*ibid*:220
John Bussell	1831?	Augusta, N along Blackwood River	?	'the bush, where unburnt, luxuriant'		Bussell 1833*a*:184
			?	'many [trees] much injured by fire'		*ibid*:185
		Blackwood River	?	'best land I had yet seen...recently burnt'	'then free from a woody bush'	Bussell 1833*b*:187
	1831?	N of Blackwood R.	?	'a country clean burnt'	'large spaces ... without underwood ... kangaroos...abundant'	*ibid*:188–9
		Geographe Bay, 'the Vasse'	?	'*un*sullied with burnt sticks'	'vegetation succulent'	*ibid*:191
Thomas Bannister	1831	SE from Perth, towards King George Sound	23 Dec.–12 Jan.	'many parts had been recently burnt, probably last year'	'this year the herbage was quite green and fresh'	Bannister 1833:102
Whale Boat crew	1831	NW of Point d'Entrecasteaux	21 Apr.	'country *not* recently burnt'	almost impenetrable	Anon.1833*b*:118
A. Collie, Surgeon	1831	King George Sound, hinterland	27 Apr.	'fire ... by which the natives seem repeatedly to have consumed the vegetable production'	Collie believes repeated fire hardens clayey soil	Collie 1833*a*:135
		Kalgan River valley	29 Apr.	channel 'filled with tall shrubs, now burnt', surrounds 'in many parts burnt'	'partly bare, partly covered with trees'	*ibid*:140–1

George Fletcher Moore	1831	Avon valley	30 Apr.	'fire had recently gone over [the] surface' of a broad belt of good soil	'wattle shrub' cleared	ibid:144
			17 Oct.	'wherever a tree has been burnt'	'patches of grass'	Moore 1884a:70
Richard Dale	1832	King George Sound hinterland, view from Toolbrunup, in Stirling Range	23 Jan.	'native fires … materially obstructed our view towards the coast'	'dense forest' and 'open country' 'driving objects of chase from their fastnesses'	Dale 1833f:163–5
			summer	'fires … periodically spread over vast tracts of country'		Dale 1834:13
			"	'natives set fire to country round for many miles'	'extreme heat … increased'	ibid:14
A. Collie	1832	King George Sound hinterland, Kalgan valley	10 Feb.	'atmosphere … thickened with the smoke of native fires'	'fine soil and feed, … good deal of pasturage'	Collie 1833b:170–1
John Bussell	1832	Augusta to the Vasse	summer	'forest blazing with native fires'	impression of heat reinforced	Shann 1926:82
George Fletcher Moore	1833	Swan River, coastal plain	2 Jan.	'a fire on the great plain'	—	Moore 1884a:156
Nancy Turner	1833	Augusta	22 Jan.	'natives burnt bush' dangerous to houses	—	McDermott 1928:17
*Capt. Chidley Irwin	early 1830s	Swan River	—	'a blazing fire'	light for corrobories	Irwin 1835:24

George Fletcher Moore	1834	Swan River	20 Feb.	'country fired by the natives... flames quite terrific and overwhelming.'	—	Moore 1884a:211
		Chittering valley	20 Mar.	'country had been recently burnt'		ibid:216
		Swan River	summer	'the natives set fire to grass and dry herbage'	grass on lake borders	ibid:219
		Avon valley	summer	'over the hills grants... are less burned, being less frequented'	'for... their hunting' by implication, areas most frequented are most exposed to casual and deliberate firing	ibid
	1836	Moore River	April	'the grass fine, whenever it had not been burned'	burnt ground associated with good grazing	Erickson 1971:2–3
	1830s	Swan River settlement	—	'after country has been burnt'	'young grass'	Moore 1884b:45
			—	'burned ground'	'progress unobstructed, tracks... easily discerned'	ibid:60
		Swan River coastal plain and 'highland' interior	*—	burial—use of fire; plus frequent lighting of fire near grave	to solace spirit of deceased	ibid:11–12
			summer	flag leaves 'burned by summer fires'	roots improved	ibid:81
			*all year	lighted bark	warmth	ibid:20–1
Lt. H. W. Bunbury	1836	Murray to the Vasse	18 Dec.	'Natives kindled a large fire'	'to announce our coming'	Bunbury 1930:74
			,,	'several fires from different spots'	answer	ibid
	*Leschenault Inlet		,,	'numerous lights'	'for attracting fish'	ibid:76
			*,,	'firestick'	fear of evil spirits	ibid

Observer	Year	Location	Date	Observation	Purpose	Reference
		Murray to the Vasse	*	'fires on a large scale' on river bank	attracting fish to spear; roasting?	*ibid*
			"	'extensive bushfires [kept] within due bounds only burning those parts they wish when the scrub becomes too thick'	country kept free from underwood, ease of tracking, elimination of obstructive scrub	*ibid*:105
	1837	Swan River to the Vasse	12 Mar.	'Natives burnt much of the country . . . all blackened and bare . . . charred trunks'	—	*ibid*:179
Nathaniel Ogle	Late 1830s	Swan River	'sometimes'	Aborigines 'set on fire dry grass'	'to capture snakes and reptiles'	Ogle 1839:63
George Fletcher Moore	*1837	Swan River, Middle Swan	27 Aug.	burial—fire in grave, beard singed	—	Moore 1884a:329
	*1838		7 May	burial—fire in grave; hair, beard and fingernail singed'	—	*ibid*:346
James Backhouse	1838	Swan River, Perth	22 Jan.	'bush . . . recently burnt . . . natives setting fire to scrub.	'to facilitate hunting and afford young herbage to the kangaroos'	Backhouse 1843:341
Georgiana Molloy	1838	Geographe Bay, the Vasse	Jan.	'a native fire' excessively mild	accelerated seed ripening	Hasluck A. 1955:157
	1841	Geographe Bay, the Vasse	7 Apr.	'surrounding native fires'	accelerated seed ripening	*ibid*:225

Observer	Date	Location	Season/Time	Observation	Purpose	Reference
Sir George Grey	1839	W of Williams	20 Jan.	'scrub . . . in some places completely destroyed by the native fires'	—	Grey 1841:I,321
	*1839	Swan River, Perth	15 June	burial—fire in grave	to draw out '*boyl-yas*'	*ibid*:II,326
*John Bussell	?	Geographe Bay, the Vasse	?	burial—fire in grave	—	*ibid*:II,332
Sir George Grey	Late 1830s	Swan River settlement	*night	natives twirl and throw lighted brand	to get rid of evil spirit supposed to cause nightmare	*ibid*:II,339–40
			*night	natives carry a light when moving after dark and set fire to bushes		
			*night	firesticks carried hunting opossums	fear of evil spirits	*ibid*:II,340
			*night	'lights' carried near shallow water	light	*ibid*:II,287
			*winter	natives stay by fire in hut during rain	to (attract and) spear fish	*ibid*
			*winter	carrying firestick	warmth	*ibid*:II,262
			*	banksia cones carried by women	warmth	*ibid*:II,262,267
			*	fungus carried by women	to transport fire	*ibid*:II,266
					to kindle fire rapidly	*ibid*
Sir George Grey	Late 1830s	Swan River, near Perth	'dry seasons', unspecified	'frequently burnt leaves' of flag	'in order to improve it'	*ibid*:II,194
				'burning the bush'	to catch smaller animals	*ibid*:II,291
			,,	'natives fire the bush'	to take wallaby and small kangaroo	*ibid*
			,,	'they fire the bushes'	driving kangaroo	*ibid*:II,270

Author	Date	Location	Time/Season	Description	Purpose/Effect	Reference
J. Lort Stokes	*1840	Swan River settlement	—	'kindle a fire'	'to avert the evil spirit' equated with powerful serpent	Stokes 1846:I,58
	1840	15 miles N of King George Sound	—	'burning the bush... in sections every year'	'destruction of snakes, lizards and small wallaby'	ibid:II,228
			—	'burning of the grass'	'to take the older animals', and to 'provide a new crop of sweeter grass'	Eyre 1845:II,299
			*	—	to 'keep monsters away'	ibid:II,257
Robert Austin	1841–3	Leschenault Estuary (Bunbury district)	*night	'fire' 'lighted firestick'	to repel evil spirits, and light to avoid snakes, etc.	Roth 1902:52
			*home camp	fire in front of entrance of each hut; whole camp arranged in crescent around fires 'lighted firestick'	light, heat and social focus	ibid:61–2
			*cold weather		warmth	ibid:64
			*wet weather	'lighted sticks'	to transport fire, when production by twirling difficult	ibid:66
Rev. John Ramsden Wollaston	1841	Swan River settlement, general	Nov.	'bush fires ... this year most extensive... caused by natives, either accidentally or intentionally'	'... for driving animals and reptiles into one spot or the margin of some river or swamp ... burnt ground ... sends up in the rainy season a sweeter crop of grass which attracts the kangaroo'	Wollaston 1841–44:13

	1848	Jarrah forest E of Perth, W of York	27 Nov.	'bush fire running through the forest burning the dry scrub'	'preparing the ground for a fresh and greener growth'	Wollaston 1848–56:79
Septimius Roe	1848	Perth to Esperance	19 Nov.	'tracts of country in which their fires were burning' 'signal smokes'	signals showed country was 'better peopled'	Roe 1852:15
		Esperance area	7 Dec.	'large smokes'	—	ibid:22
		Esperance area	15 Dec.	'tracks and fires of natives . . . burnt sticks and scrub at a brackish pool'		ibid:27
	1849	E of Stirling Range	16 Jan.	'extensively fired'	'grassy forest land'	ibid:53
		Kojonup area	20 Jan.	'extensively burnt by natives'	'grass here was extensive'	ibid:55
A. C. Gregory	1848	Approaching Murchison River	25 Sept.	'thicket burnt off by native fires'	'patch of good grass'	Gregory 1884:18
		Murchison River	26 Sept.	'bush fires . . . had burnt some large patches'	these patches were passable	ibid:18
		Murchison River	3 Oct.	'thickets . . . burnt by natives about four years previous'	impassable	ibid:20
William Henry Graham	1861	South coast W of Broke Inlet	—	'burning the ground'	getting wallabies, 'long coarse grass'	Stephens 1954:53
	1862	Kojonup	15 Dec.	'Native set my run on fire'	—	ibid:56
	*1870s	Kojonup	—	burial—thumb nail burnt off; fire by grave	to prevent dead from escaping; and for his use	Curr 1886:348

Mrs E. Hassell	1870s	Bremer Bay area	'end of the summer'	'Every year the natives burnt great tracts... When the time was ripe for the bushfires [*man carl*] the *man carl* corroborree was held... the next day the entire camp left to start their *man carl* in all directions.'	'...to make sure the grass would come up green and sweet with the first rains and to drive out the game...'	Hassell 1936:698,700
Mrs. Millett	c.1870	York area	winter	'in wet weather [they] carry a piece of smouldering wood'	warmth, and for lighting fire	Millett 1872:77
*Roger Goldsworthy	1879	York area	—	fire 'a little distance from their own'	for use of dead	Curr 1886:I,339
*W. E. Knight	1880s	Perth area	—	fire in grave, hair singed; fire apart	latter for use of dead	*ibid*:I,330
*Dick Jones	1890s?	Gingin/Moore River	—	fire near grave, with billy in tree	obviously for comfort of dead	Mrs R. Roe, Gingin
*Jesse Hammond	1890s	Kellerberrin	—	myth of burning down great tree	—	Hammond 1933:64–5

Corrections to the first edition

Two authors have been wrongly conflated by the 1975 editor: J. G. (Grahame) D. Clark and J. D. (Desmond) Clark. The entries should read:

CLARK, J. D.   1971   A re-examination of the evidence for agricultural origins in the Nile valley. In Prehistoric Society, Proceedings, v.37, pt. 2: 34–79.
CLARK, J. G. D.   1970a   Aspects of Prehistory. Berkeley, University of California Press.
——   1970b   Review of 'The prehistory of Australia" by D. J. Mulvaney, Mankind v.7, no.3: 231–232.
——   1972   Star Carr: a case study in bioarchaeology. (Addison-Wesley Modular Publications, no 10).

References

ALFORD, J. L.   1970   Extinction as a possible factor in the invention of New World agriculture. *Professional Geographer*, v.22: 120–123.
ANON.   1833a   Account of the country intervening between Augusta and Swan River. *In* Cross, J., ed. Journals of several expeditions: 110–113.
——   1833b   Report of an excursion in a whale boat, from six miles to the eastward of Ramé Point to six miles to the N.W. of Point d'Entrecasteaux, and from thence to the Murray River by land. *In* Cross, J., ed. Journals of several expeditions: 114–131.
ANELL, B.   1960   Hunting and trapping methods in Australia and Oceania. [Lund, Ohlsson]. (Studia ethnographica Upsaliensia XVIII).
ARNDT, W.   1962   The interpretation of the Delemere lightning painting and rock engravings. *Oceania*, v.32, no. 3: 163–177.
AULD, M. L.   1954   Harriett and Mary Ann King: pioneer women. *In* Western Australian Historical Society. Journal and proceedings, v.4, pt.6: 35–46.
BACKHOUSE, J.   1843   A narrative of a visit to the Australian colonies. London, Hamilton, Adams and Co.
BAIRD, A. M.   1958   Notes on the regeneration of Garden Island after the 1956 fire. *In* Royal Society of Western Australia. Journal, v.41: 102–107.
BANNISTER, T.   1833   A report of Captain Bannister's journey to King George's Sound, over land. *In* Cross, J., ed. Journals of several expeditions: 98–109.
BARBETTI, M. *and* H. ALLEN   1972   Prehistoric man at Lake Mungo, Australia, by 32,000 years BP. *Nature*, v.240, no.5375: 46–48.
BATES, D. M.   1938   The passing of the Aborigines. London, John Murray.
BAUDIN, N.   1800–3   The journal of Post Captain Nicolas Baudin Commander-in-Chief of the corvettes *Géographe* and *Naturaliste*. Translated from the French by Christine Cornell. Adelaide Libraries Board of South Australia, 1974.

BERMINGHAM, A., PACKHAM, D. R. *and* R. G. VINES 1971 The age of the petrified forest near Denmark, Western Australia. *Search*, v.2, no.11-12: 434-435.
BERNDT, R. M., *ed.* [1970] Australian Aboriginal anthropology. [Nedlands], University of Western Australia Press.
BERNDT, R. M. *and* C. H. BERNDT 1964 The world of the first Australians: an introduction to the traditional life of the Australian Aborigines. Sydney, Ure Smith.
——— 1970 Man, land & myth in north Australia: the Gunwinggu people. Sydney, Ure Smith.
BETTENAY, E. 1962 The salt lake systems and their associated aeolian features in the semi-arid regions of Western Australia. *Journal of Soil Science*, v.13: 10-17.
BIGNELL, M. 1971 First the spring: a history of the Shire of Kojonup, Western Australia. [Nedlands], University of Western Australia Press for the Kojonup Shire Council.
BINFORD, L. R. [1968] Post-Pleistocene adaptations. *In* Binford, S. R. *and* L. R. Binford, *eds.* New perspectives in archeology: 313-341.
BINFORD, S. R. *and* L. R. BINFORD, *eds.* [1968] New perspectives in archeology. Chicago, Aldine Publishing Co.
BOWLER, J. M. 1970 Alluvial terraces in the Maribyrnong valley near Keilor, Victoria. *In* National Museum of Victoria. Memoir, no.30: 15-58.
——— 1971 Pleistocene salinities and climatic change: evidence from lakes and lunettes in southeastern Australia. *In* Mulvaney, D. J. *and* J. Golson, *eds.* Aboriginal man and environment in Australia: 47-65.
BOWLER, J. M., MULVANEY, D. J., CASEY, D. A. *and* T. A. DARRAGH 1967 The Green Gully burial. *Nature*, v.213, no.5072: 152-154.
BOWLER, J. M., JONES, R., ALLEN, H. *and* A. G. THORNE 1970 Pleistocene human remains from Australia: a living site and human cremation from Lake Mungo, western New South Wales. *World Archaeology*, v.2, no.1: 39-60.
BOWLER, J. M., THORNE, A. G. *and* H. A. POLACH 1972 Pleistocene man in Australia: age and significance of the Mungo skeleton. *Nature*, v.240, no.5375: 48-50.
BRETON, W. H. 1833 Excursions in New South Wales, Western Australia and Van Diemen's Land during the years 1830, 1831, 1832 and 1833. London, Bentley.
BUCHANAN, R. H., JONES, E. *and* D. McCOURT, *eds.* 1971 Man and his habitat. London, Routledge and Kegan Paul.
BULLER-MURPHY, D. [1958] An attempt to eat the moon: and other stories recounted from the Aborigines. Melbourne, Georgian House.
BUNBURY, H. W. 1930 Early days in Western Australia. London, Oxford University Press.
BUSSELL, J. C. 1833*a* Report of an excursion to the northward from Augusta. *In* Cross, J., *ed.* Journals of several expeditions: 178-185.
——— 1833*b* Mr. Bussell's journal of an expedition to the River Vasse, from the Blackwood. *In* Cross, J., *ed.* Journals of several expeditions: 186-203.
BUTLER, W. H. 1950 Some previously unrecorded Aboriginal artefact sites near Perth, Western Australia. *Western Australian Naturalist*, v.3, no.6: 133-136.

BUTLER, W. H. *and* D. MERRILEES 1971 Remains of *Potorous platyops* (Marsupialia, Macropodidae) and other mammals from Bremer Bay, Western Australia. *In* Royal Society of Western Australia. Journal, v.54: 53–58.

BYRNE, J. C. 1848 Twelve years' wanderings in the British Colonies from 1835 to 1847. London, Bentley. 2v.

CALVERT, A. F. 1894 The Aborigines of Western Australia. London, Simpkin, Marshall, Hamilton, Kent & Co.

CASTELL, C. P. 1964 The molluscan fauna. *In* Ovey, C. D., *ed.* The Swanscombe skull: 77–83.

CHANG, K. 1970 The beginnings of agriculture in the Far East. *Antiquity*, v.44: 175–185.

CHAUNCY, P. 1878 Notes and anecdotes of the Aborigines of Australia. *In* Smyth, R. B. The Aborigines of Victoria, v.2, appendix A: 221–284.

CHURCHILL, D. M. 1959 Late Quaternary eustatic changes in the Swan River district. *In* Royal Society of Western Australia. Journal, v.42, 53–55.

—— 1968 The distribution and prehistory of *Eucalyptus diversicolor* F. Muell., *E. marginata*. Donn ex Sm., and *E. calophylla* R. Br. in relation to rainfall. *Australian Journal of Botany*, v.16: 125–151.

CLARK, J. G. D. 1970a Aspects of prehistory. Berkeley, University of California Press.

—— 1970b Review of "The prehistory of Australia" by D. J. Mulvaney. *Mankind*, v.7, no.3: 231–232.

—— 1971 A re-examination of the evidence for agricultural origins in the Nile valley. *In* Prehistoric Society. Proceedings, v.37, pt.2: 34–79.

—— 1972 Star Carr: a case study in bioarchaeology. (Addison-Wesley Modular Publications, no.10).

CLELAND, Sir J. B. 1935 The native of Central Australia and his surroundings. *In* Royal Geographical Society of Australasia, South Australian Branch. Proceedings, v.35: 66–81.

COLLIE, A. 1833a Account of an excursion to the north of King George's Sound, between the 26th of April, and the 4th of May, 1831. *In* Cross, J., *ed.* Journals of several expeditions: 132–154.

—— 1833b Account of a short excursion from Albany up French River. *In* Cross, J., *ed.* Journals of several expeditions: 168–177.

COLLIE, A. *and* W. PRESTON 1833 Observations on the coast, country &c. from Cockburn Sound to Geographe Bay, between the 17th and 30th of November 1829. *In* Cross, J., *ed.* Journals of several expeditions: 35–50.

COLLINGRIDGE, G. 1895 The discovery of Australia. Sydney, Hayes.

COWAN, Mrs. J. 1931 Some pioneer women. *In* Royal Western Australian Historical Society. Journal, v.1, no.10: 44–51.

CRAWFORD, I. M. 1968 The art of the Wandjina. Melbourne, Oxford University Press.

—— 1972 Function and change in Aboriginal rock art, Western Australia. *World Archaeology*, v.3, no.3: 301–312.

CROSS, J., *ed.* 1833 Journals of several expeditions made in Western Australia during the years 1829, 1830, 1831, and 1832; under the sanction of the Governor, Sir James Stirling, containing the latest authentic information relative to that country. London, J. Cross.

CURR, E. M. 1886–1887 The Australian race. Melbourne, Govt. Pr. 4v. in 3.

DALE, Richard   1833a   Mr. Richard Dale's first excursion to trace the Helena River, in October, 1829. *In* Cross, J., *ed.* Journals of several expeditions: 27–29.
―――― 1833b   Mr. Dale's second excursion to trace the Helena River, in December, 1829. *In* Cross, J., *ed.* Journals of several expeditions: 30–34.
―――― 1833c   Journal of an expedition under the direction of Ensign Dale to the eastward of the Darling Mountains; in August, 1831. *In* Cross, J., *ed.* Journals of several expeditions: 51–61.
―――― 1833d   Journal of another expedition to the eastward of the Darling Range, under the direction of Ensign Dale; commenced on the 25th of October, and concluded on the 7th of November, 1830. *In* Cross, J., *ed.* Journals of several expeditions: 62–72.
―――― 1833e   Letters from Mr. Dale, giving a summary description of the country passed over in going to Mount Bakewell, and, also, in an expedition to examine the country to the north and south of that place. *In* Cross, J., *ed.* Journals of several expeditions: 155–160.
―――― 1833f   Mr. Dale's journal of an expedition from King George's Sound to the Koikyennuruff Range of mountains. *In* Cross, J., *ed.* Journals of several expeditions: 161–167.
DALE, Richard   1834   Descriptive account of the panoramic view, &c. of King George's Sound, and the adjacent country. London, J. Cross.
DARWIN, C.   1859   The origin of species. London, John Murray.
DAVIDSON, D. S.   1935a   The chronology of Australian watercraft. *In* Polynesian Society. Journal, v.44: 1–16.
―――― 1935b   Archaeological problems of northern Australia. *In* Royal Anthropological Institute. Journal, v.65: 145–183.
―――― 1947   Fire-making in Australia. *American Anthropologist*, v.49, no.3: 426–437.
―――― 1948   Disposal of the dead in Western Australia. *In* American Philosophical Society. Proceedings, v.93, no.1: 71–97.
DAVIDSON, D. S. *and* F. D. McCARTHY   1957   The distribution and chronology of some important types of stone implements in Western Australia. *Anthropos*, v.52: 390–458.
DAVIES, J. L.   1964   A vegetation map of Tasmania. *Geographical Review*, v.54: 249–253.
―――― [1967]   Tasmanian landforms and Quaternary climates. *In* Jennings, J. N. *and* J. A. Mabbutt, *eds.* Landform studies from Australia and New Guinea: 1–25.
DAVIES, P. L.   1968   An 8,000 to 12,000 years old human tooth from Western Australia. *Archaeology & Physical Anthropology in Oceania*, v.3, no.1: 33–40.
DIMBLEBY, G. W.   1961   The ancient Forest of Blackamore. *Antiquity*, v.35: 123–128.
―――― 1962   The development of British heathlands and their soils. Oxford, Clarendon Press.
DORTCH, C. E.   1972   Archaeological work in the Ord Reservoir area, east Kimberley. *In* Australian Institute of Aboriginal Studies. Newsletter, v.3, no.4: 13–18.
DORTCH, C. E. *and* D. MERRILEES   1971   A salvage excavation in Devil's Lair, Western Australia. *In* Royal Society of Western Australia. Journal, v.54, pt.4: 103–113.

—— 1973 Human occupation of Devil's Lair, Western Australia during the Pleistocene. *Archaeology & Physical Anthropology in Oceania*, v.8, no.2: 89–115.

DOUGLAS, A. M., KENDRICK, G. W. and D. MERRILEES 1966 A fossil bone deposit near Perth, Western Australia, interpreted as a carnivore's den after feeding tests on living *Sarcophilus* (Marsupialia, Dasyuridae). *In* Royal Society of Western Australia. Journal, v.49; 88–90.

EDWARDS, R. 1965 Rock engravings and Aboriginal occupation at Nackara Springs in the north-east of South Australia. *In* South Australian Museum. Records, v.15, no.1: 9–27.

EDWARDS, R. *and* L. MAYNARD 1967 Prehistoric art in Koonalda Cave. *In* Royal Geographical Society of Australasia, South Australian Branch. Proceedings, v.68: 11–17.

ELKIN, A. P. 1930 The Rainbow-Serpent myth in north-west Australia. *Oceania*, v.1, no.3: 349–352.

ERICKSON, R. 1969 The Drummonds of Hawthornden. Perth, Lamb Paterson.

—— 1971 The Victoria Plains. Perth, Lamb Paterson.

ERSKINE 1833 Journal of Lieut. Ad. Erskine ... travelling from Perth to the eastward, over Darling's Range, in the month of September, 1830. *In* Cross, J., ed. Journals of several expeditions: 92–97.

ETHERIDGE, R. 1890 Notes on Australian Aboriginal stone weapons and implements. *In* Linnean Society of New South Wales. Proceedings, v.15: 251–258, 289–293, 367–372.

—— 1891 Notes on Australian Aboriginal stone weapons and implements. *In* Linnean Society of New South Wales. Proceedings, v.16: 31–43.

EYRE, E. J. 1845 Journals of expeditions of discovery into Central Australia, and overland from Adelaide to King George's Sound, in the years 1840–1; ... including an account of the manners and customs of the aborigines and the state of their relations with Europeans. London, T. and W. Boone. 2v.

FLANNERY, K. V. 1968 Archaeological systems theory and early Meso-America. *In* Meggers, B., ed. Anthropological archaeology in the Americas: 67–87. (Reprinted *in* Deetz, J., ed. Man's imprint from the past, 1971: 344–364).

—— [1969] Origins and ecological effects of early domestication in Iran and the Near East. *In* Ucko, P. J. *and* G. W. Dimbleby, eds. The domestication and exploitation of plants and animals: 73–100.

FLINDERS, M. 1814 A voyage to Terra Australis; undertaken for the purpose of completing the discovery of that vast country, and prosecuted in the years 1801, 1802, and 1803, in His Majesty's Ship The Investigator. London, G. and W. Nicol. 2v.

FRAKE, C. O. 1962 Cultural ecology and ethnography. *American Anthropologist*, v.64, pt.1: 53–59.

FREMANTLE, C. H. 1928 Diary and letters of Admiral Sir C. H. Fremantle, G.C.B., relating to the founding of the Colony of Western Australia, 1829. Ed. by Lord Cottesloe. London.

FRIEND, M. A. 1931 The diary of Mary Ann Friend. *In* Western Australian Historical Society. Journal and proceedings, v.1, pt.10: 1–11.

GARDNER, C. A. 1942 The vegetation of Western Australia. *In* Royal Society of Western Australia. Journal, v.28: xi–lxxxvii.
——— 1957 The fire factor in relation to the vegetation of Western Australia. *Western Australian Naturalist*, v.5: 116–173.
——— 1959 The vegetation of Western Australia. *In* Keast, A., Crocker, R. L. *and* C. S. Christian, eds. Biogeography and ecology in Australia: 274–282.
GENTILLI, J. [1946] Australian climates and resources. Perth, Whitcombe and Tombs.
GLAUERT, L. 1950 Provisional list of Aboriginal place names and their meanings. *In* Western Australian Historical Society. Journal and proceedings, v.4, pt.2: 83–86.
GLOVER, J. E. *and* A. E. COCKBAIN 1971 Transported Aboriginal artefact material, Perth Basin, Western Australia. *Nature*, v.234: 545–546.
GLOVER, R. 1954 Captain Symers at Albany. *In* Western Australian Historical Society. Journal and proceedings, v.4, pt.5: 74–93.
GODWIN, H. 1944*a* Neolithic forest clearance. *Nature*, v.153: 511–512.
——— 1944*b* Breckland heaths. *Nature*, v.154: 6–7.
——— 1956 The history of the British flora. Cambridge, Cambridge University Press.
GOLSON, J. 1971*a* Australian Aboriginal food plants: some ecological and culture-historical implications. *In* Mulvaney, D. J. *and* J. Golson, eds. Aboriginal man and environment in Australia: 196–238.
——— 1971*b* Both sides of the Wallace Line: Australia, New Guinea and Asian prehistory. *Archaeology & Physical Anthropology in Oceania*, v.6: 124–144.
GOODALE, J. C. 1970 An example of ritual change among the Tiwi of Melville Island. *In* Pilling, A. R. *and* R. A. Waterman, eds. Diprotodon to detribalization: 350–366.
GORMAN, C. F. 1969 Hoabinhian: a pebble-tool complex with early plant associations in south-east Asia. *In* Prehistoric Society. Proceedings, v.35: 355–358.
——— 1971 The Hoabinhian and after: subsistence patterns in southeast Asia during the late Pleistocene and Early Recent periods. *World Archaeology*, v.2, no.3: 300–320.
GOULD, R. A. 1968 Preliminary report on excavations at Puntutjarpa rockshelter, near the Warburton Ranges, Western Australia. *Archaeology & Physical Anthropology in Oceania*, v.3, no.3: 161–185.
——— [1969] Yiwara: foragers of the Australian desert. London, Collins.
——— 1971*a* Uses and effects of fire among the Western Desert Aborigines of Australia. *Mankind*, v.8, no.1: 14–24.
———1971*b* The archaeologist as ethnographer: a case from the Western Desert of Australia. *World Archaeology*, v.3, no.2: 143–177.
GOULD, R. A., KOSTER, D. A. *and* A. H. L. SONTZ 1971 The lithic assemblages of the Western Desert Aborigines of Australia. *American Antiquity*, v.36, no.2: 149–169.
GREGORY, Sir A. C. *and* F. T. GREGORY 1884 Journals of Australian explorations. Brisbane, Govt. Pr.
GREY, Sir G. 1841 Journals of two expeditions of discovery in North-West and Western Australia, during the years 1837, 38 and 39. London, T. and W. Boone. 2v.

GUILDAY, J. E. 1967 Differential extinction during late-Pleistocene and recent times. *In* Martin, P. S. *and* H. E. Wright, *eds.* Pleistocene extinctions: 121–140.

H., T. W. 1833 Journal of an expedition over General Darling's Range, 100 miles east from Swan River. *In* Cross, J., *ed.* Journals of several expeditions: 207–221.

HALE, H. M. *and* N. B. TINDALE 1930 Notes on some human remains in the lower Murray Valley, South Australia. *In* South Australian Museum. Records, v.4, no.2: 145–222.

HALLAM, S. J. 1970 Settlement round the Wash. *In* Phillips, C. W., *ed.* The Fenland in Roman times: 22–113.

—— 1971 Roof markings in the "Orchestra Shell" cave, Wanneroo, near Perth, Western Australia. *Mankind*, v.8, no.2: 90–103.

—— 1972*a* An archaeological survey of the Perth area, Western Australia: a progress report on art and artefacts, dates and demography. *In* Australian Institute of Aboriginal Studies. Newsletter, v.3, no.5: 11–19.

—— 1972*b* Comment on "Cognitive aspects of Upper Paleolithic engraving" by Alexander Marshack. *Current Anthropology*, v.13, no.3–4: 464–465.

—— 1973*a* Comment on "On the quality of evidence for the origin and dispersal of cultivated plants" by J. R. Harlan and J. M. J. de Wet. *Current Anthropology*, v.14, no.1–2: 57–58.

—— 1973*b* Ecology and demography in southwestern Australia. *In* Merrilees, D., *and others*. Aboriginal man in southwest Australia. *In* Royal Society of Western Australia. Journal, v.56, parts 1 and 2: 44–55.

—— 1974 Excavations in the Orchestra Shell Cave, Wanneroo, Western Australia. Part I. Ethnographic and environmental background. *Archaeology & Physical Anthropology in Oceania*, v.9, no.1: 66–84.

—— n.d. Part II. Archaeology. *Archaeology & Physical Anthropology in Oceania*, forthcoming.

HAMMOND, J. E. [1933] Winjan's people: the story of the south-west Australian Aborigines: ed. by Paul Hasluck. Perth, Imperial Printing Co.

—— 1936 Western pioneers: the battle well fought; ed. by O. K. Battye. Perth, Imperial Printing Co.

HARLAN, J. R. *and* J. M. J. DE WET 1973 On the quality of evidence for the origin and dispersal of cultivated plants. *Current Anthropology*, v.14, no.1–2: 51–62.

HARRIS, D. R. [1969] Agricultural systems, ecosystems and the origins of agriculture. *In* Ucko, P. J. *and* G. W. Dimbleby, *eds.* The domestication and exploitation of plants and animals: 3–15.

HARRISS, J. C. 1971 Explanation in prehistory. *In* Prehistoric Society. Proceedings, v.37, pt.1: 38–55.

HASLUCK, *Lady* A. 1955 Portrait with background: a life of Georgiana Molloy. Melbourne, Oxford University Press.

—— 1965 Thomas Peel of Swan River. Melbourne, Oxford University Press.

HASLUCK, *Sir* P. M. C. 1942 Black Australians: a survey of native policy in Western Australia, 1829–1897. Melbourne, Melbourne University Press.

HASSELL, E. 1936 Notes on the ethnology of the Wheelman tribe of southwestern Australia. Selected and edited by D. S. Davidson. *Anthropos*, v.31: 679–711.

HEARNE, T. 1970 Ecology and affinal ties among !Kung Bushmen and Coast Salish. *Mankind*, v.7, no.3: 199–204.
HEERES, J. E. 1899 The part borne by the Dutch in the discovery of Australia, 1606–1765. London, Luzac for the Royal Dutch Geographical Society.
HENTY, J. 1830 Memorandum made during a journey across the Darling Range at the Swan River Settlement, October 1830. *In* Charles Bonney Papers, v.1, item 38 [Mitchell Library (Sydney) Manuscript Collection No. A3304]
HERCUS, L. A. 1971 Eaglehawk and crow: a Madimadi version. *Mankind*, v.8, no.2: 137–140.
HIATT, B. 1969 Cremation in Aboriginal Australia. *Mankind*, v.7, no.2: 104–119.
HIGGS, E. S. *and* M. R. JARMAN 1969 The origins of agriculture: a reconsideration. *Antiquity*, v.43: 31–41.
HOLE, F. *and* K. V. FLANNERY 1967 The prehistory of southwestern Iran: a preliminary report. *In* Prehistoric Society. Proceedings, v.33: 147–206.
HOPE, G. S. *and* P. J. F. COUTTS 1971 Past and present Aboriginal food resources at Wilson's Promontory, Victoria. *Mankind*, v.8, no.2: 104–114.
HOWELL, F. C. 1960 European and northwest African Middle Pleistocene hominids. *Current Anthropology*, v.1, no.3: 195–232.
HOWITT, A. W. 1904 The native tribes of south-east Australia. London, Macmillan.
HUTCHINS, D. E. 1916 A discussion of Australian forestry, with special references to forestry in Western Australia... Perth, Govt. Pr.

IRVINE, F. R. 1970 Evidence of change in the vegetable diet of Australian Aborigines. *In* Pilling, A. R. *and* R. A. Waterman, *eds*. Diprotodon to detribalization: 278–284.
IRWIN, F. C. 1835 The state and position of Western Australia; commonly called the Swan-River Settlement. London, Simpkin, Marshall.
IVERSEN, J. 1941 Landnam i Danmarks Stenalder. Land occupation in Denmark's Stone Age. Copenhagen, Danmarks Geologiske Undersogelse. (Series 2, no.66).

JENNINGS, J. N. 1961 A preliminary report on Karst morphology of the Nullarbor Plains. Adelaide, South Australian Cave Exploration Group. (Occasional Papers, 2).
—— 1965 Man as a geological agent. *Australian Journal of Science*, v.28, no.2: 150–156.
—— 1967 Some karst areas of Australia. *In* Jennings, J. N. *and* J. A. Mabbutt, *eds*. Landform studies from Australia and New Guinea: 256–292.
—— 1971 Sea level changes and land links. *In* Mulvaney, D. J. *and* J. Golson, *eds*. Aboriginal man and environment in Australia: 1–13.
JENNINGS, J. N. *and* J. A. MABBUTT [1967] Landform studies from Australia and New Guinea. Canberra, Australian National University Press.
JOHNSTON, F. M. [1962] Knights and theodolites: a saga of surveyors. Sydney, Edwards and Shaw.

JONES, R. 1968 The geographical background to the arrival of man in Australia and Tasmania. *Archaeology & Physical Anthropology in Oceania*, v.3, no.3: 186–215.
—— 1969 Fire-stick farming. *Australian Natural History*, v.16, no.7: 224–228.
—— 1970 Tasmanian Aborigines and dogs. *Mankind*, v.7, no.4: 256–271.
—— 1971 The demography of hunters and farmers in Tasmania. *In* Mulvaney, D. J. *and* J. Golson, *eds.* Aboriginal man and environment in Australia: 270–287.

KEAST, A. 1959 The Australian environment. *In* Keast, A., Crocker, R. L. *and* C. S. Christian, *eds.* Biogeography and ecology in Australia: 15–35.
KEAST, A., CROCKER, R. L. *and* C. S. CHRISTIAN, *eds.* 1959 Biogeography and ecology in Australia. The Hague, W. Junk. (Monographiae biologicae, v.8).
KEMP, T. B. 1963 The prehistory of the Tasmanian Aborigines. *Australian Natural History*, v.14, no.8: 242–247.
KENNEDY, J. 1927 Perth in my boyhood. *In* Western Australian Historical Society. Journal and proceedings, v.1, pt.1: 7–10.
KING, A. R. n.d. The influence of colonisation on the forests and the prevalence of bush fires in Australia. Melbourne, C.S.I.R.O.
KING, P. P. 1827 Narrative of a survey of the intertropical and western coasts of Australia, performed between the years 1818 and 1822 ... with an appendix, containing various subjects relating to hydrography and natural history. London, John Murray. 2v.

LAMPERT, R. J. 1971*a* Coastal Aborigines of southeastern Australia. *In* Mulvaney, D. J. *and* J. Golson, *eds.* Aboriginal man and environment in Australia: 114–132.
—— 1971*b* Burrill Lake and Currarong: coastal sites in southern New South Wales. Canberra, Department of Prehistory, Research School of Pacific Studies, Australian National University. (Terra Australis, 1).
—— 1972 A carbon date for the Aboriginal occupation of Kangaroo Island, South Australia. *Mankind*, v.8, no.3: 223–224.
LANDOR, E. W. 1847 The bushman; or, life in a new country. London, Richard Bentley.
LAWRENCE, R. J. 1968 Aboriginal habitat and economy. Canberra, Dept. of Geography, School of General Studies, Australian National University. (Occasional papers, 6).
LEICHHARDT, L. 1847 Journal of an overland expedition in Australia, from Moreton Bay to Port Essington ... during the years 1844–1845. London, T. and W. Boone.
LE SOUEF, W. H. D. [1907] Wild life in Australia. Christchurch, N.Z., Whitcombe and Tombs.
LONG, J. P. M. 1970 Change in an Aboriginal community in Central Australia. *In* Pilling, A. R. *and* R. A. Waterman, *eds.* Diprotodon to detribalization: 318–322.
LUNDELIUS, E. L. 1960 Post-Pleistocene faunal succession in Western Australia and its climatic interpretation. *In* International Geological Congress. Report of the Twenty-first Session, Norden. Pt. IV: Chronology and climatology of the Quaternary: 142–153.

McARTHUR, W. M. 1957 Plant ecology of the coastal islands near Fremantle, W.A. In Royal Society of Western Australia. Journal, v.40: 46–64.

McARTHUR, W. M. and E. BETTENAY 1960 The development and distribution of the soils of the Swan coastal plain, Western Australia. Melbourne, C.S.I.R.O. (Soil publication no.16).

McBRYDE, I. 1964 The linear engravings of the Clarence valley, northern New South Wales. Oceania, v.34, no.3: 201–210.

—— 1966 Radiocarbon dates for northern New South Wales. Antiquity, v.40, no.160: 285–292.

—— 1968 Archaeological investigations in the Graman district. Archaeology & Physical Anthropology in Oceania, v.3, no.2: 77–93.

McCONNEL, U. H. 1931 The Rainbow-Serpent in north Queensland. Oceania, v.1, no.3: 347–349.

McDERMOTT, J. M. 1928 Augusta in 1833 [Selections from the diary of Nancy Ann Elizabeth Turner, Jan. to Dec. 1833]. In Western Australian Historical Society. Journal and proceedings, v.1, pt.4: 17–29.

MABBUTT, J. A. 1971 The Australian arid zone as a prehistoric environment. In Mulvaney, D. J. and J. Golson, eds. Aboriginal man and environment in Australia: 66–79.

MADDOCK, K. J. [1970]a Myths of the acquisition of fire in northern and eastern Australia. In Berndt, R. M., ed. Australian Aboriginal anthropology: 174–199.

—— 1970b Imagery and social structure at two Dalabon rock art sites. Anthropological Forum, v.2, no.4: 444–463.

MAJOR, R. H., ed. 1859 Early voyages to Terra Australis, now called Australia: a collection of documents, and extracts from early manuscript maps, illustrative of the history of discovery on the coasts of that vast island, from the beginning of the sixteenth century to the time of Captain Cook. London, Hakluyt Society.

MARSHACK, A. 1970a New techniques in the analysis and interpretation of Mesolithic notation and symbolic art. Valcamonica Symposium. Capo di Ponte, Centro di Studi Preistorici.

—— 1970b The baton of Montgaudier. Natural History, v.79: 56–63.

—— 1972a The roots of civilisation. New York, McGraw-Hill.

—— 1972b Cognitive aspects of Upper Palaeolithic engraving. Current Anthropology, v.13, no.3–4: 445–477.

MARTIN, P. S. 1966 Africa & Pleistocene overkill. Nature, v.212: 339–342.

—— 1967 Pleistocene overkill. In Martin, P. S. and H. E. Wright, eds. Pleistocene extinctions: 75–120.

—— 1973 The discovery of America. Science, v.179: 969–974.

MARTIN, P. S. and H. E. WRIGHT, eds. 1967 Pleistocene extinctions: the search for a cause. Yale, University Press.

MEGAW, J. V. S. 1967 Archaeology, art and Aborigines: a survey of historical sources and later Australian prehistory. In Royal Australian Historical Society. Journal, v.53, pt.4: 277–294.

MEGGITT, M. J. [1962] Desert people: a study of the Walbiri Aborigines of Central Australia. [Sydney], Angus and Robertson.

MENZIES, A. 1791 Journal, [folio] 43–74. [Mitchell Library (Sydney) Manuscript Collection No. B1135]

MERRILEES, D. 1968 Man the destroyer: late Quaternary changes in the Australian marsupial fauna. *In* Royal Society of Western Australia. Journal, v.51: 1–24.

MILLETT, Mrs. E. 1872 An Australian parsonage: or the settler and the savage in Western Australia. London, Stanford.

MITCHELL, Sir T. L. 1848 Journal of an expedition into the interior of tropical Australia, in search of a route from Sydney to the Gulf of Carpentaria. London, Longman.

MOGEY, J. 1971 Society, man and environment. *In* Buchanan, R. H., Jones, E. *and* D. McCourt, *eds*. Man and his habitat: 79–92.

MOORE, G. F. 1884*a* Diary of ten years eventful life of an early settler in Western Australia. London, Walbrook.

—— 1884*b* A descriptive vocabulary of the language in common use amongst the Aborigines of Western Australia; with copious meanings, embodying much interesting information regarding the habits, manners, and customs of the natives, and the natural history of the country. London, William S. Orr and Co. First printed 1842. [Reprinted in 1884, in the same covers as his "Diary", paginated separately]

MOUNTFORD, C. P. [1958] The Tiwi: their art, myth and ceremony. London, Phoenix House.

MOUNTFORD, C. P. *and* E. J. BRANDL 1968 Aboriginal cave paintings and rock markings at Ingaladdi rock shelter, Willeroo, Northern Territory of Australia. *In* South Australian Museum. Records, v.15, no.4: 679–692.

MULCAHY, M. J. 1967 Landscapes, laterites and soils in southwestern Australia. *In* Jennings, J. N. *and* J. A. Mabbutt, *eds*. Landform studies from Australia and New Guinea: 211–230.

MULVANEY, D. J. 1964 The Pleistocene colonization of Australia. *Antiquity*, v.38, no.152: 263–267.

—— [1969] The prehistory of Australia. London, Thames and Hudson. (Ancient peoples and places, no.65).

—— 1970 Green Gully revisited: the later excavations. *In* National Museum of Victoria. Memoirs, v.30: 59–77.

—— 1971*a* Aboriginal social evolution: a retrospective view. *In* Mulvaney, D. J. *and* J. Golson, *eds*. Aboriginal man and environment in Australia: 368–380.

—— 1971*b* Discovering man's place in nature. [Sydney], Sydney University Press for Australian Academy of the Humanities.

MULVANEY, D. J. *and* J. GOLSON, *eds*. 1971 Aboriginal man and environment in Australia. Canberra, Australian National University Press.

MULVANEY, D. J. *and* E. B. JOYCE 1965 Archaeological and geomorphological investigations on Mt. Moffatt Station, Queensland, Australia. *In* Prehistoric Society. Proceedings, v.31: 147–212.

MULVANEY, D. J. *and* R. P. SOEJONO 1971 Archaeology in Sulawesi, Indonesia. *Antiquity*, v.45, no.177: 26–33.

MURRAY-GORDON, A. E. 1952 Pioneering days in the eastern wheatbelt. *In* Western Australian Historical Society. Journal and proceedings, v.4, pt.4: 76–88.

NARR, K. J. 1956 Early food-producing populations. *In* Thomas, W. L., *ed*. Man's role in changing the face of the earth: 134–151.

NATIONAL MUSEUM OF VICTORIA 1970 Memoir no.30: The Green Gully burial. Melbourne, National Museum of Victoria.

NIND, S. 1831 Description of the natives of King George's Sound (Swan River Colony) and adjoining country. *In* Royal Geographical Society. Journal, v.1: 21–51.

OAKLEY, K. P. 1952 The culture of Swanscombe Man. *In* Geological Association. Proceedings, v.63: 283–290.

—— 1956 The earliest firemakers. *Antiquity*, v.30: 102–107.

—— 1961 On man's use of fire, with comments on tool-making and hunting. *In* Washburn, S. L., *ed.* The social life of early man: 176–193.

—— 1964 The evidence of fire at Swanscombe. *In* Ovey, C. D. *ed.* The Swanscombe skull: 63–66.

OGLE, N. 1839 The colony of Western Australia: a manual for emigrants to that settlement or its dependencies. London, James Fraser.

OVEY, C. D., *ed.* 1964 The Swanscombe skull: a survey of research on a Pleistocene site. London, Royal Anthropological Institute. (Occasional papers, 20).

PEACOCK, B. A. V. 1971 Early cultural development in south-east Asia with special reference to the Malay Peninsula. *Archaeology & Physical Anthropology in Oceania*, v.6, no.2: 107–123.

PEARCE, R. H. 1973 Uniformity of the Australian backed blade tradition. *Mankind*, v.9, no.2: 89–95.

—— n.d. The spatial and temporal distribution of Australian backed blades. *Mankind*, forthcoming.

PEARSON, M. C. 1956 A pollen-analytical investigation of a Bronze Age barrow at Swarkeston. *In* Derbyshire Archaeological & Natural Historical Society. Journal: 23–25.

PERON, F. A. *and* L. FREYCINET 1807 Voyage de découvertes aux Terres Australes exécuté sur les corvettes le Géographe, le Naturaliste, et la goelette le Casuarina, Pendant les années 1800, 1801, 1802, 1803 et 1804... Paris, Imprimerie Impériale.

PHILLIPS, C. W., *ed.* 1970 The Fenland in Roman times: studies of a major area of peasant colonization with a gazetteer covering all known sites and finds. London, Royal Geographical Society. (Research series, no.5.)

PILLING, A. R. *and* R. A. WATERMAN 1970 Diprotodon to detribalization: studies of change among the Australian Aborigines. East Lansing, Michigan State University Press.

PRESTON, W. 1833a A journal of the proceedings of a party of officers and men, belonging to His Majesty's Ship Sulphur, landed on the 8th of September, 1829, for the purpose of crossing the Darling Range of mountains, under the orders of Lieutenant Preston, R. N. *In* Cross, J., *ed.* Journals of several expeditions: 6–13.

—— 1833b Journal of an expedition under the command of Lieutenant Preston, to explore the coast to the northward of Swan River. *In* Cross, J., *ed.* Journals of several expeditions: 73–79.

PROUDFOOT, B. 1971 Man's occupance of the soil. *In* Buchanan, R. H., Jones, E. *and* D. McCourt, *eds.* Man and his habitat: 8–33.

RADCLIFFE-BROWN, A. R. 1926 The Rainbow-Serpent myth of Australia. *In* Royal Anthropological Institute. Journal, v.56: 19–25.

―― 1930 The Rainbow-Serpent myth in south-east Australia. *Oceania*, v.1, no.3: 342–347.
RIDE, W. D. L. 1958 The edge-ground axes of south-western Australia. *Western Australian Naturalist*, v.6, no.7: 162–179.
ROE, J. S. 1833 Government notice relative to Port Leschenault. *In* Cross, J., ed. Journals of several expeditions: 80–88.
―― 1852 Report of an expedition under the Surveyor-General, Mr. J. S. Roe, to the south-eastward of Perth, in Western Australia, between the months of September, 1848, and February, 1849, to the Hon. the Colonial Secretary. Communicated by the Colonial Office. *In* Royal Geographical Society. Journal, v.22: 1–57.
ROTH, H. L. 1899 The Aborigines of Tasmania. 2d ed. Halifax, King.
ROTH, W. E. 1902 Notes of savage life in the early days of West Australian settlement. *In* Royal Society of Queensland. Proceedings, v.17: 45–69.
SAUER, C. O. 1956 The agency of man on earth. *In* Thomas, W. L., ed. Man's role in changing the face of the earth: 49–69.
―― 1971 Plants, animals and man. *In* Buchanan, R. H., Jones, E. *and* D. McCourt, eds. Man and his habitat: 314–361.
SCHWARZ, D. W. 1956 Demographic changes in the early periods of Cohonina prehistory. *In* Willey, G., ed. Prehistoric settlement patterns in the New World: 26–31.
SERVENTY, V. N. 1952 Cave paintings near York and Hyden. *Western Australian Naturalist*, v.3, no.6: 121–130.
SHANN, E. O. G. 1926 Cattle Chosen: the story of the first group settlement in Western Australia 1829 to 1841. London, Oxford University Press.
SINGH, G. 1971 The Indus Valley culture: seen in the context of post-glacial climatic and ecological studies in north-west India. *Archaeology & Physical Anthropology in Oceania*, v.6, no.2: 177–189.
SMART, W. C. n.d. Mandurah and Pinjarrah: history of Thomas Peel and the Peel Estate, 1829–1865. Perth, Paterson and Brokensha.
SMITH, A. G. 1970 The influence of Mesolithic and Neolithic man on British vegetation. *In* Walker, D. *and* R. G. West, eds. Studies in the vegetational history of the British Isles. Cambridge, Cambridge University Press.
SMYTH, R. B. 1878 The Aborigines of Victoria: with notes relating to the habits of the natives of other parts of Australia and Tasmania. Melbourne, Govt. Pr. 2v.
SOLHEIM, W. G. 1969 Reworking southeast Asian prehistory. *Paideuma*, v.15: 126–139.
―― 1972 An earlier agricultural revolution. *Scientific American*, v.226, no.4: 34–41.
SPARROW, J. G. *and* E. P. NEY 1971 Lightning observations by satellite. *Nature*, v.232: 540–541.
SPAULDING, A. C. 1960 The dimensions of archaeology. *In* Deetz, J. Man's imprint from the past, 1971: 22–39.
SPENCER, *Sir* W. B. *and* F. J. GILLEN 1904 The northern tribes of Central Australia. London, Macmillan.
STANNER, W. E. H. 1961 On Aboriginal religion: IV. The design-plan of a riteless myth. *Oceania*, v.31, no.4: 233–258.

—— 1965 Aboriginal territorial organization: estate, range, domain and regime. *Oceania*, v.36, no.1: 1–26.

STEPHENS, R. 1954 Fairfield and its founder: William Henry Graham. *In* Western Australian Historical Society. Journal and proceedings, v.4, pt.5: 47–81.

STEWART, O. C. 1956 Fire as the first great force employed by man. *In* Thomas, W. L., *ed.* Man's role in changing the face of the earth: 115–133.

STIRLING, J. 1827 Letter to Governor Darling. From H.M.S. Success, 1827: with enclosures—No. 1 Narrative of operations; No. 2 Observations on the soil, etc. [by C. Fraser]. *Historical Records of Australia*, ser. 3, v.6, 1923: 551–584.

STOCKTON, E. D. 1970 An archaeological survey of the Blue Mountains. *Mankind*, v.7, no.4; 295–301.

STOKES, J. L. 1846 Discoveries in Australia; with an account of the coasts and rivers explored and surveyed during the voyage of H.M.S. Beagle in the years 1837–38–39–40–41–42–43. London, T. and W. Boone. 2v.

STORR, G. M. 1957 Quokkas and the vegetation of Rottnest Island. Typescript. Submitted as a fourth-year thesis, Zoology Dept., University of Western Australia.

STORR, G. M., GREEN, J. W. *and* D. M. CHURCHILL 1959 The vegetation of Rottnest Island. *In* Royal Society of Western Australia. Journal, v.42; 70–71.

SUTCLIFFE, A. J. 1964 The mammalian fauna. *In* Ovey, C. D., *ed.* The Swanscombe skull: 85–111.

SYMPOSIUM 1971 Controlled burning in West Australian forests. Symposium organised by the Royal Society of Western Australia, 19 April 1971.

TALBOT, L. 1973 Karri thickets, before settlement. *Forest Notes*, v.II, no.2: 6–17.

TEN RAA, W. F. E. R. 1971 Dead art and living society: a study of rock-paintings in a social context. *Mankind*, v.8, no.1: 42–58.

THOMAS, W. L., *ed.* 1956 Man's role in changing the face of the earth. Chicago, Chicago University Press.

THOMSON, D. F. 1939 The seasonal factor in human culture: illustrated from the life of a contemporary nomadic group. *In* Prehistoric Society. Proceedings, v.5, pt. 2: 209–221.

TINDALE, N. B. 1959 Ecology of primitive Aboriginal man in Australia. *In* Keast, A., Crocker, R. L. *and* C. S. Christian, *eds.* Biogeography and ecology in Australia: 36–51.

TINDALE, N. B. *and* C. P. MOUNTFORD 1926 Native markings on rocks at Morowie, South Australia. *In* Royal Society of South Australia. Transactions, v.50: 156–159.

UCKO, P. J. *and* G. W. DIMBLEBY [1969] Context and development of studies of domestication. *In* Ucko, P. J. *and* G. W. Dimbleby, *eds.* The domestication and exploitation of plants and animals: xvii-xxi.

UCKO, P. J. *and* G. W. DIMBLEBY, *eds.* [1969] The domestication and exploitation of plants and animals. London, Duckworth.

VANCOUVER, G. 1801 A voyage of discovery to the north Pacific Ocean and round the world, performed in the years 1790, 1791, 1792, 1793, 1794 and

1795 in the Discovery, sloop of war and armed tender, Chatham, under the command of Captain George Vancouver. London, John Stockdale. 3v.

VITA-FINZI, C. 1969 The Mediterranean valleys: geological changes in historical times. Cambridge, Cambridge University Press.

VITA-FINZI, C. *and* E. S. HIGGS 1970 Prehistoric economy in the Mount Carmel area of Palestine: site catchment analysis. *In* Prehistoric Society. Proceedings, v.36: 1–37.

VLAMINGH, W. de 1696–1697 Extract from the Journal of a voyage made to the unexplored South Land... in the years 1696 and 1697. *In* Major, R. H., *ed.* Early voyages to Terra Australis, 1859: 120–133.

VOLKERSEN, S. 1658 Description of the west coast of the South Land, by the Captain Samuel Volkersen of the pink, "Waeckende Boey", which sailed from Batavia on the first of January 1658,... Translated from a Dutch MS. in the Royal Archives at The Hague. *In* Major, R. H., *ed.* Early voyages to Terra Australis, 1859: 89–90.

WALLACE, J. R. 1966 Fire in the jarrah forest environment. *In* Royal Society of Western Australia. Journal, v.49: 33–44.

WASHBURN, S. L., *ed.* 1961 Social life of early man. [New York], Wenner-Gren Foundation for Anthropological Research. (Viking Fund publications in anthropology, no.31).

WENDORF, F., RUSHDI SAID *and* R. SCHILD 1970 Egyptian prehistory: some new concepts. *Science*, v.169: 1161–1171.

WEST, R. G. 1956 The Quaternary deposits at Hoxne, Suffolk. *In* Royal Society Philosophical Transactions, ser. B, v.239: 265–356.

WEST, R. G. *and* C. B. M. McBURNEY 1954 The Quaternary deposits at Hoxne, Suffolk and their archaeology. *In* Prehistoric Society. Proceedings, v.20: 131–154.

WHITE, C. 1967 Early stone axes in Arnhem Land. *Antiquity*, v.41, no.162: 149–152.

—— 1971 Man and environment in north-west Arnhem Land. *In* Mulvaney, D. J. *and* J. Golson, *eds.* Aboriginal man and environment in Australia: 141–157.

WHITE, J. P. 1971 New Guinea and Australian prehistory: the 'Neolithic problem'. *In* Mulvaney, D. J. *and* J. Golson, *eds.* Aboriginal man and environment in Australia: 182–195.

WHITE, J. P., CROOK, K. A. W. *and* B. P. RUXTON 1970 Kosipe: a late Pleistocene site in the Papuan Highlands. *In* Prehistoric Society. Proceedings, v.36: 152–170.

WHITTLESEY, D. 1929 Sequent occupance. *In* Association of American Geographers. Annals, v.19: 162–165.

WILLEY, G. R., *ed.* 1956 Prehistoric settlement patterns in the New World. New York, Wenner-Gren Foundation for Anthropological Research. (Viking Fund publications in anthropology, no.23).

WILLEY, G. R. *and* P. PHILLIPS 1958 Theory and method in American archaeology. Chicago, Chicago University Press.

WILSON, T. B. 1835 Narrative of a voyage round the world: comprehending an account of the wreck of the ship "Governor Ready", in Torres Straits; a description of the British settlements on the coasts of New Holland, more particularly Raffles Bay, Melville Island, Swan River, and King George's

Sound; also, the manners and customs of the Aboriginal tribes... London, Sherwood, Gilbert and Piper.

WOLLASTON, J. R. 1841–1844 Picton journal: being volume 1 of the journals and diaries (1841–1856) of Revd. John Ramsden Wollaston, M. A., Archdeacon of Western Australia, 1849–1856. Collected by Rev. Canon A. Burton. Edited with introduction and notes by Canon Burton and Rev. Percy U. Henn. [Perth, Paterson Brokensha, 1948].

—— 1848–1856 Albany journals: being volume 2 of the journals and diaries (1841–1856) of Revd. John Ramsden Wollaston, M.A., Archdeacon of Western Australia, 1849–1856. Collected by Rev. Canon A. Burton. Edited with notes by Canon Percy U. Henn. Perth, Paterson Brokensha [1954].

WRIGHT, G. A. 1971 Origins of food production in southwestern Asia: a survey of ideas. *Current Anthropology*, v.12, no.4–5: 447–477.

WRIGHT, R. V. S. 1971a The archaeology of Koonalda Cave. *In* Mulvaney, D. J. *and* J. Golson, *eds.* Aboriginal man and environment in Australia: 105–113.

WRIGHT, R. V. S., *ed.* 1971b Archaeology of the Gallus site, Koonalda Cave. Canberra, Australian Institute of Aboriginal Studies. (Australian Aboriginal studies, 26; Prehistory series, 5).

Index

Aboriginal camps *see* camps
Aboriginal ecological concepts, vocabulary 37, 38, 39, 40, 41, 43, 45, 46, 68, 97
Aboriginal property in land *see* usage rights
Aborigines
  absence of 16, 21, 22, 26, 27, 48, 62
  as friends, guides 21, 67, 68, 69, 70, 71, 72, 73, 74, 76, 77, 83, 109
  encountered 21, 24, 26, 29, 43, 60, 61 62, 66, 70, 73, 75, 108, 109
  numbers 13, 22, 29, 60, 64, 66, 67, 69, 70, 73, 74, 108, 109
  traces of 16, 17, 21, 22, 23, 24, 25, 27, 61, 62, 64, 65, 66, 68, 69, 70, 71, 74, 79, 106
  see also art; camps; fires; industries; etc.
Acanthocarpus 49
Acacia 49, 52, 53, 57, 59, 63
Acheulian 1
activities, of men, women 32, 33, 34
  see also patterns of activity
'Adaptive Phase' 11, 104
adze, hafted 11, 100, 101, 104
  see also industries, 'small tool'
aeolian limestone *see* limestone
Africa 2, 8, 9, 88
agglomeration; aggregation *see* groups; seasonal agglomeration
agriculture 3, 5, 9, 10, 11, 12, 15, 49, 50, 57, 59, 63, 64, 65
  see also 'firestick farming'; 'proto-horticulture'
Albany *see* King George Sound
Alford, J. L. 9, 10

Allen, H. 5, 99
alluvial plain (Pinjarra Plain) 51, 52, 53, 55, 56, 57, 58, 59, 60, 61, 77, 106, 108, 111
annulus *see* semi-arid annulus
ant-hill 87, 95
April 39, 40, 63
  see also autumn; seasonal activities
archaeological excavation, sites, survey
  see excavation; surface survey
arid centre, central areas 10, 11, 31, 77, 110
Armstrong 37
Arndt, W. 93
Arnhem Land 6, 9, 82, 85, 93, 95, 107
art 11, 12, 78, 83, 85, 86, 87, 91, 93, 94, 95, 96, 97, 98, 113
artifact assemblages *see* industries
Arundel Terrace 5, 17
assemblages of people *see* groups
Atherton tableland 50
August 36, 38, 62, 63, 74, 99
  see also seasonal activities; winter
Augusta x, 25, 26, 27, 35, 59, 69, 70, 71, 102, 108, 109
Austin, Robert 43, 44, 81
Australian core tool and scraper tradition
  see industries
Australian Institute of Aboriginal Studies xi, 94, 99
autumn 30, 31, 36, 39, 40
  see also April; March; May; seasonal activities
Avon River 23, 99
Avon valley ix, x, 23, 24, 43, 56, 61, 62, 64, 75, 77, 79, 86, 94, 99, 100, 106, 109, 110
  see also Aborigines, traces; population

axe; axe-adze; ground stone axe   5, 6, 10, 93, 98–99
axe-hammer   *see Kodja*

backed blades   *see* crystal quartz; industries, backed-blade
Backhouse, James   41, 42
Badgee-Badgee; Badji-Badji   73
Baird, Alison   49, 50
bag
  women's   32
  men's   92
  mythical   87, 96
baked clays   5
Balbuk, Fanny   67
Balgarrup   74
Balgor   37
Balranald, great tree/fire myth   89
bandicoots   30, 32, 33, 36, 38, 48
Banksia   33, 44. 45, 52, 53, 54, 57, 59, 60, 69, 102, 103, 111
Bannister, Capt. Thomas   23, 27, 62, 69
Bannister (the area)   26
baobab trees   12
'Baramba'   60, 61
Barbetti, M.   5, 99
'barde' grubs   77
barter   *see* groups
Bassendean Sands, Dunes   *see* sandplain, west coastal
Bates, Daisy   21, 67, 82, 83, 89
battues   *see* drives, kangaroo; fire drives
Battye Library   13, 14, 58
Beagle, H.M.S.   33, 81
beard, singed   *see* fire in burials
beating out fire   33
  see also fire management
Bell Rock Range   94
Belmont   22
'Berkshire Valley'   74
Berndt, C. H. and R. M.   87, 95, 96
Bettenay, E.   34, 51, 52, 53, 66
Beverley   64
Bibra Lake   67
Bibulmun   83
Bidi   46, 68
  see also paths
Bignell, M.   6, 74
Big Water   112
billy, over fire for corpse   81
Bindoon   13, 72
Binford, L. R.   2, 4, 9
bio-mass   6, 10, 11–12, 107, 111
birds   23, 28, 30, 39
  crows   87
  ducks   30, 69
  hawks   30
  parrots   30
  pigeons   30
  swans   30, 61, 69
  teal   69
  waterfowl   39, 52, 61, 69, 77, 111
  young   30, 39
birds in myths   82, 83, 87, 88, 89, 97
  see also Brown Tree-creeper; crow; hawk; *karrgain*; kestrel; swallows
Birok   39
  see also December; January; summer
blackboy   45, 53
  see also grass tree
Blackwood River   25, 27, 53, 54, 55, 64, 65, 110
bladelets   *see* industries, backed-blade
blades   *see* industries, backed-blade; lunates; waisted blades
blood letting, sprinkling   91–96
  see also chest-cutting; crystal quartz; industries, backed-blade; quartz splinters
Boggy Lake   103
Bohn   14
Bokyt   37
  see also unburnt countryside
Bolgart   73
Boreal climate   2
bores, peat   101–103
Borneo   9
botanists
  Aborigines as   15
    see also Aboriginal ecological concepts, vocabulary
  European   *see* Drummond; Fraser; Molloy, Georgiana
Bowler, J. M.   5, 10, 79, 98, 99, 100
boyl-yas   80, 91, 92
  see also crystals; quartz
bracket fungus   *see* fungus
Brown Tree-Creeper   89
  see also birds in myths
'broad spectrum' exploitation   9, 11
Brockmans   72
brushwood
  barriers   47
  burnt in grave   80
  see also bush; firing
Buller-Murphy, Deborah   83, 112
Bullsbrook   53
Bunbury, Lieut.   35, 42, 47, 48, 54, 56, 59, 60, 66, 69, 70, 108, 109
Bunbury (W.A.)   24, 43, 44, 45, 65, 67, 69, 81
burials   *see* fire in burials
burning   *see* fire; fires; firing
burnt bush, scrub, shrubs, underwood   25, 26, 27, 33, 35, 36, 41, 43, 44
burnt countryside, ground, vegetation   17, 22, 24, 25, 27, 35, 37, 38, 42, 48, 52, 60, 65, 68, 74, 75, 82, 88, 97, 103, 112
  see also Nappal; *Yanbart*

burnt grass   17, 35, 63
  see also firing grassland
burnt layers   *see* baked clays; carbon; charcoal
burnt patches   *see* burnt bush; bush, thick; firing, patchy
burnt trees   17, 21, 24, 25, 32, 35, 62, 88, 89, 97, 112
  see also Yanbart
Burnur, Burnuro   39
  see also autumn; February; March
Burrill Lake rock shelter   7, 99
bush, thick, unburnt   11, 16, 17, 19, 21, 22, 25, 26, 27, 41, 46, 48, 49, 52, 54, 56, 57, 59, 61, 62, 64, 74
  see also Mundak
bushfires   *see* fires; firing
Bussell, John and Bessie   25, 70, 71, 80
Busselton   24, 25, 67
  see also Vasse
Byeen, the   73
Byrne, J. C.   76
By-yu   *see* Zamia

cake, of pounded root   *see* cooking; reed
Callabonna, Lake   6
Callitris   49, 52
Calvert, A. F.   89
camp fires   16, 17, 21, 22, 24, 25, 32, 33, 43, 44, 62, 75, 80, 81
camps   3, 46, 49, 52, 62, 68, 72, 75, 76, 80, 88
camps
  deserted   12–13, 16, 17, 22, 23, 61
  post-contact   37, 62, 67, 72, 88
  see also huts
Canning Desert   7, 50
Canning River   24, 53, 57, 59, 64, 67, 72, 77, 108
canoes   22, 31
canopy, forest, opened by severe burn   55
Capel River   60, 70
Cape Naturaliste   25, 109
Cape York   9, 30, 38, 98
carbon, carbonised wood   *see* charcoal
Castell, C. P.   2
Castor and Pollux   87, 89
Casuarina   50, 52, 53
cattle   14, 15, 71, 75
'Cattle Chosen'   71
causeway, Heirisson Island   59, 66, 67
caves
  associated myths and rituals   85–88, 91–97
  associated with mythological serpent   81–85, 93–97
    see also earth-sky myths; serpent myths
  Harvey estuary   84, 96

New South Wales   93
Nullarbor   83, 84, 96, 100
Swan coastal plain   9, 96
Yanchep area   83
see also Cutta-Cutta; Dale's Cave; Devil's Lair; Drover's Cave; Frieze Cave; Ingaladdi; Kenniff Cave; Kintore; Koonalda Cave; Mammoth Cave; 'Orchestra Shell' cave; Puntutjarpa; *Yun-de-lup*; Wedge's Cave
Celebes   9
centre   *see* arid centre
ceremonies   *see* corroborees
Chang, K. C.   5
charcoal   1, 2, 4, 5, 7, 79, 80, 83, 94, 95, 96, 99, 101, 102, 103
  see also carbon; fire in ritual
Chauncy, Philip Snell   13, 14, 38, 39, 44, 58, 77, 86, 87, 92, 108
Cheriton   72
chert (Eocene fossiliferous; silicified limestone) artifacts, industry   84, 96, 100, 101, 103–104
  see also Glover, J.; Koonalda Cave
chest painting   94
chest cutting, cicatrices, 'rain-cuts', scars   92, 93, 95, 96
  see also industries, backed-blade; crystal quartz; quartz splinters
Chingi   83
  see also Jinga; evil spirits; serpent myths
Chittering valley   99
chopper, chopper/scraper traditions   *see* industries
Churchill, D.   7, 49, 50, 102, 103, 104, 112
cicatrices   *see* chest cutting
Claise Brook   66
Claremont burial   80
Clarence (W.A.)   35
Clarence valley sites (N.S.W.)   93
Clark, J.G.D.   4, 38, 44
clearance
  Aboriginal   *see* firing, effects; usage patterns, rights
  Africa, Asia   4, 5
  by Europeans   ix, 1–3, 48–50
cleared zones   *see* zones of easy movement
Cleland, *Sir* J. B.   15, 77
Cleveland Hills   2
Clifton, Algernon   45
Clinch, James   74
cloaks   *see* kangaroo skin
coastal activities, tribes   23, 24, 26, 30, 31, 34
  see also autumn; fishing; interior; summer
coastal dunes   *see* dunes; sand-dunes
coastal plain
  south   25–26

west   14, 24, 26, 34, 37, 39, 40, 43,
    51–53, 56–60, 64, 66, 67, 77, 96, 99,
    100, 103, 105, 111
  see also alluvial plain; dunes; limestone;
    sandplain; sea level rise
cobbler   40, 67, 69
Cockbain   84, 100, 103
Cockburn Sound   112
Collie, Mr   24, 27, 28, 68
Collie River   70, 109
Collingridge   16, 17
commons   see sandheath
communities   see groups
conflict   see Europeans, conflict with
    Aborigines
contact   see European contact
cooking   14, 32, 33, 39
cooking fires   see campfires
corroborees   22, 42, 44, 70, 109
Crawford, Dr Ian   12, 80, 85
crayfish   32, 39, 69
cremations   79, 98
crevices   see holes
crop
  European   22
  of grass   see grass
  of roots   12–14, 39, 72, 77
crops threatened by fire   35, 37, 41, 75
Cross, J.   55
crossing   see fords
crow, in myth   87
crystal facet as blade backing   92
crystal quartz   92, 95, 96, 97
crystals
  in myth   89, 90, 91
  of calcite   93
  of quartz   91, 92, 93, 94, 96, 97
  see also boyl-yas; rain-stones
cultivation   see agriculture; crop; 'firestick
    farming'; resource management
Curr, E. M.   80, 82, 83, 93
Cutta-Cutta   93

Dale, Richard   26, 28, 30, 32, 61, 62, 64,
    68, 86, 87, 94
Dale's Cave   85–89, 94–97
  see also earth–sky myths
dalgert   36
Dandelup River   57, 60
Darling, Governor   vii, 23, 56
Darling Range, Scarp   ix, 14, 21, 23, 24,
    26, 27, 52, 53, 55, 56, 57, 59, 61, 62, 63,
    64, 68, 99, 100, 108
Darling River   5
Darradup   54, 55
Darwin, Charles   3
dates   5, 6, 7, 10, 11, 83, 92, 96, 97, 99, 100,
    101, 102, 103, 104, 106
Davidson, D. S.   10, 22, 44, 45, 79, 93, 99

Davies, J. L.   7, 50
Davies, P. L.   99
de Burgh, W.   61
December   23, 24, 29, 30, 39, 60, 61, 65, 68,
    69, 83, 108
  see also seasonal activities; summer
deforestation   1, 2, 3, 34
  see also firing, effects and uses;
    fires, bush, 'native'
Delamere   93
demography   see population
Denmark   2
desert   x, 7, 10, 50, 77, 100, 101, 104, 107
detrital laterites   see 'Older Laterites'
devegetation   see deforestation; firing,
    effects and uses
Devil's Lair   5, 11, 99, 101, 102
Devon Downs   93
de Wet, J. M. J.   5, 10
digging grounds   see roots
digging stick   32, 82, 87
  see also ant-hill in myth
dilly-bag   92, 96
  see also bag; sacred objects
Dimbleby, G. W.   2, 4, 9
dingo   11, 12, 68
Dioscorea   see yam
Diprotodon   6
disease   see illness
dispersion   see seasonal dispersion
distribution
  Aboriginal   see population
  European   see European distribution
district, tribal   see territory
Djanni   45
Djubak   30, 38, 39
domestic animals   17
  see also cattle; sheep
domestication   3, 11
Doo(r)da Mya   85
Dortch, Charles   5, 8, 11, 98, 99, 101, 102
drays   73
drive, fire   see fire drive
drive, kangaroo   15, 19, 28, 30, 32, 35, 36,
    37, 38, 64, 68
Drover's Cave   102
Drummond, James   72, 73, 76, 86
dry season   see autumn; summer
ducks   30, 69
Duidgee   73
  see also Toodyay
dunes, coastal   7, 17, 21, 22, 25, 26, 48, 50,
    51, 52, 103, 104
  see also Quindalup dunes; sand-dunes
Dutch explorers   16
  see also Vlamingh; Volkersen

earth-apertures   see caves; holes; earth–sky
    myths

earthquake myths, Great Shaking 112
earth–sky myths 82, 85, 86, 87, 88–89, 91, 95, 96
East Perth 66
ecological balance, disequilibrium, stability, stress 3, 4, 6, 8, 9, 10, 48, 49, 50, 104
  see also grazing pressure; stress
ecological concepts *see* Aboriginal ecological concepts
ecological systems *see* ecosystems
ecological ties, usage *see* territories; usage
ecological zones *see* geomorphic zones
economies, ecosystems, generalised and specialised 6, 9, 10, 11, 76
ecosystems, impoverishment and improvement 3, 4, 6, 10, 12, 46, 49, 104, 105, 110, 111
Edwards, R. 93, 96
eggs 30, 87
Elkin, A. P. 92
Ellen Brook 14, 21, 24, 58
emus 30
encampments *see* camps
Eocene *see* caves; chert; Koonalda; limestone; Wilson Bluff limestone
Erickson, R. 63, 68, 73, 84, 86, 109
erosion by wind denudation 7, 50, 103
Erskine, Lieut. 26, 61
Esperance 45, 65, 69, 70
estuaries, inlets 25, 26, 40, 46, 52, 64, 69, 70, 71, 108, 109
  see also Harvey; Leschenault; Murray; Nornalup; Swan; Vasse; etc.
estuarine products 22, 30, 31, 40, 52, 69, 105, 109, 111
  see also fish; lakes
Etheridge, R. 92
ethnoarchaeology, ethnographic evidence, ethnohistory 31, 98
eucalypts 17, 53, 57, 59, 62, 102
Eucalyptus calophylla *see* marri
Eucalyptus diversicolor *see* karri
Eucalyptus marginata *see* jarrah
Eucla 82
European contact 16, 21, 22, 34, 35, 37, 60, 61, 62, 63, 66, 67, 69, 77, 105, 106, 107, 111
European distribution, population 63, 64, 71, 75, 76, 77, 108
European forestry 33, 54–55
Europeans
  clearance by ix, 1–3, 6, 27, 47–50, 57, 60, 62, 63, 64, 103, 111
  conflict with Aborigines 60, 71, 72, 75, 76
  firing by 22, 24, 33, 44, 54, 55
  see also paths; Rottnest Island
European settlers, settlement ix, 11, 13, 14, 23, 25, 26, 29, 35, 49, 50, 52, 53, 54, 55, 60, 63–65, 67, 68, 70, 71, 72–77
European usage, based on Aboriginal usage vii, 13, 41, 47–48, 55, 63, 65, 66–78, 111, 113
European usurpation x, 13, 14, 15, 41, 42, 55, 65, 67, 71, 72–77, 78
evil spirits 43, 69, 80–83, 89, 90
  see also fire, to protect against evil spirits; serpent myth
excavation, archaeological ix, 1, 4, 5, 6, 7, 11, 78, 79, 80, 83, 91–96, 99, 102, 104
exploitation patterns *see* patterns of exploitation; territory; usage
explorers *see* Dutch explorers; French explorers; etc.
extinction, giant marsupials *see* megafauna
Eyre, John 14, 15, 32, 39, 42, 43, 81, 92, 107

fabricators 92, 106
farming *see* agriculture
fauna *see* birds; fish; frogs; mammals; megafauna; reptiles
Fauré 19
February (*Burnur*) 29, 30, 39
  see also seasonal activities; summer
felling *see* Europeans; litter
Fertility Mother in myth and ritual 82, 87, 95, 96
  see also earth-sky myths; Sun Woman; womb in myth
fire
  evidence from caves 5, 79, 94, 95, 99, 102
  evidence from peat bores 102, 103, 104
  (figurative use) *see* hearths
  for cooking *see* campfires; cooking
  for light 43, 44, 70, 81
  for warmth 44, 70
  gentle, mild 25, 33, 54, 102
  in burials 79, 80, 81, 97, 98, 113
  in frequented localities 3, 37, 44, 45, 46, 68–69, 71
  in ritual 44, 78, 79, 85, 90, 91, 93, 94, 95, 96, 97, 98
  see also charcoal
  intense 25, 32, 33, 55, 102
  Kalla *see* hearths; *Kalla*
  near grave 80–81
  to protect against evil spirits 79, 80, 81, 90, 97
  see also fire in burials; firestick
  see also burnt bush, etc; campfires; fires; firing; hearths; *Kalla*
fire carrying 33, 43, 44, 45
  see also Banksia; *Djanni;* firestick
fire climax vegetation 2, 50, 53, 54, 55, 110–111

fire drives 2, 3, 19, 28, 30, 32, 33, 35, 36,
    38, 41, 42
  see also drive, kangaroo
fire-making
  by friction 44, 45
  by fire-drill 44, 45
  by fire-saw 45
  by percussion 44
fire management
  Aboriginal 14, 19, 32, 33, 42, 45, 47–48,
    54, 55, 75, 76
  see also firing, systematic
  European 54, 55
fire myths 82, 84, 85, 86, 87, 88, 89, 90, 91,
    94, 95, 96, 97, 98, 112, 113
  see also birds; digging stick; Great Tree;
    serpent; stars; sun; Sun Woman;
    womb
fire-resistance 2, 49, 50, 53, 54, 55, 65,
    103, 110–111
  see also Banksia; mallee; regeneration;
    tussock grass
fires
  Aboriginal see fires, 'native'; 'smokes'
  accidental 33, 42, 45, 49, 54, 69, 75, 102
  Acheulian 1
  bush 25, 42, 43, 47, 65, 70, 102
  by rivers 26, 62, 69, 108–9
  camp see campfires
  extensive 2, 11, 14, 16, 19, 28, 32, 35, 47,
    48, 65, 74, 75
  extinguished 17, 21
  interglacial 1, 2
  late Glacial 1
  'native' 14, 15, 17, 19, 22, 24, 25, 26, 27,
    28, 35, 36, 37, 38, 42, 45, 48, 60, 61,
    62, 64, 65, 74, 75, 76, 87, 88
  seen from the sea 16, 21, 22, 24, 71
  see also 'smokes'
fire signal 21
firestick 22, 32, 33, 42, 43, 44, 45, 69, 70, 81
'firestick farming' vii, 8, 12, 111
fire to protect against evil spirits 79, 80,
    81, 90, 97
  see also fire in burials; firestick
firing
  absence of 16, 25, 26, 47, 50, 74
  by men 32, 33, 36, 87
  by women 32, 33, 36, 87
  controlled, deliberate, regulated see
    fire management; firing, systematic
  effects and uses
    clearing campsites 3, 46
    clearance vii, 1, 2, 3, 5, 17, 20, 21, 24,
      25, 27, 33, 38, 41, 45, 46, 47, 48,
      49, 50, 52, 60, 65, 68, 69, 70, 76
    collecting small game 19, 30, 32, 33,
      36, 49
    devegetation 7, 8, 34, 50, 52, 103, 104,
      110

  see also sand-dunes, mobile
  driving game 3, 19, 28, 30, 32, 35, 36,
    38, 41, 42, 49
  geomorphic 7, 14, 104, 105
  heat see fire for warmth
  improving collecting grounds 14, 39,
    52
  improving grass, grazing, green
    herbage, pasture vii, 3, 14, 15,
    19, 25, 32, 34, 39, 41, 42, 43, 45, 49,
    55, 75, 111
  on population 34, 50, 107, 111
  on vegetation 28, 50, 66
  see also megafauna; pyrophylic
    vegetation; salinity; sclerophyll
    forest; sedgeland; vegetational
    change
European see Europeans, firing by
extensive, large scale 2, 4, 14, 17, 19, 33
frequent 19, 24, 27, 28, 45–46, 47, 54,
    55, 56, 70, 101, 102, 107
grassland 7, 15, 27, 33, 35. 36, 37
infrequent 16, 27, 46, 47, 54, 55, 102, 107
  see also firing, absence
patchy 14, 17, 27, 64, 68, 69, 75
  see also firing, swamps; firing, waterhole
    surrounds
periodic, regular, by consecutive portions,
    firing régime see fire management;
    firing, systematic
season 29, 30, 31, 39, 40
small scale, restricted 32
swamps 33, 39, 52, 77
systematic 8, 14, 19, 32, 33, 42, 46, 48,
    49, 54, 68, 69, 75, 102, 105, 107, 110,
    111, 112
threat to European property 35, 37, 41,
    75
waterhole surrounds 46, 65, 75
  see also grass patches
woodland 33
fish 2, 6, 22, 30, 31, 39, 40, 52, 68, 69, 71,
    77, 87, 111
  drying, roasting, storage 31, 69
  shoals 30, 31, 39
  spearing 23, 31, 32, 39, 67, 69
  weirs 4, 31, 39, 46, 69, 109
fishing by torchlight 43, 69
fishing season 23, 24, 29, 30, 31
  see also cobbler; mullet; salmon;
    schnapper; tailor-fish
flag, flagroots see reed
flake see industries, flake
Flannery, K. V. 2, 3, 4, 6, 9, 15
Flinders Bay Swamp 103
Flinders, Capt. Matthew 16, 19, 21, 22, 33
flood myths 112
flora 1, 2, 9, 10, 12, 15, 37, 40, 49, 52, 53,
    54, 63, 74, 76, 77, 110, 111, 113
  see also Aboriginal ecological concepts

Flores 9
food *see* birds; cooking; fish; mammals; roots
foothills of Darling Scarp 51, 53, 108
 see also Ridge Hill Shelf
footprints 16
fords 60, 67, 68, 69, 70
forest 1, 2, 26, 53, 56, 57, 108
 dense 27, 28, 54, 61, 67, 68, 69, 75, 110, 113
 jarrah (mahogany) x, 24, 25, 26, 27, 42, 50, 53, 54, 55, 61, 62, 64, 74, 110
 karri (blue gum) 25, 26, 27, 55, 70, 103, 110
 open *see* open forest; open woodland
 rain 50
 sclerophyll 50
 southwestern triangle of x, 26, 107, 111
 see also parklike countryside; savannah
forest floor *see* litter
forest management
 by Aborigines *see* fire management; firing, systematic
 by European foresters 45, 50, 54, 55
fossiliferous chert *see* chert
fowl *see* birds
Frake, C. O. 38, 78, 113
France 2
Fraser, Charles vii, 53, 56, 66
Fraser Ranges myth 89
Fremantle 35, 52, 57, 67, 80
Fremantle, Capt. Charles H. 117
French explorers 19-21, 48, 66, 67, 71
 see also Fauré; Freycinet; Peron
fresh growth, fresh new grass *see* young growth
Freycinet 19, 21, 66, 79
Friend, Mary Ann 35, 36
Frieze Cave ix, 79, 85, 86, 88, 89, 91, 92, 93, 94, 95, 96, 97, 101, 104
frogs 39, 52, 77
fuel 3, 49
fungus, as tinder 44, 45

Gambarang 39
 see also November; October; spring
game 2, 3, 6, 8, 9, 10, 11, 19, 28, 30, 32, 33, 35, 36, 38, 41, 42, 49, 64, 69
 see also food; mammals; megafauna
garden vii, 22
Garden Island 21, 48, 49, 50, 62, 112
Gardner, C. 7, 26, 33, 50, 53, 54, 63, 64, 110
Gardner River 26
Geelvink 16
Geographe Bay 19, 21, 24, 53, 56, 60, 66, 71, 79, 108, 110
Géographe, Le 19
geomorphic effects *see* firing, effects
geomorphic zones x, 51, 52, 53, 56-64

 see also alluvial plain; coastal plain; dunes, coastal; limestone, aeolian; 'Older Laterites'; sandplain; sandplain and saltlake country; 'Younger Laterites'
Geran 39
giant tree in myth *see* great tree in myth
Gilgie, land-spirit 83
gilgies 52, 67
 see also crayfish
Gingin 13, 61, 72, 99, 108
Gingin Brook 60, 81
Gipping glaciation 1
Glover, J. 84, 100, 103
Glover, R. 74
Godwin, H. 3
Golson, J. 5, 9, 11, 98, 113
Gongan 46, 68
 see also paths; sandy areas
Gorman, C. F. 5, 10
Gould, R. 7, 11, 94, 100, 104
Grahame, W. H. 75
grain 4, 63
grass, grassland, good grass ix, 1, 15, 17, 25, 26, 27, 28, 33, 37, 38, 45, 46, 50, 59, 60, 61, 62, 63, 64, 65, 68, 69, 70, 71, 73, 74, 75, 111
grass 'crop' 14, 15, 19, 42, 75, 111
grass patches 28, 46, 62, 68, 69, 73, 74, 75
 see also cattle; parklike countryside; pasture; sheep; spinifex; sedgeland
grass tree 25, 32, 44, 45
 see also blackboy
gravels, lateritic *see* 'Older Laterites'; 'Younger Laterites'
grazing *see* grass; pasture; pastoralism
grazing improvement *see* firing, effects
grazing pressure 3, 48, 49, 50, 64
grazing tracts *see* grass, good
great tree in myth 88, 89, 112
Great Shaking *see* earthquake myths
'Greater Australia' 4, 5, 6, 7, 9, 10, 101
Gregory, A. C. and F. T. 74, 75
Green Gully 100
Greenough River 12
Grevillea 95
Grey, *Sir* George 12, 13, 14, 26, 27, 36, 39, 41, 42, 43, 44, 45, 52, 55, 60, 67, 77, 80, 81, 82, 83, 86, 91, 92
grinding *see* grindstones; reeds; roots
grindstones 4
group size 13, 22, 29, 30, 31, 40, 60, 64, 66, 67, 69, 70, 73, 74, 108, 109
groups for barter, ceremonies, firing, fishing; large 29, 30, 31, 34, 42
 see also autumn; seasonal agglomeration; summer
growth of fresh new grass *see* young growth
Guilday, J. E. 8
Guildford 22, 53, 57, 68

Gumba 83
   see also serpent myth
gum
   edible 42
   for tools 92
gum trees *see* eucalypts; jarrah; karri; marri
Gwambygine *see* Dale's Cave; Frieze Cave
hafted tools 92, 100, 101, 104
   see also adze; axe; industries,
      backed-blade; *Kodja*; 'waisted
      blades'
Hakea 45, 56
   see also Djanni
Hallam, S. J. 10, 31, 34, 38, 77, 83, 84, 92,
   95, 98, 99, 102, 105, 106
Hammond, J. 26, 45, 67, 68, 88, 89
hand-axes *see* industries
hand stencils 85, 86, 94
Harlan, J. R. 5, 10
Harris, D. R. 9, 10
harvesting *see* crop
Harvey 53, 55, 110
Harvey estuary, River 26, 27, 46, 53, 67,
   69, 84, 108
Hasluck, *Lady A.* 25, 35, 60, 70, 71
Hasluck, *Sir* Paul 64, 77, 88, 108
Hassell, E. 31, 35, 45, 80
hawk in myth 89
hawks *see* birds
Hawthornden 73
hazel 2
Hearne, T. 31
hearth
   domestic 5, 99
      see also campfires
   figurative (*Kalla*) 43, 112
heaths 3, 26, 53, 64
   see also sandheath
heaven *see* earth–sky myths
heavenly bodies in myth *see* moon; stars;
   sun
Heirisson Island 19–21, 66, 67
Helena River 24, 55, 57, 61, 62
Henty, J. 26, 61
herbivores 3, 5, 6, 46, 50, 53, 111
Hercus, L. A. 89
Hiatt, Betty 79, 98
Higgs, E. 12, 29, 31
Hillman (surveyor) 74
Hoffman Hill 27
Hole, F. 2, 6, 9
holes and crevices, in myth and ritual 87,
   88, 94, 95, 96, 97
Hope, G. S. 40, 50
'horsehoofs' *see* industries, steep-edge
   scraper
horticulture 10
   see also agriculture
Hotham River ix, 26, 63, 64
Howell, F. C. 1

Howitt, A. W. 87, 89
Hoxne 1, 2
hunting *see* drive; emu; kangaroo;
   pitfalls
hunting territory *see* territory,
   exploitative; usage rights
hut over grave 80
huts, shelters 12, 16, 17, 29, 37, 39, 43, 44,
   49, 61, 64, 66, 68, 69, 109
   see also campfires; camps
Hutchins, D. E. 54, 55
Hutt, Governor 37, 71
Hutt River 12
Hyde Park Lake 67

'iguanas' 39, 48, 81
illness 91
increase ceremonies 95, 96
   see also Grevillea; rain-making
Indonesian Islands 98
Indo-Pacific region 4
Indus Valley 4
industries
   Australian core tool and scraper 8, 100
   backed-blade 4, 11, 12, 91, 92, 95, 96,
      97, 100, 101, 104, 106
      see also Frieze Cave; Puntutjarpa
   blade 4, 5, 92
   chopper and flake; chopper/scraper;
      pebble/chopping tool 4, 5, 99
   flake 4, 99
   hand-axe 1
   microlithic 4, 12, 92, 93, 96
   'small tool' 8, 11, 12, 100, 101
   steep-edge scraper 11, 98, 99, 100, 101,
      106
Ingaladdi 100
inland from coast, 'interior' 23, 30
   see also seasonal movement; winter
inland zone, east of jarrah belt 26, 27, 34,
   52, 62, 63, 74, 75, 108, 110, 111, 112
   see also arid centre; savannah
inlets *see* estuaries
interior *see* inland
'Inventive Phase' 11, 104
Ireland 2
Irvine, F. R. 12
Irwin, Capt. C. 26, 39, 43, 44, 57, 58, 62,
   65, 108, 109
islands 22
   see also Garden Island; Heirisson Island;
      Mondrain Island; Rottnest Island
Iversen, J. 2, 3

January 23, 24, 29, 30, 39, 65
   see also summer
jarrah (mahogany) ix, x, 6, 23, 24, 25, 26,
   27, 43, 50, 52, 53, 54, 55, 56, 57, 58, 59,
   60, 61, 62, 64, 65, 70, 74, 75, 77, 102,

103, 105, 110
  see also forest, jarrah
Java   9
Jennings, J. N.   4, 14, 98, 100, 107
Jilakin rock   75
Jilba   38
  see also August; September; spring
Jinga, '*jingee*'   81, 88–89
  see also serpent myths
Johnston, F. M.   45
Jones, Dick   81
Jones, Rhys   5, 8, 12, 76, 77, 100, 110
July   40
  see also winter
June   40
  see also winter

Kalgan River, valley   27, 68
Kalla   43, 112
  see also hearth; usage rights
Kambarang   39
kangaroo   14, 15, 25, 41, 42, 63–64, 70
kangaroo as food source   23, 30, 32, 33, 35, 36, 38, 48
kangaroo drive   *see* drive, kangaroo
kangaroo rats   48
kangaroo skin bags   *see* bag
kangaroo skin cloaks   33, 45
kangaroo spearing, stalking in wet   30, 32
kangaroos
  numbers   36, 60, 64, 68, 70
  traces of   22, 25
  see also pitfalls
karrgain (blue pigeon) myth   89
karri   x, 25, 26, 27, 55, 70, 75, 103, 107, 110
  see also forest, karri
Kellerberrin   84, 88, 89, 90
Kelmscott   67
Kemp, T.   68, 76
Kennedy, James   67
Kenniff Cave   99–100
kestrel   82, 87
Kimberleys   12, 48, 85, 88, 94, 95, 98, 110
King, Capt. P. P.   21, 22
King George Sound   x, 17, 19, 21, 22, 23, 24, 25, 27, 28, 29, 33, 34, 36, 38, 40, 41, 44, 56, 62, 63, 64, 65, 68, 69, 74, 80, 100, 102, 108, 109, 110
King River   68
Kintore   93
Kodja   99
Kojonup   6, 63, 74, 75, 80, 86
Koonalda Cave   83, 84, 95, 96
  see also art; caves; limestone, Eocene; Nullarbor plain; serpent myths; serpentine markings
Kosipe   6, 7
Kulumput   93
Kundyl   37
Kun-go   46

  see also paths
Kunmanggur   82
  see also serpent myths

Lachlan River   5
Lake Callabonna   6
Lake Menindee   5
Lake Monger   67, 88
Lake Mungo   5, 6, 79, 99
Lake Neerabup (Neerabub)   39, 84
lakes   *see* water sources
Lampert, R.   7, 99, 100
Landor, E. W.   ix, 15, 36, 42, 46, 52, 57, 59, 63, 64, 66, 67, 73, 83
land-use
  Aboriginal   vii, 14, 15, 19, 31, 37, 38, 41, 42, 43, 46, 60, 62, 65, 66–71, 75, 76, 77, 78, 112–113
  European   vii, 41, 52–53, 57, 59, 60, 61, 62, 63, 66–71, 72–77
  see also patterns of exploitation; usage patterns; usage rights
laterites, lateritic gravels   *see* 'Older Laterites'; 'Younger Laterites'
'lawns'   *see* grass; parklike countryside
Lefroy, Gerald   73, 74, 76
Leichhardt   75
Leschenault estuary   24, 26, 64, 67, 69, 70, 108, 109
light, use of fire for   43, 44, 70, 81
Lightning Brothers   93
Lightning Snake   *see* serpent
lightning in myth   82, 85, 91, 93, 96, 97
  see also rain-making; serpent myths
lightning strikes   7, 54, 102
limestone
  aeolian, west coastal   48, 51, 52, 54, 56, 57, 60, 61, 77, 83, 84, 95, 99, 105, 106
  denuded   52, 57
  Eocene   84, 96, 100, 101, 103–104
    see also Koonalda Cave
  Pleistocene   *see* limestone, aeolian
  thickly wooded   82–83, 84
limestone caves   *see* caves; serpent myths; serpentine markings
linear markings   93, 95, 96
  see also parallel dash motif; parallel grooves
lithology   100, 101, 103
  see also chert; limestone; quartz
litter on forest floor   19, 26, 27, 47, 54, 55
lizards   32, 33, 39
Long, J. P. M.   11, 12
Lowestoft glaciation   1
lunates   4
  see also industries, backed-blade, microlithic
Lundelius   5, 99, 102

McArthur, W.   34, 48, 49, 51, 52, 53, 66
McBryde, Isabel   93, 94, 100, 101
McBurney, C. B. M.   1
McCarthy, F. D.   10, 99
McConnel, U. H.   88
McDermott, J. M.   35
Maddock, Kenneth   82, 85, 87, 89, 96
Magdalenian   2
Maggoro   40
   see also July; June; winter
mahogany   *see* jarrah
Malaysia   9
mallee   26, 50, 53, 54, 65
   see also pyrophylic vegetation;
      regeneration from underground
      parts
mallet   53
mammals   *see* cattle; marsupials;
   megafauna; sheep
Mammoth Cave   5, 99, 101, 102
March   23, 24, 30, 37, 39
   see also autumn
Margaret River   25
margins   *see* peripheral areas
marri   25, 53, 65, 74, 103
Marshack, A.   38, 78, 93, 96, 113
marsupials   *see* bandicoots; dalgert;
   Kangaroo; opossum; quokka; wallaby
marsupials, giant   *see* megafauna
Martin, P. S.   8, 9
Maryborough   87, 88
May   30, 35, 39, 40, 50
   see also autumn; *Geran*; *Wan-Yarang*
meanders   *see* serpentine markings
megafauna   5, 6, 8, 9, 10, 50
Megaw, J. V. S.   98
Meggitt, M. J.   8, 31, 110
Melaleuca   49, 52, 69, 73, 102
Menindee   *see* Lake Menindee
Menzies, Archibald   17
Merrilees, D.   5, 6, 8, 10, 11, 98, 99, 101,
   102, 103
Mesolithic   2, 93
Miago   81
microliths, geometric   96
   see also industries, backed-blade,
      microlithic
Middle Swan   37, 53, 79–80
Miellup Lagoons   69
Milky Way in myth   83, 89
   see also earth–sky myths
Millett, Mrs   43, 92
mining   *see* quarrying
Mitchell, *Sir* Thomas   14
Mogey, J.   37
Molloy, Capt. and Georgiana   25, 70, 71
Mondrain Island   22, 33
Monger's Lake   *see* Lake Monger
moon in art   85, 86, 87
moon in myth   85, 86, 87, 88, 89, 95, 96, 97

   see also Dale's Cave; earth–sky myths;
      Tiwi
Moon's House   *see* Dale's Cave
Moore, George Fletcher   ix, x, 26, 36, 37,
   38, 39, 41, 43, 45, 46, 57, 62, 63, 65, 68,
   79, 81, 82, 86, 91, 108, 109, 112
Moore River   53, 60, 63, 67, 73, 77, 81, 103,
   104, 106, 108, 109, 110
Morowie   93
Moulack   84
   see also serpent myths
Mount Bakewell   62
Mount Carmel, Palestine   29, 34
Mountford, C. P.   87, 93
movement   *see* patterns of movement;
   seasonal movement; zones of easy
   movement
movement between earth and sky, heaven
   see earth–sky myths
Mudja   14
Mulcahy, M. J.   23, 53, 63, 74
mullet   39, 69
   see also fish
Mullion   89
   see also serpent myths
Mulvaney, D. J.   10, 11, 98, 100, 104
Mundak   46
Mundijong   53
Mungo, Lake   *see* Lake Mungo
Murchison River, area, district   12, 45, 74
Murinbata   12, 82
Murra Murra   73
Murray River, S.A.   12, 93, 113
Murray River, delta, W.A.   24, 47, 53, 57,
   59, 60, 64, 67, 69, 70, 77, 80, 106, 108,
   109
Murray Aborigines   60, 80, 108
mussels   *see* shellfish
myths   *see* ant-hill; birds; digging-stick;
   earth–sky; fire; lightning; Milky Way;
   moon; rainbow; Rainbow Serpent;
   serpent; sun; stars; woman; womb

Nackara Springs   93
Nannup Cave   *see* Devil's Lair
Nappal, burnt ground   38
Narr, K. J.   2
Narrik   38
'natives'   *see* Aborigines
Naturaliste, La   19
Naturaliste, Cape   25
near-cultivation   *see* 'protohorticulture';
   'firestick farming'
net   *see* bag
network   spatial, social   3, 31, 49, 67, 68, 77
New England   93, 101
new growth after burning   *see* young
   growth
New Guinea   4, 6, 7, 9, 98

New Holland 16, 107
New Norcia x, 63, 73
   see also Salvado
Nijptang 16
Nind, Scott 22, 29–33, 36, 42, 91
Nile valley 4
Nornalup Inlet 26
Northam x, 63, 64, 99
North America 2, 4, 8, 9
Northcliffe 25, 69
November 24, 30, 39
   see also Gambarang; seasonal activities; spring
Nullarbor plain 82, 84, 96, 100
numbers *see* Aborigines, numbers; group size; population
nuts 77

Oakley, K. P. 1, 2
ochre 92, 94, 95
October 30, 39
   see also Djubak; Gambarang; Jilba; seasonal activities; spring
Ogle, Nathaniel 26, 36, 65, 108
Old Bunbury Road, Old Coast Road 70
   see also paths
'Older Laterites' ix, x, 23, 26, 53, 56, 61, 62, 99, 110
open country x, 28, 33, 53, 55, 56, 57, 59, 60, 61, 62, 63, 64, 68, 70, 73, 74
   see also zones of easy movement
open forest, woodland 14, 19, 22, 24, 26, 27, 47, 54, 55, 56, 58, 59, 61, 62, 65, 68
   see also parklike countryside; savannah
opening up of country 2, 3, 5, 6, 46, 47–49, 53, 63, 65, 68, 70, 76, 110, 111
opening up of country by fire *see* firing, effects
   see also Europeans, clearance by; grazing pressure; quokka; Rottnest Island
opossum 23, 30, 33, 36, 43, 48
'Orchestra Shell' cave 79, 83, 84, 95, 96, 102
Ovey, C. D. 1
owner, ownership *see* usage rights
Oyster Harbour 17, 19, 22
oysters *see* shellfish

pads *see* paths
Palestine *see* Mount Carmel
parallel dash motif 85, 93, 94, 95, 96
   see also chest; parallel grooves; splash spots
parallel grooves 93
   see also parallel dash motif; rain-making; 'rain-cuts'
paraphernalia *see* sacred objects
parklike countryside ix, 25, 53, 56, 57, 58, 59, 60, 62, 64, 70
   see also grass; pasture; savannah
park-tundra 1
parrots *see* birds
pastoralism 3, 63, 66
pasture ix, 47, 63, 65, 72, 73, 107
pasture, good x, 19, 26, 47, 53, 55, 61, 62, 63, 69, 70, 71, 73, 74, 108, 111
   see also grass; parklike countryside
pasture improvement *see* firing, effects
pasture management *see* land-use
paths 12, 21, 25, 30, 46, 65–71, 75, 77, 86
   see also Bidi; Gongan; Kun-go; zones of easy movement
patterns of activity *see* movement; seasonal activities; usage patterns
patterns of grouping 31, 46
patterns of exploitation 10, 11, 12, 13, 14, 15, 23–24, 29, 30, 31, 37, 38, 40, 41–43, 46, 57, 63, 68, 70, 75, 77, 102, 104, 105, 107, 110, 111, 113
   see also seasonal activities; usage patterns
patterns of movement 21, 31, 40, 46, 70
   see also network; paths; seasonal movement; zones of easy movement
Pearce, R. 11, 12, 92, 100
Pearson, M. C. 4
peat bores 102–104
pebble/chopping tool cultures 99
Peel Inlet 24
Peel, Thomas 35
Pelsart 16
penis *see* blood-letting; serpentine penis
percussion 44
   see also fire-making
peripheral areas, margins (of Australia) 6, 10, 12
Peron 19, 21, 66, 79
Perth, Perth Area 14, 26, 27, 31, 34, 35, 36, 41, 52, 55, 57, 59, 65, 66, 67, 77, 79, 80, 83, 84, 95, 99, 104, 108–109
Perth Basin 100
Perth water supply, lakes, swamps, wells 66, 67
   see also Swan coastal plain; Swan River, area centred on
phases, early, middle, late and final 106
   see also 'Adaptive Phase'; dates; 'Inventive Phase'
Phillips 73
piedmont of Darling Scarp *see* alluvial plain
pigeons *see* birds
pine tree in myth 89
   see also great tree in myth
Pinjarra 53, 56, 57, 59, 60, 67, 70
Pinjarra Plain *see* alluvial plain
pitfalls 30
plant diet, exploitation, utilisation 5, 6, 10, 11, 13, 30, 72, 77, 105
   see also Bohn; Djubak; Kundyl; Mudja;

reed; *Wan-yarang*; *Warran*;
  woorine; *Yanjidi*; *Yun-jid*; yam
Pleiades 87
  see also stars in myth
Pleistocene 1–8, 10, 11, 12, 38, 82, 96, 98,
  99, 100, 101, 102
ploughing 62, 63, 74
Point d'Entrecasteaux 26
pollen sequence, radiocarbon dates 1,
  102, 103
Pollux *see* Castor and Pollux
pools *see* water sources
population, Aboriginal, at contact
  Albany area 29
  central Australia 77, 110
  Greenough 13
  jarrah, karri forest 27
  Kimberleys 110
  South-west 10, 12, 34, 69, 71, 72, 74, 76,
    77, 104–110
  Tasmania 76, 110
population, Aboriginal, growth, trends 6,
  9–12, 34, 104–111
population, European *see* European
  distribution
population, herbivore 10
population, Pleistocene and post-
  Pleistocene 6, 9–11
population pressure, stress *see* stress,
  demographic
Porongorups 27, 68, 69
post-Pleistocene 2, 4, 7, 38, 83
pounding, roots *see* reed roots
Preston, Lieut. 24, 25
Princess Royal Harbour 68
property, Aboriginal *see* hearth; *Kalla*;
  territory; usage rights
'proto-horticulture' 5, 12–15
  see also 'firestick farming'
Proudfoot, B. 3
Pukara 94–95
Puntutjarpa 7, 100, 101, 104
pyrophylic, pyrophylous vegetation *see*
  fire climax vegetation

quarrying 96, 100
Quartania *see* coastal plain, west
quartz 61, 106
  see also industries, backed-blade
quartz barbs, saw teeth, skin cutters,
    splinters 91, 92, 95, 106
  ritual use *see* blood letting; *boyl-yas*;
    chest cutting; crystal quartz;
    crystals
Quindalup dunes 48, 51, 52
  see also dunes, coastal
quokka 49, 50

Radcliffe-Brown, A. R. 84, 85, 92, 96

radiating lines, splay, engraved, painted
  83, 94
rainbow in myth 82, 83, 85
Rainbow Serpent 12, 83, 84, 85, 95, 96
  see also serpent myths
rain forest *see* forest
rain-making, 'rain-cuts' 93, 94, 96
  see also chest cutting; Rainbow Serpent
rain stones 93
rainy season *see* winter; fire for warmth;
  huts
range *see* seasonal movement; territory;
  usage rights
reed (flag) 12, 14, 39, 52, 59, 73, 79
  see also Duidgee
reed roots, pounding, roasting, ca!:es 14, 39
  see also cooking
reeds
  burning, cutting 4, 14, 39, 52
  ritual patterns of burnt reeds 79
regeneration of flora 49, 50, 53, 55
  see also Garden Island; mallee; Rottnest
    Island
regrowth following fire 45, 53–55
  see also young growth after burning
reptiles *see* iguanas; lizards; snakes
resource management, utilisation 12, 34,
  46, 76
  see also agriculture; crop; usage patterns
resources 46, 52, 53, 72, 74, 107
  see also seasonal resources
Ridge Hill Shelf 51
  see also foothills of the Darling Scarp
Ride, W. D. L. 10, 98, 99
ringbarking 55, 57
ritual 11, 12, 31, 44, 77, 78, 79, 84, 85, 88,
  90–98, 101, 113
ritual assemblages *see* corroborees;
  groups; seasonal agglomeration, etc.
rituals involving fire *see* fire in ritual
roasting *see* cooking
Roberts, Glen and Mervyn 54
Rockingham 67
rock-piles 94
Roe, Mrs Robin 13, 61, 72, 80, 81, 99
Roe, Septimius 60, 65, 74
roots 30, 38, 68, 77, 113
roots, digging, digging grounds 12–13, 14,
  32, 46, 58, 72, 113
roots, flag (*Typha*) *see* reed; reeds
roots, *Dioscorea, Warran, warrang,
  warrine, woorine, wyrang see* yam
  see also Djubak
Roper River 89, 90, 91
Roth, H. L. 68
Roth, W. E. 22, 43, 44–45, 81, 92
Rottnest Island 16, 19, 21, 48–50, 52, 62,
  112
  see also earthquake myths; flood myths;
    quokka; sea-level rise

routes *see* paths
rushes *see* reed; reeds

Sabina River 71
sacred objects, paraphernalia 92, 93, 95, 97
 see also bag; crystal quartz; ochre
sacred hiding places
 see holes and crevices
salinity, salinisation 6, 107, 111
salmon 39
 see also fish
saltbush 6
salt-lake country *see* sandplain
Salvado, Bishop Dom 43, 73
sandalwood tracks 75-76
 see also paths
sand-dunes
 grassy 16, 21
 mobile 7, 50, 103, 104
 see also dunes, coastal
sandheath 26, 53, 54, 64
 see also heath
sandhills 53, 60
 adjacent to swamp 34, 52, 57
 see also dunes; sand-dunes; sandplain; sandy areas
sandplain and salt-lake country 26, 53, 54, 64
sandplain, west coastal (Bassendean Sands) 34, 39, 51, 52, 54, 56, 57, 59, 60, 61, 66, 77, 99, 106, 108, 111
 see also coastal plain, west
sandy areas 27, 46, 59, 60, 61
sandy areas, Aboriginal preference for 49, 52, 53
 see also Gongan
Sauer, C. O. 2, 4
savannah, African 2
savannah woodland, Australian x, 6, 10, 50, 53, 63, 64, 111
Scandinavia 2
scarification *see* industries, backed-blade; chest cutting; quartz
scattered trees *see* trees
scattering *see* group size; seasonal agglomeration and dispersion
schnapper 39, 69
 see also fish
sclerophyll forest 50
Scott River 83, 102, 103
scratchings *see* linear markings; parallel grooves; radiating lines; serpentine markings
scrub *see* bush
Scully 73
sea-level, low 98
sea-level rise 10, 16, 19, 21, 48, 98, 100, 101, 104, 112
seasonal activities, movement, resources 23-24, 29-31, 34, 35-40, 42, 44, 46, 65, 68, 107, 113
seasonal agglomeration and dispersion, grouping and scattering 29-31, 34, 42, 108, 109, 113
secondary growth *see* regrowth
Seddon, George 14
sedgeland 50
 see also grassland
semi-arid annulus, areas, land, sector, zone 6, 10, 11, 111
September 30, 38
 see also seasonal activities; spring
serpent myths; serpent, mythological 12, 81-89, 93-97
 see also Chingi; evil spirits; *Gumba*; *Jinga*; *Kunmanggur*; *Moulack*; *Mullion*; *Wagal*; etc.
serpent in art 85, 93-95
 see also serpentine frieze, markings
serpent ritual 94-96
serpentine frieze of parallel dashes *see* parallel dash motif
serpentine markings 83, 84, 94-95
 see also linear markings; parallel dash motif; parallel grooves
serpentine penis 87
Serpentine River 53, 57, 108
Serventy, V. N. 94
settlement, settlers *see* European settlers
Shann, E. O. G. 25, 71
Shark Bay 16
sheep, pasture for ix, 15, 47, 62, 63, 73, 74
shellfish 6, 27, 39
Shenton Park Lake 67
shoals *see* fish
shrubland 16, 21, 22, 27, 50, 57, 62, 64
 see also firing, effects and uses
silicified limestone *see* chert
site-clustering 104
sites, archaeological *see* excavation; surface survey
skilfulness, skills, Aboriginal 30
sky in myth *see* earth-sky myths; moon; stars; sun
'small tool' industries, traditions *see* industries, 'small tool'
Smart, William 80
Smith, A. G. 2, 3, 50
'smokes' 16-17, 21, 22, 24-25, 28, 61
 see also fires
Smyth, R. Brough 87
snakes 32, 35, 36, 38, 42, 47, 48, 81, 82, 84, 85, 86
snakes, mythological *see* serpent myth
soak-well *see* water sources
soils *see* geomorphic zones; salinity; sandy areas
Solheim, W. G. 5, 10

sorcerers *see boyl-yas*
South Australia 39, 93
South-east Asia 5, 9, 10
South-west of Western Australia, scope x
Spaulding, A. C. 31
spearing *see* emus; fish; kangaroos
spears 30, 31, 32, 33, 39, 88
Spearwood Dunes 48, 51, 52, 57
  see also limestone, aeolian
Spencer, *Sir* W. B. 89
spinifex 7, 50
  see also grass
spirits *see* evil spirits
splash spots 85
  see also parallel dash motif; serpent in art
splay, engraved *see* radiating lines
spring 29, 30, 38
  see also Gambarang; Jilba; November; October; seasonal activities; September
springs *see* water sources
springs, grass patches around *see* grass patches
stalking *see* kangaroo
Stanner, W. E. H. 12, 31, 110
'Stanton Springs' 84
Star Carr 4, 38, 44
stars 38
stars in myth 83, 87, 88, 89, 90, 91, 94, 95, 97
  see also earth–sky myths
steep-edge scraper, steep scrapers *see* industries, steep-edge scraper
Stephens, R. 75
steppe 3, 6, 10
Stewart, O. C. 2
sting-ray in myth 87
  see also serpent myths
Stipa see tussock grass
Stirling, Capt. James vii, 21, 22, 23, 24, 43, 53, 56, 66, 108, 109
Stirling Range 28, 65, 68
Stokes, J. 33, 48, 77, 81
stones, rounded *see* sacred objects
Storr, G. M. 49
stress, demographic; population pressure 4, 6, 9–11, 34, 82, 104–107, 110, 111
  among large marsupials 5, 8, 50, 111
  among quokkas 49, 50
  see also ecological balance; population; quokka
sugar *see wama*
Sulphur, H.M.S. 24
Sumatra 9
summer 23, 24, 29, 30, 31, 35, 36, 37, 39, 40, 54, 60, 67, 70, 96
  see also Burnur; December; February; January; seasonal activities
'sun' in art 87, 94
sun in myth 81, 88, 95, 97
Sun Woman 87, 88, 95

  see also Fertility Mother
surface sites, surface survey, archaeological sites ix, x, 10, 31, 61, 72, 78, 84, 99, 100, 101, 103–104, 105–106, 108
Sutcliffe, A. J. 1
swallows, nests in Frieze Cave, Dale's Cave 94, 97
swamp products 34, 35, 39, 40, 105, 106, 107, 108
  see also birds; frogs; gilgies; reeds; shellfish; tortoises
swamps 12, 25, 35, 35, 38, 39, 40, 42, 52, 53, 57, 59, 60, 66, 67, 70, 71, 73, 77, 83, 99, 101, 102, 103, 106, 108, 111, 112
  see also water sources; Boggy Lake, Flinders Bay, Scott River and Weld Swamps
sandhills adjacent to 25, 66
  see also surface survey
tea-tree *see Melaleuca*
Swan coastal plain *see* coastal plain, west
Swan River
  area centred on x, 27, 31, 34, 35–40, 41, 48, 52, 53, 56–59, 64, 67, 73, 106, 108, 109
  estuary x, 13, 14, 19, 21, 22, 23, 24, 33, 35, 39, 43, 52, 56, 57, 58, 62, 64, 66, 67, 80
  exploratory trips vii, x, 16, 22, 23, 24, 53, 56, 66, 67
Swan River Colony, Settlement 23, 35, 77, 81, 91, 112
swans 30, 61, 69
Swanscombe 1, 2
swidden agriculture 113
symbol *see* art; myth; ritual
symbolic ties, usage *see* territory
Symer, Capt. 74

tailor-fish 39, 69
  see also fish
Taiwan 5
Tasman 16
Tasmania 2, 3, 4, 6, 7, 8, 50, 64, 68, 76, 77, 79, 82, 87, 89, 98, 100, 101, 110, 113
tea-tree *see Melaleuca;* swamp
ten Raa, W.F.E.R. 88
tension *see* stress, demographic
termite mound *see* ant-hill
territory
  exploitative use, hunting 31, 32, 34, 41, 42, 43, 65, 107, 113
  ritual and symbolic ties to, usage of 31, 97, 113
  see also usage rights
Thailand 5
thick scrub, thicket *see* bush, thick
Thomson, D. F. 30, 38
throwing sticks 39

Timor 9
Tindale, N. 7, 50, 93
tinder 44, 45
Tiwi 12
Tooat 52, 70
Toodyay 10, 13, 63, 64, 72, 86, 108, 109
Toolbrunup 28
torch 44, 45
  see also Banksia; grass tree
tortoises 23, 39
tracks *see* paths
traditions *see* industries
transport *see* drays; movement
transport, river 77
trees *see* individual species
  see also burnt trees; firing; forest
tree-clumps, dispersed, scattered 25, 57, 59, 60, 62, 63, 70
  see also parklike countryside
trees in myth *see* great tree; pine tree
tuart 52, 70
Turner, Nancy Ann Elizabeth 35
turtles 39, 52, 77
tussock grass (*Stipa*) 49
  see also Rottnest Island; quokkas
Typha see reed

Ucko, P. J. 9
unburnt countryside, ground 25, 26, 37, 38
  see also Bokyt; *Narrik*
underground caverns *see* caves; serpent
undergrowth, underwood 32, 53, 54
  absence of 17, 19, 24, 26, 46, 47, 56, 62
  thick 26–27, 47, 57
  see also bush; burnt bush
Upper Palaeolithic 2, 93
Upper Swan 57, 58
usage patterns vii, 9–15, 19, 21, 31, 38, 41–43, 65, 66–71, 75–77, 78, 97, 107, 110, 113
  see also land-use; patterns of exploitation
usage rights 15, 32, 34, 41, 42, 43, 65, 75, 107, 113
  see also hearth; *Kalla*; territory
usage, European *see* European usage; land-use; Rottnest Island
usurpation *see* European usurpation
uterus *see* womb in myth, ritual

Vancouver, Capt. 17, 19, 22, 24, 41
Van Diemen's Land 47
  see also Tasmania
Vasse (Busselton), district, estuary, Port, river 24, 25, 35, 47, 60, 64, 69, 70, 71, 79, 80, 108, 109
vegetable diet *see* plant diet
vegetation 18, 19, 20, 21, 37, 38, 48, 50, 52, 53, 64, 66, 82, 104, 111
  see also flora

vegetational change 1–8, 14–15, 20, 24, 26–28, 34, 35, 36, 45–48, 50, 54, 55, 56, 66, 101–105, 110
  see also firing, effects; opening up of country; peat-bores
vein opening *see* blood letting; quartz splinters
Vergulde Draeck 16
Victoria Plains x, 13, 56, 63, 64, 72, 74 108
'virgin' forest 7, 55
Vita-Finzi, C. 4, 29, 31, 34
Vlamingh, Wilhelm de 16, 17, 66
vocabulary *see* Aboriginal ecological concepts; and individual words
Volkersen, Capt. Samuel 16, 19, 48
votive deposits *see* sacred objects
vulva *see* womb in myth, ritual

Waeckende Boey 16
Wagal 82, 83, 84
  see also serpent myths
'waisted blades' 6
Walebing 74
wallaby 32, 33, 38, 49
Wallace, J. R. 33, 50, 53
Walter Brook 66
Walyunga 62, 99
wama (sugar) 95
Wandjinas 85, 87
  see also lightning in myth; parallel dash motif; rain-making
wandoo 53
  see also savannah
Wan-yarang 39
  see also April; autumn; *Geran*; May
warran, warrang, warrine see yam
water 46, 82, 83, 84, 85, 95
water sources
  lakes 39, 52, 60, 67, 83, 108, 111
  pools 39, 61, 66, 67, 73, 83
  springs 43, 55, 66, 67, 68, 69, 71, 72, 73
  waterholes 66, 67, 68, 73, 74, 75, 81, 84
  wells 7, 12, 21, 26, 66, 67, 68, 69, 71, 74, 75, 76, 81
  see also grass patches; swamps
waterholes, watersnakes, sacred 81, 84, 94–95
  see also ritual; sacred objects; serpent
wattle 57, 59, 63, 74
  see also bush
Waugal see Wagal
Weber's line 98
Wedge's Cave 102
weirs *see* fish weirs
Weld Swamp 102, 103, 105
wells *see* water sources
Weseltje 16
West, R. G. 1
Western Desert 7, 77, 100, 101, 104, 107

'wet', wet season *see* winter
Whajack 80
White, Carmel 7, 10
White, Peter 6, 7, 11
wild fowl *see* birds
Willandra Creek 5, 6, 10
Willeroo 93
William Bay 103–105
Williams 26, 63, 86
Wilson, T. B. 22, 68
Wilson Bluff limestone 100
Wilson's Promontory 50
winter 23, 29, 30, 36, 38, 40, 44
　see also fire for warmth; huts; kangaroo; seasonal activities, agglomeration and dispersion
woggal, woggle see Wagal
Wollaston, John 42, 43, 45, 72, 86
womb in myth, ritual 82, 87, 88, 95, 96
　see also Sun-Woman; Wuradjeri; waterholes, sacred
women in myth 82, 83, 87, 88, 89, 95
　see also Fertility Mother; Sun-Woman
Woodbridge 57
wooded zone, woodland 1, 2, 17, 25, 48, 50, 52, 57, 58, 59, 61, 62, 63, 107, 111
　see also open forest
wood-working 11
　see also adze; industries
woorine see yam
work 13
work of firing 14, 32, 33, 55, 107
Wright, G. A. 4
Wright, R. V. S. 82, 84, 96
Wuradjeri myth 87
wyrang see yam

Yagan x
yam gathering 12
yam grounds x, 12, 13, 72, 74
yam holes ('*warran*', '*warrine*', '*woorine*' holes) 12, 13, 14, 72, 74
yams at Bindoon, Gingin 13, 72
yamstick *see* digging stick
Yanbart, ground where vegetation has been burnt 38
Yanchep 83
Yanjidi see reed (flag)
Yarra River 87
Yeinart 73
Yirda Meening 83
Yoolgan 73
York ix, x, 10, 15, 36, 55, 56, 62, 63, 64, 73, 74, 77, 79, 80, 84, 86, 94, 108, 110
York gum 53, 63, 74
Yorkshire 2
young growth after burning 14, 15, 19, 25, 35, 37, 41, 42, 43, 45, 49, 54, 55, 75
　see also Balgor; *Kundyl*
'Younger Laterites' x, 53, 63, 64, 74
Yule 73
Yulika 71
Yun-de-lup 83
Yun-jid, Yun-tid see reed (flag)

Zamia (*By-yu*) 39, 53
zones of easy movement 3, 6, 17, 46, 49, 52, 68, 70
　see also opening up of country

Fire and Hearth:
Afterword to the revised edition

I summarise briefly the new understandings of Aboriginal landscape burning brought by new investigations and published sources over the forty years since *Fire and Hearth* was written, as well as the debates and controversies that have flared and died. I then treat the very considerable new work done on the prehistoric global and Australian contexts for both domestic and landscape fire. (Some of this writing has to be rather technical, and some readers may wish to skip these sections.) But these sections address important questions: What has been the role of fire in shaping man? How long has man shaped the face of the Earth, particularly in Australia? Finally, can we learn from the labour and skill that Australia's first people devoted to land care?

Burning in the Southwest in European Records

Working the Land

The notion of *terra nullius* rested on the assumption that Aboriginal people had not put labour into land. We now have an outstandingly informative eyewitness account that shows Aboriginal people working intensively on the care of the terrain. The recently translated journals of the eighteenth century D'Entrecasteaux expedition (Duyker and Duyker 2001) give an unparalleled close-up view of a single episode of 'burning off' and its timing, spacing and labour force.

In December 1792, two French vessels, *La Recherche* and *L'Esperance*, commanded by Bruny D'Entrecasteaux, sailed eastward along the south coast of Western Australia, searching for La Perouse. On 16 December, a party from *L'Esperance* landed in what is now Esperance Bay, and 'moved closer to some fires that were lighting up suddenly from place to place'. There was no lightning to ignite these fires. 'On following days we saw some natives [who] had probably set the dried bushes on fire', wrote D'Entrecasteaux (Duyker and Duyker 2001: 113–114).

During a foray onshore, the vessel's naturalist, Monsieur Riche, became separated from his companions and was left ashore over two nights. He penetrated inland, where 'whirlwinds of smoke' had been sighted in various parts of the interior, apparently at a short distance from the coast. 'I walked towards one of these smoke columns, which did not seem very distant', wrote Riche. But 'moving inland I realized... appearances had been deceptive'. After three hours he was no nearer his goal:

> I saw many places where the natives had made fires, and there were several columns of smoke rising around me. I approached one of these fires, which seemed to have been crowded with activity; but when I arrived the natives had gone... They set fire to a field covered with bushes, and spread the flames until everything has been consumed [then] leave the fire to extinguish itself during the night, and transport themselves to another place... Next day, I saw several natives, who from morning to night were busy poking their fire... When I approached them they went away, and when I retired, they again returned to their fires.

Riche is observing deliberate, controlled, systematic firing of the bush, each patch limited in extent, implying fire of limited intensity, and each part of an ongoing coverage. Each day's burn was controlled by a group of men starting ignitions within sight of each other. Yesterday's patch was no more than a short walk away.

More than one group was at work over the wider region. Riche later wrote of 'the natives, whose fires I could see in the distance, spending the whole day...occupied with their fire... I have not counted more than thirty fires in a circumference of at least ten leagues [50 or 60 kilometres] in diameter.' Thus, many bands of firers were at work over around 3,000 square kilometres (Duyker and Duyker 2001: 119–124).

Labillardiere, Riche's fellow naturalist from *La Recherche*, joined the search for his lost colleague. He reported, 'the natives had recently made fires in many places which we passed. They frequently set fire to the dried grass'. The search party passed 'many [burnt] places' in the space of a few hours, so each patch must have been quite small. These southern fires were not countrywide conflagrations lit by summer lightning, but a controlled, fine-grained mosaic of deliberate small-patch burns. To fit these descriptions one has to envisage individual ignitions expanding to burns some tens or hundreds of metres across, in clutches with no more than a few hundred metres between components, and some kilometres between each cluster and its neighbour.

We have few such descriptions of an entire series of burns, on a countrywide scale, carried out over a number of days. In January 1802, on a foray inland to Frenchman's Peak just northeast of Cape Le Grand, Robert Brown, botanist on Flinders' *Investigator*, had no doubt that 'smokes of nine fires' indicated 'the country set on fire in nine different places by the natives' (Brown 1801–1805: 96, 99, 113). In late January 1818, King's survey expedition, on their way from Port Jackson to the northwest, put in at King George Sound for ten days. Alan Cunningham gathered plants. He avoided 'a tract of bushland...lately fired by natives', and found the country still 'in flames around us in various patches'. A few days later 'several new smokes...indicated the presence of natives'; five days later one side of Princess Royal Harbour was 'recently fired by natives', and 'smokes of natives' were seen to the north and west while 'fresh native fires' were around Oyster Harbour. Cunningham had witnessed an extensive programme of controlled but widely scattered burns, on the scale of those observed by Riche ten years before. As King's expedition departed they saw 'one great blaze of flame, having been kindled by the natives...running before the wind illuminating all around' (Cunningham 1818 in Lee 1925: 313–325).

In mid-January 1827 at King George Sound, Major Edmund Lockyer, in command of the military contingent, was more specific: 'Yesterday was counted twelve large Smokes or Fires at the back of our Encampment about two miles apart forming a complete semicircle... From so many fires there must be assembled a number of Natives' (Lockyer 1826–1827: 11).

Burning programmes lasting days or weeks may have been the norm. In February 1842, at Grassdale in the Avon Valley, Eliza Brown observed it took several days for Mount Matilda to burn over. It 'presented the appearance of a most beautiful illumination for several successive evenings, much to Mr Brown's satisfaction...for the ensuring of a much more luxuriant crop of grass, and this I suppose is the reason why the natives are allowed to pursue their custom' (Cowan 1977: 38).

These examples are comparable with Aboriginal burning regimes observed in the 'top end' in the 1970s and 1980s by archaeologist Rhys Jones and his wife Betty Meahan; ecologist Chris Haynes; and anthropologist Hank Lewis (Lewis 1985; Lewis and Ferguson 1988). Rhys reported (Jones 1973) that during the dry season, an average of three foraging parties from a band of around forty people set out, each party lighting perhaps ten fires. Rhys estimated tens of ignitions per day for a band terrain 30 kilometres across, and deduced thousands of ignitions per year for the area (but see below, p. 174).

Haynes mapped, week by week, areas that had been burned. It is clear from his published maps (although they do not show each individual burn) that early season control burns can have been no more than tens or hundreds of metres across (Haynes 1983). Early burns were planned to protect valued resources, including yam patches and swamps, and repeated as the swamp dried out, previous burns acting as firebreaks. Some areas were preserved for hotter late season hunting fires, which would be prevented from becoming dangerous by prior burning. Finally larger areas of little-valued savannah woodland – 'rubbish country' – were burned at random late in the season.

In all these accounts, the Aborigines' persistence and hard work, using virtually all the available manpower of their small communities, are remarkable, as is their fine control of low intensity burns. This was already clear in accounts available in 1975, but not in such detail. Lieutenant Bunbury in 1836 wondered how thick and impenetrable the country between the Murray and the Vasse would become without burning, and concluded, 'We might ourselves burn the bush but we could never do it with the same judgement and good effect as the Natives, who keep the fire within due bounds, only burning those parts they wish, when the scrub becomes too thick, or they have any other object to gain by it' (Bunbury and Morrell 1936: 105; Hallam 1975: 47–48). Stokes, ashore from *HMS Beagle* in 1840, observed 'natives...burning the bush, which they do in sections every year', able to 'guide or stop the running flame...armed with large green boughs' (Stokes 1846: II, 228; Hallam 1975: 33). In all these accounts, we see Aborigines encouraging, spreading, maintaining, reviving, guiding, controlling fire, and *working* their land. It is clear how much planning, skill and sheer hard work go into management burns carried out over a sequence of years.

'Fire is for kangaroos', Mick Kubarkku told David Bowman in the Northern Territory. 'Just like when we plant a vegetable garden, the new grass comes up...and the kangaroos crawl across, eating the grass' (Bowman, Garde and Saulwick 2001). Right of tenure applies to worked pastures, as to worked gardens. If labour invested is the ultimate basis of ownership, there was no *terra nullius*, land that nobody had laboured over, in Australia.

Controls on Burns and Ceremonies

Controls on burning were enmeshed within Aboriginal 'law' and ecological lore. This is made evident in the journals of Captain Collett Barker, commandant of the military detachment at King George Sound from 1829 to 1831 (published in an annotated edition by Mulvaney and Green 1992).

In January 1830, Captain Barker told of 'a great [ceremonial] assembly at King River from all parts of the country, from Will's country [to the north], and other places at a great distance'. Barker's Aboriginal friend, Mokare, knew the visitors were coming 'by the appearance of distant fires', and told Barker, 'the blacks had plenty of kangaroo…killed by the fires'. Large gatherings were essential for hunting by fire drives, and fire drives were essential to support large gatherings. The 'great assemblage' continued through the last week of January into the first days of February (Mulvaney and Green: 249–254).

In November 1830, the King George Sound men again began to think of burns and ceremonial gatherings, but it was January 1831 before the fires of the northern Wills men once more approached. On 4 January, Mokare's companions hoped 'to burn for Wallabi, which they begin on a grand scale tomorrow'. On 7 January, there was 'much burning in different parts', and by 10 January, men were still 'burning for Wallabi'. On 13 January, Nakinah and others asked to borrow a boat 'to burn for Wallabi at Bald Head'. But 'he did not know the exact day as it depended on Coolbun's arrival, whose ground it was, & their starting there without him would be considered stealing… They also required his presence to burn at King George [Sound]'. By 18 January, the others 'were becoming impatient for Coolbun', who was not well, and on 19 January, Coolbun finally went out by boat with a group that landed to start 'large fires'. But on 21 January, Mokare borrowed a boat to go 'to burn for Wallabi', promising this would not be stealing because he would make only 'a little fire'. However, a 'large fire' appeared, which Coolbun said was 'on his ground', and others expressed indignation as another 'smoke' appeared (Mulvaney and Green: 377–386).

The timing of gatherings should be decided by the appropriate elders in light of their ritual responsibilities (law) and ecological knowledge (lore) about the readiness of the vegetation and availability of resources. Storable plants like processed zamia fruit, plant gums, yam tubers and reed rhizomes, and fish supplies from 'weirs' on Oyster Harbour and the Kalgan River, were more reliable than large game, and thus were prerequisites for a great assembly. The experienced elder/owner, not a young man like Mokare, should decide which patches should be burned for small game, which should be burned as part of an ongoing sequence of control burning, and which should be reserved for the great fire drives, enabled by, and enabling, great gatherings of neighbours for ceremonial and social purposes.

In March 1835, George Fletcher Moore witnessed a similar controversy on the Swan, in central Perth (Moore 1835, in Moore 1884: 259–260; and in Cameron 2006: 375). After the deaths of the respected elder Midgegoroo and his son Yagan, 'the country…belongs now of right to two young lads (brothers), and a son of Yagan. Some trespasser went upon this ground, lighted their fires, and chased the wallabees [sic]'. Some ritual assembly was in the offing: 'There was a large meeting of natives at the time'. The outcome was not as clear cut as at the Sound, for these youngsters did not command the unquestioned authority of an elder like Coolbun: 'A general row commenced, and no less than fifteen were wounded with spears in different parts of the legs'. The wounding was formal rather than mortal, to enforce recognised rules and assert and establish tenure where it was seemingly 'up for grabs'.

The linkage of fire, firing rights, attachment of kin to land, land ownership and rights in resources and ritual is made even clearer by the subtle shades of meaning of words for fire. 'The blacks', explained Captain Barker in 1830, 'to express home or resting place...say such a one's fire'. A family may make their 'fire' under a rock or a bush or near to the water, and it is the fire, rather than any structure, that constitutes 'home'. Moore, in September 1833, talked with his northern friend Weeip, who told him that he could not accompany Moore to Perth, 'for he has so many black men enemies...he is unwilling to go much from "his fire" [where] he has many women and children under his protection' (Moore in Cameron 2006: 277). As Gene Kelly tells us, '*Karl* not only describes fire, but also our immediate nuclear family', while '*karlup*, the name given to my home country', is 'literally...the place of my fire, my family place, my home' (Kelly 1999).

The ritual/ecological control by 'Aboriginal men of high degree' became very clear when, in 1847, Bishop Rosendo Salvado surveyed a track from New Norcia to Perth. His Aboriginal companions negotiated formally with the local landholders along the route, sitting thigh to thigh for long minutes, 'the most profound silence reigning throughout the entire ceremony'. Then the oldest Bindoon leader addressed his New Norcia counterpart: '*Nichia n'agna cala...*' or 'Here is my *fire*, now it is yours too. I stay here; you come and go, then you come back to go away and come again' (Salvado in Stormon 1977: 66). *Cala* was land held in sacred trust. Access to any part of that tenement was ceded only with the utmost solemnity. Neighbours were guests, granted privileges and roles; usage rights in the resources of a landscape ('ownership' or 'tenure' in European legal terms) were vested in the local community, which took the onus of responsibility and labour. This principle can almost certainly be applied more widely through space and time (cf. Mellars 1976).

Fire was important in ceremonial cycles (Nicholson 1981). In February 1830, William Taylor Jay saw, across the Murray River, a striking ceremony enacted, with 'twenty or thirty dancing each with a stick flaming a vivid blue light in their hands which they waved to and fro as they passed each other sending forth a kind of wild chaunt [sic]... The scene appeared magic, the lights were so beautifully and so dexterously waved around and across each other' (Jay 1830). On the Swan in March 1830, Mary Ann

Friend recorded that 'families residing at Preston Point used occasionally to see the Natives on the opposite side of the water; they used at night to kindle huge fires and dance round in the most fantastic manner' (Friend 1830). In September 1833, George Fletcher Moore heard of 'great gatherings of the natives, corroborees and visitings', including 'strangers from "waylo far away" [to the north]...great dancing...a great meeting to go kang'roo hunting'. He was invited to go and see the proceedings 'not far from Mr Bull's', on the Upper Swan, where the Ellen Brook enters. Moore and Bull set out on a long walk 'to find their fire', the focus of reception for all visitors. Their hosts, 'with burning brands in their hands', met them, and, evading *warran* holes, 'lighted us to their quarters whence we found about 30 men and 20 women & children resting around a number of fires, one fire to each family party'. But ceremonies on previous nights, and a big meal of kangaroo, had left the gathering too exhausted to continue (Moore 1833, in Cameron 2006: 280). Ceremonial gatherings enabled and necessitated fire drives to provision the assemblage; fire brands and small fires lit the scene. Similarly, in March 1836, Charles Darwin, onshore from the *Beagle* at King George Sound, described preparation for a corroboree: 'As soon as it grew dark, small fires were lighted' by which the men could see to paint themselves. Then 'as soon as all was ready, large fires were kept blazing, round which the women and children were collected as spectators' to dances imitating the movements of the kangaroo and the emu (Darwin 1845: 455; Armstrong 1985: 17–18).

Fire also had an important role in funerary observances. At a burial in May 1835, the beard was singed, fire was used to strip the nail from the right little finger, brushwood was burned in the grave and, after the grave had been refilled, 'a piece of fire was left burning in front of the mound' (Moore 1838, in Moore 1884: 346–347; Cameron 2006: 442). In September 1837, old Gear conducted a burial ceremony for Yellagonga on Tanner's land, just north of Moore's Millendon grant: 'He lighted a fire in the grave, singed off part of the beard...' (Moore 1837 in Moore 1884: 329; Cameron 2006: 431). In the Gantheaume Bay area (now Geraldton), for some time after burial, 'a fire is daily lighted on the grave' (Oldfield 1864: 245; 2005 reprint: 27). Thus, fire is closely linked to ceremony and ritual throughout each individual's life cycle, from womb to tomb. The respected elders responsible for ceremony were also responsible for the sacred duty of burning.

Under Aboriginal lore and law, a close attachment to land, which Europeans call 'property', 'ownership' or 'tenure', involved knowledge, rights and duties. The right to hold ceremonies was linked to the responsibility to hold the fire drives that enabled those ceremonies and to conduct burning programmes that left that option open. Fire was an important component in funerary, cleansing and increase rituals, and was itself a sacred activity.

Fire Regimes: Season, Frequency, Intensity and Extent of Burns

Since *Fire and Hearth* appeared in 1975, a series of important symposia and monographs have brought together bushfire data and interpretation from ecologists, foresters and others involved in recent practise and theory of land management (Gill *et al.* 1981; Ford 1985; Rose 1995; Whelan 1995; Bradstock *et al.* 2002; Mackay, Lindenmayer *et al.* 2003; Lindenmayer and Franklin 2003; Abbott and Burrows 2003; Adams and Attiwill 2011; Bradstock *et al.* 2012). Most have included Aboriginal burning under their aegis, and palaeobotanists, prehistorians and historians among their contributors. These publications should be consulted to understand the implications of past firing regimes for the ecology of subsequent landscapes. The work of Ian Abbott and David Ward has been most important in working out syntheses between past data and present ecology. Both have been involved in forest management and in tracing past regimes from historical records, correlated with Ward's work on grasstrees (see below).

Ecological effects are brought about not by single fires, but by fire *regimes*, or sequences of fires, with a range of *seasonality, frequency, intensity, extent* and *local landscape patterning* (Gammage's 'templates').

Data on *season* for firing are tabulated very thoroughly by Ian Abbott (2003: 122). Over half his records of Aboriginal fires occur in December or January; November to February includes nearly 80% of fire records, while 94% lie between October and March. Abbott's listed records of fires may include a few domestic fires (perhaps the few in winter), but there is no doubt his figures reflect Aboriginal firing procedures.

We can take as a sample of such data the letters and diaries of George Fletcher Moore, based on his land grant of Millendon, east of the Upper Swan as it runs south towards Guildford (see map in Cameron 2006: xiv). On 26 January 1832, 'fire...seems to be raging between this and the hills... The country all around Guildford has been burned'; on 27 January, 'Mr Tanner is ploughing long furrows to guard against fire. Great smoke and consequent alarm'; on 27 February, 'Got to Guildford. Country on fire' and on 29 April, 'The flat on the other side of the river was on fire yesterday'. In 1833, Moore was away from the Swan for most of February. But in 1834, he wrote on 16 January, 'Bush on fire in many places', and on 20 February, 'The country has been fired by natives, and we have been obliged to use great efforts to save our houses and property'. In March, Moore was obliged to assart his sheep on the land of a neighbour, 'not being able to keep them on my own grant, which has been so recently burnt'. An excursion in April 'up a long winding valley of bays, swamps and lakes [the Chittering Valley]' found some grass on the borders of wetlands, but here also 'the country had been recently burned'. In 1835, on 13 January, he wrote, 'The natives just now are making their fires in the bush to kill kangaroos, etc.' so that between 17 and 23 January there were 'native fires in all directions' and Moore and his shepherd had to explore the hills, 'hardly knowing where to find as much pasture as will support life in them'. As late as 26 March, there was a melee in Perth over an unauthorised fire drive (see above, pp. 163–4). Following hiatuses in the journal for the summers of 1836 and 1837, Moore wrote in 1838, on 12 February, 'Country was on fire each side of the road' as he rode between Perth and Millendon, and again on 26 March 1840, 'The country is all on fire between Perth and this' (Moore 1884: 214, 216, 259–260; Moore in Cameron 2006: 90–110, 310–318, 368–375, 437, 483). Most of these fires were in late summer, and it is not possible to say how frequently any one spot would be burned. Bush burns became so familiar that they were rarely mentioned, and neither was their native origin. Patrick Armstrong (1978) and David Ward (2010) gathered several references to fires in the heart of what is now the metropolitan area of Perth. These also (see pp. 172–3) were late summer fires.

Frequency is the most contentious issue. Rhys Jones maintained (1973) that Aborigines increased 'frequency' of burning by several orders of magnitude. David Horton (1982, 2000, 2003) argued they could have no such effect. This apparently unresolvable disagreement should warn us to define our terms. Jones was talking about frequency of *ignitions*; Horton was talking about average frequency of burns at any one spot, the *fire return frequency*. But 10,000 ignitions, each affecting on average an area of 100 metres across, burn only as much country as one vast wildfire extending 10 kilometres in each direction. People can increase frequency of *ignition* by several orders of magnitude without increasing average *fire return frequency* much or at all. But the change would have a massive effect on landscape and biota.

We cannot deduce average *fire return interval* or its inverse, average *fire return frequency*, without records of fire occurrence and extent for a large stretch of country over a long span of years. No such written records exist for the nineteenth century. But the pattern of multiple ignitions and close spacing, observed by Riche and others on the south coast, would fit the model provided by Haynes' mapping of 'top end' burning two centuries later and account for Rhys Jones' observations on ignition frequency.

Abbott (2003) has argued for an average *fire return interval* of two to four years for the Swan Coastal Plain woodlands and for the Avon Valley. The historical data he presents are too sparse to be conclusive. A record of one fire in 1838 and another in 1840 on the Swan Coastal Plain between Perth and Upper Swan (as above) is not sufficient to assure us that a two-year interval would have been the norm. We know neither the completeness of the record nor the extent of each fire, nor how often that spacing might have been repeated (see Moore's records above).

Paradoxically, general estimates, given as considered opinions by careful observers, are probably more reliable than unsystematic observations. Lieutenant Bunbury, writing in 1836 about the region around the settlement later named after him, wrote of 'periodical extensive bush fires...destroying every two or three years the dead leaves, plants, sticks, timber, etc.' (Bunbury and Morrell 1930: 105). Thomas Turner, tracing the Blackwood River northward from its estuary in September 1834, stated that over 'the greater part of our journey the bush was burnt last season by the natives consequently not bad walking' (Turner 1834). Does this imply that more than half the forest was being burned every year? Singleton, resident magistrate for the Murray District, thought that half the sandy country of the coastal plain was burned each year. From the Avon Valley, east of the forest belt, the botanist James Drummond told Hooker of 'triennial or quaternal burnings' in the 1840s; similarly, Gilbert from Northam spoke of 'intervals of three years' (Ward 2001; Ward and Underwood 2003; Abbott 2003: 125–126). John Septimus Roe (1835: 478) referred to 'the annual fires in the dry season' across forested lateritic gravels, but he may have meant no more than fire somewhere in that region each summer.

Dr David Ward has introduced a different type of record into the debate – the annual growth rings of grasstrees, with dark bands indicating burning events (Ward and Sneewjagt 1999; Ward 2001, 2009, 2010). On the face of the Darling Scarp northeast of Perth, in the John Forrest National Park, Ward sampled almost two hundred grasstrees, on ridge tops, valley sides, and creek banks. Before about 1860, fire had come through three to five times per decade (that is, once every two or three years, agreeing with Gilbert and Singleton). Frequency dropped in the late nineteenth century, and again in the 1950s and 1960s, to once every five to ten years. By the end of the twentieth century there were decades between fires, giving an unprecedented build-up of fuel (Ward 2001). Ward also sampled hundreds of grasstrees in the Wungong catchment, within the jarrah forest of the Darling Range southeast of Perth. Again, pre-European fires, in the eighteenth and early nineteenth century, recurred every three or four years, but from the mid-nineteenth century frequency dropped to less than one per decade (Ward 2010: 130–135, figures 6.16–6.18). The present objective for prescribed burns in the jarrah forest is one every eight years, but that is rarely achieved.

It has been objected that perhaps grasstrees were fired selectively. In the Avon Valley in September 1831, Moore recorded, 'Man sets fire to the tops of grass trees' (Moore 1831 in Cameron 2006: 50), and in the course of a march from Albany in July 1833, Alfred Hillman wrote somewhat mysteriously, 'Mopie set fire to a blackboy to prevent the rain falling at night as it has been doing all morning' (Hillman 1833: 330)! It seems very unlikely that such ignitions could unduly affect Ward's statistics, gathered from many hundreds of trees.

Dr Ian Abbott has assembled evidence from interviews with over 200 old bush residents; a third gave estimates of fire intervals for the early twentieth century (drawn up as a frequency histogram in Ward 2010: 136, figure 6.19). By then jarrah burned every four or five years, but some south coast localities much less frequently, supporting the near end of the grasstree record.

In general, grasstree, historical and oral data converge on an average fire return period through the jarrah forest of around two or three years under Aboriginal regimes (Ward 2001; Ward and Underwood 2003; Ward 2010; Lamont, Ward et al. 2003). But whatever the mean interval, the variance about the mean seems likely to be huge. A much wider sampling programme of grasstree analyses, for different ecological zones and different topographic and resource units within those zones, is needed to modify or amplify the broad-brush picture given by historical records.

Anecdotal accounts imply that the average interval in the southwest was likely to differ between major zones (karri forest, coastal plain, jarrah forest and Avon Valley) according to their relative usage by Aboriginal populations (cf. Christensen and Annell 1985; Lamont, Ward et al. 2003; Hassell and Dodson 2003). Thus, an Aboriginal group would frequent, and burn, the coastal plain wetlands much more than the forested lateritic uplands. Interval would also vary significantly between different parts of a zone – say, between wide valley routes or lake surrounds, and the bulk of the forested plateau they intersect. Kelly points out variation on a much more local scale. For instance, to maintain the close growth necessary for long spear shafts, spearwood thickets would be *protected* from normal cool fires, and burned intensively only at longer intervals (Kelly 1999).

Thus, combining these data from the south with ethnographic evidence from the north, it seems some areas were regularly burned early, while other zones were subject to more extensive and random later fires. This resulted in a systematic difference between frequent burns in one vicinity and sparse burns over a neighbouring swathe, with deliberate special treatment of small resource locales. Additionally, an element of random variation was important, because it superimposed an additional heterogeneity on landscape. Regimes differed between adjacent areas: protective zones burned frequently and early; unburnt protected zones; moderately burnt pasture enclaves, yards and corridors (often with well-defined boundaries); and wider, less frequented, less burnt 'rubbish' areas of forest, woodland and 'bush'. There was no one universal frequency.

Intensity is an inverse function of frequency, and is in turn correlated with extent. Conversely, descriptions of low intensity fires carry implications about previous fire history. From Riche near Esperance to Barker, Nind and Stokes around King George Sound, there are striking descriptions of fires so mild they could be guided, with flames licking gently around unharmed trees. Walkinshaw Cowan, landing in Fremantle in 1839 and riding to Perth, saw that 'the frequent burning of the bush by the natives had cleared the forest of all underwood', and encountered during his ride 'fires in the Bush through which we sometimes had to ride as they crossed the path' (Cowan n.d.: 10–11). Frequent burning had indeed tamed fire in the bush between Fremantle and Perth. I know of no descriptions of loss of life in bushfires in the early decades of colonial settlement.

Extent of individual fires was very small by today's standards, and varied enormously through the terrain of any one Aboriginal group. The Riche descriptions suggest the range for areas of burnt patches lies between fractions of a hectare and hundreds of hectares. Ian Abbott sums up, 'Size is rarely quantified by observers but could reasonably be inferred to follow a log-normal statistical distribution, with most fires "small" and a few fires "large"' (Abbott 2003: 126). It may now be impossible to confirm this. Similar 'average return frequency' can mask vital differences between rare vast conflagrations and huge numbers of smaller burns, from many tiny, protective, early burns to a few wide, late season, casual spreads.

Even less are we able to quantify patchiness *within* the burn. The lower the intensity, the more uneven the burn is likely to have been. Surveyor John Septimus Roe moved north in 1835 from King George Sound through 'country…recently burnt by the natives to a great extent, and [which] in many situations was still on fire' where 'grass was occasionally met with in positions which had escaped the conflagrations' (Roe 1835: 414). Such small-scale patchy burns posed no threat to those elements in the vegetation that need a long hiatus between fires.

Ecosystem manipulation was not confined to maintaining openness, increasing diversity and improving pasture. In the environmental mosaic were certain focal points: waterholes where the herbage was kept fresh, patches of root crop to access and foster, swamps and stands of spearwood to be guarded against destructive burns, and fruit trees and bushes around caves, rock shelters and shell middens. Roger Cribb (1996) calls the fostering of such a productive landscape 'domiculture', 'integration of certain kinds of plants into a modified ecosystem within and surrounding human settlements'. People maintained resources around the locations they frequented, with implications of custodianship, territoriality, 'ownership' and responsibility for care and maintenance, with burns as part of that onus.

Templates, planned local landscape patterns proposed by Bill Gammage, may add another dimension to the hierarchy of fire regime schemes. In *The Biggest Estate on Earth*, Gammage (2011) gives a detailed treatment of the many varieties of data (journals, letters, papers, books, maps, paintings, etc.) that can be used to elucidate fire as observed at contact and deduces that Aborigines imposed layouts as detailed as those of any farming estate, with planned rotations. I shall question this controversial hypothesis later.

Debates

There have been many controversies, ranging from gracious to less than gracious, on firing and its implications since humans first occupied the continent.

Dr Phyllis Nicholson (1981) doubted the value of data on Aboriginal burns from historical sources, because there is 'no way of knowing' which observations of smoke or fire were cooking fires and which were bushfires. And how could observers know whether bush burns were humanly lit? These difficulties are exaggerated. They do not apply to all maritime observations, and rarely to records of land explorers and subsequent long-term settlers. Some of the earliest European visitors to the west ran a constant chorus of 'fires but no people' (e.g., Vlaminghe in Robert 1972, *passim*; Vlaminghe in Schilder 1985, *passim*), but the Dutchmen who made forays up the Swan River (in the last days of 1696 and the first week of 1697) knew from wells, footprints and cooking fires that people were not far away (cf. Hallam 1983), and it was clear which fires were domestic.

By contrast, one can pick out, almost at random, from recently published or republished explorers' journals, many more instances where landscape burns are observed as being due to Aboriginal ignition. At the end of May 1801, Captain Baudin, commanding the *Geographe* and the *Naturaliste*, sailed north from Cape Leeuwin and in early June lay anchored in Geographe Bay. He assumed the many fires observed meant that the country was inhabited. They were 'too big and spreading' for people to gather round them, thus proving to be bushfires rather than campfires, and indeed 'thick clouds of smoke' were rising all along the coast. A foray ashore led to an encounter with a man busy spearing fish, three spears in one hand and a fire brand in the other. Baudin concluded, 'There were so many traces of fire everywhere, and the paths were so well-worn, that it looked to me as if this place were much frequented' (Baudin 1800–1803: 168–175). Numbers of fires reflected numbers of people.

When Captain Fremantle came ashore in May 1829 to found permanent European settlement, he met a group of natives, one of whom, again, had 'a spear in one hand and a firebrand in the other' (Fremantle 1829). Although Aboriginal people could make fire by percussion, sawing or drilling, the process was laborious (Nicholson 1981; Blake and Welch 2006). They preferred to retain a smouldering brand – in the southwest a banksia cone and in the midwest 'a bundle of smouldering bark' (Oldfield 1864: 283) – to light sequences of fires.

Once permanently ashore, settlers knew very well whether fires were humanly lit (I know of no reported lightning ignitions), whether Aborigines were responsible, and usually whether fires were domestic hearths or bush burns. There are plenty of records of fires adjacent to huts, which are clearly domestic. Thus, George Fletcher Moore, on a lengthy hunting expedition from Millendon in December 1832, came upon 'nine native huts... Each hut had had its fires', and around them were remnants of meals of kangaroo and yabby and shavings from spear-making (Moore in Cameron 2006: 190).

But everywhere first intruders encountered traces of the natives 'burning trees and the country' (Fremantle 1829). In December 1831, northeast of the Porongurups, surveyor Raphael Clint led his party 'in the direction of a large fire in hopes of meeting the natives to show us water' (Clint 1831). Dr Alexander Collie wrote in 1831 of 'the fires with which the natives have continually consumed the vegetable productions' and observed near Moorillup, 'much frequented by natives', a broad belt where 'fire has recently gone over its surface' (Collie 1831). In May 1832, he described a valley near Mount Barker 'with trees sufficiently wide apart to admit of agriculture without any clearing', where 'the grass has not escaped the spreading conflagration of the natives' (Collie 1832). When in January 1835 surveyor Hillman's party traced the Bannister River, each fire they saw could be ascribed unambiguously to Aborigines: 'The country appeared to be on fire, and around us were recent traces of natives'; 'the country around was burned or then burning...recent traces of natives'; and 'the bush in our rear suddenly on fire in many places... We now heard the voices of natives' (Harris 1835).

Later, many attributions to fires as due to Aboriginal bush burns were recorded in the press, especially those close to the centres of the urban communities on the Swan. (I omit deliberate firings of European assets, and burns found to be due to other agencies.) *Perth Gazette* reported fire across Mount Eliza [Kings Park] after 'natives had breakfasted on the spot', as well as a continuous blaze on the banks of the Melville Water. In February 1834, Aborigines fired bush on Shaw's grant [where the Swan River emerges from the scarp], but the burn got out of hand and crossed the river. By 1835, settlers were back burning as a precaution against Aboriginal burns around them. In March, settlers bemoaned the fires 'ignited by natives for the purpose of hunting', including a large fire at 'the flats' [by Heirrisson Island, adjacent to the present CBD], and another destructive blaze at Bull's Creek [a southern tributary of the Canning River near today's Murdoch University]. In March 1836, settlers still complained of the heat exacerbated by 'natives fires around us'. In 1838, 'native bush fires' were 'very destructive around Perth' in February, and there is an unusual mention in July of 'bush fires' in 'the Canning district'. By then, burns had almost ceased to be a matter for remark, but in 1841, the *Gazette* reported 'many bush fires round Perth in the last week' and, to remedy this situation, discouraged the lighting of fires on the town outskirts.* It

---

* Perth Gazette 3/01/1833, 10/01/1835, 07/03/1835, 05/03/1836, 10/02/1838, 28/07/1838, 28/03/1841.

is hard to claim uncertainty when the reports come from the local settler community, by now closely familiar with their predecessors close by. By the mid-century, only newcomers continued to remark on 'scorched and blackened...trees', and even for them 'the blackened trunks of the gum trees...are at first rather striking but the novelty soon wears off' (Richardson's journals 1859, in Richardson 1990: 79,91).

Nor does the supposed difficulty of attribution apply to all observation by mariners. They too may see the expansion of a fire front, or a linear sequence of ignitions. For instance, in November 1829, an exploring party in two whaleboats commanded by Lieutenant Preston saw 'smoke in many places between Port Vasse and Port Leschenault [Busselton and Bunbury]... and heard the natives shouting on the beach'. Later, mired in the shallows of the Peel Inlet, 'we had a distant view of the Flames of several fires among the trees and shrubs in Western Australia. We have no doubt they owe their production to the natives' (Preston 1829: 95–103).

Tabulating data from six voyages around our coasts, I judged that of 151 observations of smoke, forty-eight were uncertain, thirty-four were domestic and sixty-nine were almost certainly bush burns. That is, about 46% of the maritime observations *do* provide the supposedly missing evidence of landscape burns, while 32% were uncertain. From a sample of thirty-six land-based records of smokes, 55% could be identified as bush burns, and only 28% were unassignable. Taking sea and land observations together, almost half could be assigned to the landscape category, while for less than a third was there 'no way of knowing' (Hallam 2002).

It has bothered some writers that large amounts of charcoal, signifying intense burns, have been put forward as evidence for Aboriginal *advent*, as at Lake George (Singh, Kershaw and Clark 1981; Singh and Geissler 1985) and in offshore bores (Kershaw 1994; Kershaw et al. 2002); whilst high charcoal has been taken to signify Aboriginal *absence* from Kangaroo Island. There is no inconsistency here. Both before and after initial Aboriginal settlement, parts of the continent experienced long periods devoid of regular burns, which led to fuel build-up and fierce fires, whether these were initiated by lightning or by Aborigines.

It is beyond the limits of this essay to consider the debates about the effect of firing on the demise of megafauna, but the lack of environmental correlation seems to be swinging opinion towards Aboriginal hunting (McGlone 2012). Conversely, the effect of the demise of megafauna on the need for firing has also seemed controversial. Tim Flannery (1990, 1994) suggested that it was not Aboriginal burning that led to the demise of the megafauna, but the demise of the megafauna that led to Aboriginal burning. With no megafauna, scrub grew unchecked, and thus initiated the need for firing. Although this seemed far-fetched, more recent studies support Flannery's hypothesis. From the arid centre (the Lake Eyre basin and the Murray/Darling region) analyses of eggshell fragments have shown that, while the emu *Dromaius*, with a wide dietary spectrum of grasses and woody bush, survives to the present, another flightless bird, *Genyornis*, concentrating on once abundant grasses, became extinct around 45,000 years ago. This implies replacement of nutritious grasses by chenopod scrub and spinifex around that time as the prelude to human burns (Miller et al. 2005; Bowman et al. 2012). A recent analysis of spores of dung-dwelling fungi in volcanic lake deposits in Lynch's Crater in Queensland showed that a sudden drop in spore count, marking the loss of the megafauna, *preceded* a rise in charcoal and massive vegetation change (Rule et al. 2012). Megafauna loss *preceded* firing and its effects. However, it remains more likely that megafaunal demise increased, rather than initiated Aboriginal use of landscape burns.

Bill Gammage (2012: 325–342 and *passim*) discusses the controversy sparked by 'deniers' of Aboriginal burning, particularly David Horton and Bill Lines, and refutes them at length. I shall merely point out some basic misunderstandings.

Horton (1982, 2000, 2003) maintained that, as a matter of elementary logic, Aboriginal firing could have had *no* effect, good or bad, on Australian landscapes (though he does not apply this same logic to European, management burns). He argued that a particular ecological unit would only burn when it was ripe to burn, and not *more* frequently. The gap in Horton's logic is that a patch could burn *less* frequently. Lightning does not necessarily strike the moment a particular locality will support a fire. 'In the pre-human past, when lightning was the major ignition source, many "suitable" fire conditions may have passed without a fire for the lack of a dry lightning storm', says a standard textbook on fire ecology (Whelan 1995: 29). Human presence, even without deliberate ignition, increases the statistical chances that actual intervals between fires will approach more closely to minimum possible intervals. Changes in regime will change the flammability of what is there to burn.

Horton dismissed as ludicrous Rhys Jones' claim that Aboriginal burning increased the frequency of fires by several degrees of magnitude. But Jones was not talking of the frequency of return of fire to any one spot, but frequency of ignition, which is completely different (see above, p. 167). It is possible to increase numbers of ignitions without changing the average fire return frequency, if each ignition spreads only over a tiny area.

Those who do not accept Horton's dismissal of the significance of Aboriginal burning do *not* maintain, as he implies, that there were no bushfires in Australia before, and independent of, human intervention. Rather, human intervention changed the *average extent* and *average ignition frequency* of fire, and therefore its intensity and its effects. Those effects included the composition of the vegetation of each locality (Jones 1968, 1969; Hallam 1975, 1985, 2002; Bowman 1998, 2003; Burrows and Christensen 1990; Burrows et al. 2000; Bird 2008).

A further debate concerns the relative role of climate and Aborigines (and Europeans), through burning or attempts to prevent burning, in shaping Australian vegetation systems on the widest spatial and temporal scales. This was an issue raised by Duncan Merrilees in 1968, but only recently have data become sufficient to hope to return to his questions. There is general agreement that increasing climatic dryness, from the Miocene onwards, resulted in an increase in burning and its consequences over time (Bowman 1998, 2000; Kershaw et al. 2002). This, with superimposed Aboriginal burning over a timescale of tens of thousands of years, could and did affect the species composition, demographic composition and distribution of Australian vegetation systems (Bowman 1998, 2000; Bowman et al. 2012), instigating self-reinforcing spiral feedbacks affecting openness and flammability.

It has become increasingly apparent that the overall Aboriginal impact on Australia over tens of millennia has been massive. David Bowman discusses this in a lengthy paper on the botanical/ecological impact of Aboriginal burning (Bowman 1998) and in a book appropriately titled *Islands of Green in a Land of Fire* (Bowman 2000). He points out that deciduous vine thicket rainforest occupies a tiny proportion of its potential geographical range in the 'top end', and he looks at the patchiness and sharp boundaries of remnant rainforest, asking what controls its extent. After careful and lengthy discussion, Bowman concludes, as Jackson did half a century ago for Tasmanian rainforests and sedgelands, that fire frequency has been an important component in establishing and maintaining present vegetation patterns, and that Aboriginal burning has modified that frequency. While rejecting speculation that eucalypt speciation might be due to Aboriginal burns, Bowman did see the changed frequency and distribution of burns as affecting the distribution of vegetation types, and realised the degree of close ecological knowledge involved. Thus, Aborigines achieved the very specific fire regimes required to support healthy populations of cypress pines (*Callitris*), which can be killed by either too frequent or too infrequent burning (Bowman 1998).

Bowman saw Aboriginal people as playing 'an important part in the making of a flammable Australia', for instance by nibbling into rainforest over time and substituting sclerophyll. He also argued that human intervention altered the 'grain' of vegetation in the direction of greater patchiness and diversity. He sees this diversity threatened by the demise of Aboriginal traditions and the transition to European fire management (or, in the truly arid areas, *lack* of fire management) as 'a major ecological and evolutionary event...of the same significance as the Pleistocene colonisation of Australia' (Bowman 2003; Bowman et al. 2012: 36–39).

Bowman also queried whether the overall increase in total burning might have been sufficient to affect not only vegetation, but also climate (Bowman 2002). Modelling has since indicated the strong probability that the scale of burning was sufficient to delay the onset of the monsoon in the 'top end' (Notaro, Wyrwoll and Chen 2011). Thus, in a rising spiral, firing and its ecological consequences would produce drier conditions conducive to more fires.

Throughout Australia it was the mosaic of small, deliberate pre-European burns that kept the landscape sufficiently fuel-free and diverse to avert huge fires (figure 2.4 in Bowman et al. 2012). In the Western Desert, recent air photographic coverage has shown that vast tracts that had not been burned for more than thirty years have been reduced to sameness by one huge conflagration, contrasting with the complex palimpsest of burns under indigenous custodianship shown on earlier photographs (Burrows and Christensen 1990; Burrows, Burbidge and Fuller 2000; Pyne 2001; Bird et al. 2008). Paradoxically, indigenous burns both contributed to rising trends in burning and aridity on a continental long-term scale and averted catastrophic fires locally in the short term.

As controversial as Horton's denial that Aboriginal burning brought any change is Bill Gammage's (2011) assertion that Aborigines created artificial landscapes, 'templates' laid out with a degree of detailed deliberation that no one previously envisaged. He deduces that Aboriginal people 'coupled preferred feed and shelter by refining grass, forests, belts, clumps and clearings into templates...maintained for centuries...offering abundance, predictability, continuity and choice... Together they rotated growth in planned sequences, some to harvest, some to lure and locate' (Gammage 2011: 211). Aboriginal managers, he avers, over spans of many years, used fine control of burning procedures to initiate and maintain differences between adjacent tracts, where there were no pre-existing differences of geology, soil, slope, elevation, aspect, etc. Gammage envisages 'tongues of forest' left to 'bite into grassland...to let hunters ambush prey' and 'clumps' of trees providing patches of shade cover, while the entire surrounding grassland was burned too frequently for saplings to grow (Gammage 2011: 59 and *passim*). The whole pattern of a group's terrain, he argues, thus became a 'template', a total planned landscape, requiring different rotations for different areas to keep that diversity. Gammage's argument here is circular and unconvincing. The verdict must be 'not proven'.

On the other hand, it is difficult to deny the 'unnaturalness' of many Australian landscapes. Would Bussell or Bunbury or Moore doubt that 'an English gentleman's park' was an artificial creation? Why then does it never seem to have occurred to them that in the Vasse, the Swan Coastal Plain and the Avon Valley (which they so described) they might be looking at equally artificial creations? Capability Brown achieved 'wild' landscapes by meticulous planning. Had this happened here?

A very debatable contention is that the universality of unnatural landscapes 'made a continent a single estate' (Gammage 2011: 280).

Gammage also asserts (2011: 288) that 'agriculture [the cultivation of fields] spread more widely than now', if we take a managed crop as the criterion of a field. This is well argued: 'So people burnt, tilled, planted, transplanted, watered, irrigated, thinned, cropped, stored and traded... What farm process did they miss?' (Gammage 2011: 301). But Europeans find it difficult to get used to an idea so foreign to their assumptions, and undoubtedly controversy will continue.

Gammage underlines for us the massive impact of the human diaspora on Australian landscapes. There is much new evidence from world prehistory that indicates this may be true of all global landscapes, long before those developments we label 'farming'.

Global Context

'The greatest discovery ever made by man'?

Darwin considered the 'discovery of fire probably the greatest ever made by man, excepting language' (Darwin 1871: 72), important for making plant roots and tubers more digestible and toxic foods innocuous. Levi-Strauss in 1964 showed that myths worldwide regarded obtaining fire and cooking food as *the* criteria of being human (*The Raw and the Cooked*, cited in Goudsblom 1992: 2). Richard Wrangham has returned to Darwin's theme, relating the significance of fire and cooking to the evolution and spread of humanity (Wrangham 1999, 2009).

Wrangham sees not just a meat diet, but a *cooked* meat diet as making possible the relative enlargement of that calorifically expensive organ, the brain, and the concomitant decline of the huge jaw apparatus previously needed for processing raw flesh and tubers. In our genus, *Homo*, the whole skull was remodelled, with the diminution of the jaws and teeth, masticatory muscles and skull buttressing (Wrangham 2009; cf. Stringer 2012: 138–141). Wrangham goes much further, concluding, 'Humans are biologically adapted to eating cooked food', and that those biological adaptations extend to reduced gut, mandatory bipedalism, faster terrestrial movement, larger body size, slower maturation, longer life, availability of older people to support young families, social cohesion and relatively larger brain and cranial capacities. In a somewhat circular argument he sees all these characteristics of even the earliest *Homo* societies as evidence they already possessed fire, making possible cooking to satisfy the energy demands of a big brain and giving a social focus around which the complexities of technology, kinship and ritual, story and song could thrive (Wrangham 2009; Wrangham and Carmody 2010).

To trace the global picture, we need to look for evidence of hearth fire and bushfire, from the first African hominins and the origins of our genus almost two million years ago, through multiple waves of spread, with successive ripples reaching Southeast Asia and Australia. We can now be certain that, whenever they came, first Australians would be familiar with controlling both hearth fire and bushfire.

On a global scale, most of the acceptable evidence for the antiquity of fires lit by humans comes from hearth fires rather than landscape fires. Multiple ash layers in a cave represent human hearths, lit and relit over centuries, millennia or tens of millennia. Such evidence of fire has been found abundantly in occupation sites of the last hundred thousand years, associated frequently with Neanderthal and other archaic forms, and almost universally with modern forms of *Homo sapiens* (Balter 2004; Roebroeks and Villa 2011). If a structural hearth constitutes the criterion of anthropogenic fire, then we lack such evidence before the Neanderthals (James 1989). Even if we use wider criteria, some apparently ashy deposits initially identified as hearths have failed more sophisticated analyses. Consequently, standards of proof have become continually more stringent. Do we have valid evidence that earlier hominins used fire?

African Beginnings

The oldest records of anthropogenic fire come from Africa, the birthplace of our hominid group among the primates.

As long ago as 1948 Raymond Dart claimed Australopithecine fire in the 'Cave of Hearts'. But his supposed charring was manganese staining. Although Swartkrans Cave in the Transvaal (Brain and Sillen 1988) may also show hominid use of fire from before a million years ago, the first stringent validation of evidence for fire is the result of innovative methods used in Wonderwoek Cave in South Africa (Beaumont 2011; Berna *et al.* 2012; Roberts and Bird 2012). Analysis of the microstructure of the cave sediments and examination of stone tools, burnt bone and ash plant remains show that the makers of Acheulian artefact assemblages, members of our own genus, *Homo*, were lighting fires 30 metres inside the cave around a million years ago. *Homo erectus* is the earliest universally acknowledged fire monger in southern Africa.

Proof is more difficult to obtain on open campsites. However, even when ash and charcoal from a hearth have been dispersed or degraded, the baked sediment underneath may have survived to show an anomalous magnetic signature. At Koobi Fora and Chesowanja in Kenya, patches of reddish orange earth in lacustrine and riverine deposits, containing stone artefact clusters around one and a half million years old, provided initially debatable evidence of earlier hearths. Mike Barbetti, who had done palaeomagnetic work on Aboriginal campsites around Lake Mungo in southeast Australia (Clark and Barbetti 1982), applied magnetic surveying to these much earlier sites in Africa (Barbetti 1986). R. V. Bellomo showed by experiment that multiple-burn hearths exhibit clear magnetic anomalies, whereas single campfires, grass fires, brush fires, forest fires and stump fires cannot be identified as humanly caused events. His archaeomagnetic studies (plus phytolith analysis) showed that fires of easily ignitable palm wood had been kindled and rekindled at Koobi Fora (Bellomo 1994). Similarly, at Chesowanja, by Lake Baringo, beneath basalt potassium-argon dated to 1.4 million years ago, alternating lenses of burnt material suggest repeated returns to the same location (Gowlett *et al.* 1981; Clark and Harris 1985). In Ethiopia, at Gadeb and in the Middle Awash Valley, patches of intensely reddened clay may be due to smouldering tree stumps. But, all in all, 'these [east African] studies have removed all doubt that even early *Homo erectus* had the technological capability of cooking foodstuffs' (Rowlett 1999), and pushed the probability of hominin control of fire back to around one and a half million years ago.

The importance of fire to the social life of hominins and their global landscape impact has been realised since the 1950s (e.g., Oakley 1956). But African evidence in the 1980s showed that control of fire, and gathering of family around the protective hearth, enabled our relatively defenceless hominid forebears to live on the ground in open African savannahs, despite large carnivores. Desmond Clark saw the use of fire, perhaps conserved from wildfires, stored in smouldering stumps, carried as fire brands, and focussed in campfires, as 'fundamental to humanity' (Clark and Harris 1985).

Some hint that the use of fire may have extended from a domestic to a landscape scale comes from faunal studies showing the prevalence in Africa over the last two million years of antelopes adapted to secondary grasslands. These grasslands, maintained by fires, which may well have been ignited, deliberately or not, by people (Boaz and Ciochon 2004: 120).

Fire Beyond Africa

The 'Cave of Hearts' and Choukoutien showed that mere visual examination will not suffice for recognising hearths. The difficulties of identifying burnt material dictated that more rigorous techniques should be applied to analyse intact depositional structures.

Impeccable evidence for human hearth fires comes from Gesher Benot Ya'aqov, on the shore of paleo-Lake Hula in Israel. Small burnt flint fragments were a tiny component of the total stone artefact assemblage, but they comprised the majority in specific clusters, the locations of Acheulian hearths. Only a small percentage of the wood, bark and fruits were burnt, very unlikely to be due to indiscriminate wildfires. Fuels included ash, olive and wild barley and other grasses (Goren-Inbar *et al.* 2004), perhaps indicating open areas of landscape. The age, however, is less certain. Burnt flint artefacts do not occur until 4 metres *above* the 800,000-year magnetic boundary.

The 7.5-metre sedimentary sequence at Qesem Cave, also in Israel, was stringently investigated using microscopic analyses of thin sections through consolidated deposit to examine microstructure; infrared spectroscopy to determine whether the black colour of bones was due to manganese or to pyrolysed collagen; oxygen and carbon isotope measurements to identify wood ash (and even its species components); and thermoluminescence to confirm that calcined bones had been burned. The deposits were shown to consist predominantly of massive lithified wood ash accumulations, containing large quantities of burnt bone fragments, fine black charcoal, stone artefacts and clay lumps, reddened by heat. The analyses confirmed 'the extensive and repeated use of fire' from roughly 400,000 to around 200,000 years ago. Hominins had repeatedly and habitually built small campfires within the cave, sitting around these hearths to skin and butcher fallow deer, aurochs and horse, disarticulate bones and cut off the meat, extract marrow, cook animal and plant foods, eat, make and repair tools (Karkanas *et al.* 2007; Dennell 2009: 307–308) besides, no doubt, chatting, singing and telling tales.

There are less stringently analysed evidences of the use of domestic fire in Europe from 400,000 or 500,000 years ago onward, e.g., at Boxgrove in Sussex, Atapuerca in Spain, and La Cotte, Terra Amata, Schöningen, Bilzingsleben and Vertesszollos (James 1989). Although people had been around in northwest Europe for 800,000 years, evidence of fire becomes apparent only during a warm phase, around 400,000 years ago, known as Marine Isotope Stage 11 (Roebroeks and Villa 2011). Even in interglacial periods, the cold winters would present a problem for survival. Sites are few, so the apparent absence of fire may be 'an issue of taphonomy and recovery rather than a real absence' (Pettitt and White 2012: 55). Pre-*sapiens* members of our genus *Homo* could already control fire, and were dispersing that skill through the Old World.

But did they burn the bush? The best evidence for landscape burns still comes from East Anglia (cf. Hallam 1975: 1). At Beeches Pit, fire had burned several thousand flint artefacts, including hand axes and flaking debris, in interglacial lake sediments of MIS11 (see p. 185) around 400,000 years ago. There were several phases of occupation, shifting location from lakeside to channel bank. This was a home base to which people returned repeatedly. Burnt flints and charred bones at all phases, plus hearths (lens-shaped accumulations of burnt material 20 centimetres thick) showed repeated burning over a period. Three such hearths intersected and succeeded one another, with a later hearth 25 metres away, indicating that the wider locality attracted occupation over a long period. A widespread dark horizon containing burnt material is interpreted as detritus from a regional forest fire (Gowlett *et al.* 2005; Pettitt and White 2012: 81–85). The pollen record shows the surrounding closed temperate oak woodland was interrupted by a brief phase of deforestation, probably contemporary with similar episodes at other East Anglian localities, including Hoxne and Marks Tey (Pettitt and White 2012: 68–73, 78–85). Thus, Beeches Pit shows both domestic fire for warmth in cold winters plus bushfire moulding biota during an early northern interglacial period.

Early Fire in Eastern Asia

Early hominins dispersed across the ancient grasslands of Asia, northwest to the Caucasus and southeast to Java (part of the Southeast Asian landmass at times of low sea level) before 1.8 million years ago, before the Sahara, Sinai and Arabia dried out to present extensive desert barriers (Dennell 2009).

From the huge site of Zhoukoudian (Choukoutien), 'home of Pekin man', archaeologists (starting with Davidson Black, Pierre Teilhard de Chardin and Henri Breuil in the 1930s) have long claimed evidence of fire: burnt bone and stone, charcoal and supposedly thick ash deposits (Dennell 2009: 411–413). Despite some doubts (Binford and Ho 1985; Binford and Stone 1986), it was widely accepted that the use of fire enabled colonisers to penetrate so far north. But micromorphological analyses (Weiner *et al.* 1998) reinterpreted so-called 'ash' layers in the remnant 'western section' as redeposited loess, washed in from adjacent hillsides and lacking the abundant phytoliths that would be found in wood ash. Carbonaceous material was the remains of plants from water-laid sediments. Nonetheless, re-examination of Breuil's original samples confirmed burnt bone and burnt wood, and samples from the exposed profile included significant proportions of burnt flakes and hammerstones, burnt bone, burnt ostrich shell, burnt redbud wood and burnt hackberry seeds. Some bones, heated while fresh, showed that large mammals were also cooked, and other older bones became heated as the substrate of fires (Boaz and Ciochon 2004: 100–102). Probably the remaining 'west section' once lay deep inside the cave, and more fires would have been lit nearer the mouth of the cave in deposits long removed (Dennell 2009: 411–413). Fire enabled people to live in this cave from approximately 700,000 to 400,000 years ago, though not often during the coldest phases (Boaz and Ciochon 2004: 113–119).

From around 800,000 years ago, human movement through Asia and towards Australia would have been subject to alternations between glacial and interglacial periods and more arid and moister phases, with concomitant fall and rise of sea levels (Dennell 2009: 77–81, 200–202; figures 3.25, 5.9,

6.2, 7.12). At times of low sea level people could walk dry-shod as far as the eastern end of Java. Hominins journeyed remarkably early beyond the furthest extent of mainland Southeast Asia and moved from island to island along the Indonesian arc, reaching Flores before one million years ago (Morwood *et al.* 1998; Dennell 2009: 428–432; Falk 2011: 185–186). It is perhaps surprising that strong southward ocean currents, through several deep channels between those islands, did not carry some early watercraft to an extended Greater Australia (Dennell 2009: figure 10.10) at dates much earlier than those now validated.

Also on Flores, by the recent span of 95,000 to 17,000 years ago, strange non-*sapiens* hominins, so-called 'Hobbits', were using fire in Liang Bua Cave. Mike Morwood's team have excavated charcoal, charred bones, clusters of fire-cracked rocks and an arrangement of burnt pebbles that may have been part of a hearth. Here these small people gathered to knap tools, using them to butcher *Stegodon* and formidable Komodo dragons (Morwood *et al.* 2004; Falk 2011: 88). Did they learn to use fire from *sapiens* neighbours, or bring it with them as part of a much earlier diaspora?

Sapiens Approaches Australia

On present evidence, that last crossing, bringing anthropogenic fire to Australia, was made only by modern *Homo sapiens* during the last fifty or sixty thousand years. During the lengthy fluctuations of the last glaciation, global sea levels fell as low as 150 metres below present levels. Mainland Southeast Asia extended to include what are now the islands of Sumatra, Borneo and Java in a landmass known as Sunda. Dry land stretched across what are now the Bass Strait, Gulf of Carpentaria and Torres Strait, creating Sahul or Greater Australia. It was never possible to enter Australia dry-shod from Asia, for between Sunda and Sahul stretched a chain of Indonesian islands always separated by very deep water with strong currents. Recent investigations show that, over more than 50,000 years, humanly controlled fire in Sunda, and the intermediate islands, has included bush burns.

'Hell Trench', located in the West Mouth of the Niah Cave on Borneo, first excavated in the 1950s and '60s by Tom and Barbara Harrison of the Sarawak Museum, produced the earliest *Homo sapiens* skull in the region, dating around 40,000 years old. Recently, Graeme Barker of Cambridge and an array of collaborators (Barker 2005; Barker *et al.* 2002, 2007; Higham *et al.* 2009) investigated the baulks left by previous excavators and elucidated human activity dating from recent back to more than 46,000 years ago. People were butchering pigs, monkeys and lizards and exploiting fruit, nuts, yams, taro and sago pith, several of which required lengthy processing. Burnt bone occurring in hearth clusters, burnt soil, abundant micro-charcoal and a peak in magnetic susceptibility indicate intense local burning.

The Niah pollen record shows vegetation very different from the humid rainforest that now surrounds the cave. Forest taxa were predominantly those of dry forest. Nonarboreal pollen from grasses, plantain and *Cyperaceae* indicates disturbed and open areas that would have provided good habitats for tubers (such as yams, *Dioscorea*), given access to fruit and nut trees and sago palms as sources of starchy pith, and attracted game. The high frequency of trees known to be first colonists after fires indicates burnt and regenerating woodland and the cyclical advance and retreat of forest, brought about by repeated human landscape burns. *Sapiens* colonists moving into Southeast Asia were already creating mosaic landscapes, rotating forest burns and detoxifying plants, thus extracting high-energy carbohydrates from rainforest biomes.

In the Sula Sea (east of Borneo, west of the Philippines and south of the China Sea), a 36-metre piston core through foraminiferal ooze showed cycles of micro-charcoal abundance during glacial periods. Starting 60,000 years ago, there was a steep rise in micro-charcoal, peaking at 50,000 years ago with double any previous density. It is attributed to anthropogenic burning superimposed on the previous natural cycles (Beaufort *et al.* 2003). Like the Niah pollen record, this very different evidence shows modern humans, by at least 50,000 years ago, using landscape burns for hunting and clearing. In a positive feedback cycle, they unintentionally reinforced the glacial weakening of the regional summer monsoon in Southeast Asia, thus further increasing dryness.

It has long been orthodox, despite contrary evidence (Bowdler 1983), that tropical and temperate rainforests were little used by early peoples, and could not be control burned. Evidence is now emerging that this was not so. Did landscape burning make its way into and through the rainforests of northern Sahul?

Australian Context

Controlled Fire in the North of Greater Australia

The best evidence of vegetation manipulation in the approaches to Australia comes from New Guinea, once an equatorial projection from Greater Australia. In the 1970s, Peter White excavated artefact scatters at Kosipe in the Ivane Valley, 2000 metres above sea level in the New Guinea highlands (White *et al.* 1970). Geoff Hope investigated pollen and charcoal from the adjacent swamp, showing that grassy openings were being created in the forest at least 30,000 years ago, maximising the nut crop from high-altitude *Pandanus* (Hope and Golson 1995). Despite contentions that an increase in fire events over the Malesian region related primarily to climate change (Haberle, Hope, and van der Kaar 2001), more recent investigations have extended the evidence of early human manipulation and exploitation of forest products. A group of sites in the Ivane Valley around Kosipe were occupied almost 50,000 years ago. Charred *Pandanus* nut shells, starch grains adhering to stone artefacts and an increase in microscopic charcoal in the adjacent swamps between 41,000 and 38,000 years ago, all indicate vegetal manipulation that included landscape burns, creating openings within the forest (Summerhayes *et al.* 2010).

The Huon Peninsula lies on the northeast coast of New Guinea, where strong intermittent coastal uplift has resulted in a 'staircase' of coastal terraces. The many stone axe heads on some of these terraces must be older than the overlying volcanic deposits, which have potassium-argon ages of more than 40,000 years (Groube *et al.* 1986; Groube 1989). These heavy, 'waisted' axe heads have been hafted and intensively used. Many show damage scars or have snapped at the 'waist', probably while being used for ringbarking, branch trimming or root clearance. Pollen records in the region show forest disturbance by 30,000 years ago, and fire and axes would have enabled people to open up the canopy, create clearings and clear encroaching trees to encourage the growth of sago and *Pandanus*, taro, bananas, yams and nutritious green vegetables. The first colonists had barely entered a larger Australia before they began to use fire as a tool to modify vegetation, tackling both high-altitude open zones and also the lowland forests of the Huon Peninsula.

Confirmation comes from the rainforests of West New Britain (part of the Bismarck Archipelago), where a consistent stratigraphic picture is presented over a wide area. Discrete patches of 35,000-year-old occupation debris are preserved under airborne volcanic tephra in inland valleys, about 500 metres above sea level and 30km inland around Yambon, where flint was exploited. The charcoal-rich occupation layers and the high proportion of fire-crackled flint artefacts on some sites imply a pattern of land use similar to recently dispersed and shifting hamlets (Pavlides and Gosden 1994).

Rainforest penetration also extended southwest into what became, as postglacial sea levels rose, the north of mainland Australia.

Controversial Early Fire in Mainland Australia

The Australian continent shows plenty of evidence for fires *not* lit by Aborigines: charcoal from fires dating from 2.6 million years ago in Pliocene lake deposits in the northern part of the west coastal plain (Hassell and Dodson 2003); charcoal in late Pliocene/early Pleistocene deposits of the Swan Coastal Plain (George Kendrick, personal communication, September 2003; Kendrick, Wyrwoll and Szabo 1991); and charcoal off the Queensland coast dating from 1.4 million years ago (Kershaw *et al*. 2002), all long before the advent of people. Conversely, the pollen record from Kangaroo Island (Singh, Kershaw and Clark 1981) shows intense burns *after* Aboriginal access ceased. European mariners recorded thick vegetation, then explosively intense fires, on other uninhabited islands (Hassell and Dodson 2003; Hallam 1975, 2002).

Some charcoal records, however, show high peaks, seriously considered by their investigators as likely to be due to humans, at dates regarded as too early for *sapiens* colonisation. Should these records automatically be considered as 'false leads' (Hiscock 2008: 27) to early human presence in Australia?

In Darwin Crater in Tasmania, drilling through Pleistocene lake clays to levels dating back to over 700,000 years ago, showed a long sequence of alternating colder and warmer phases and a very high charcoal peak in the penultimate glaciation, around 180 to 160 thousand years ago. William Jackson suggested that this evidence might represent human occupation, but his 'extraordinary claim' was emphatically rejected (Colhoun and van der Geer 1988).

Stages of alternating cold and warmth, recorded in deep sea bores as Marine Isotope Stages MIS19 to MIS1 – that is, eight or nine climatic cycles from treeless glacial maxima (MIS18, MIS16, MIS14, etc.) to warmer interglacial periods (MIS19, MIS17, MIS15, etc.) – now form the accepted chronological framework for world prehistory (e.g., Dennell 2009: *passim*; Mooney *et al*. 2012). Two long pollen and charcoal sequences (from Lake George and Offshore Bore 820 off the Queensland coast) show sudden increases in charcoal during the last interglacial period, MIS5, around 120,000 years ago. Are these increases due to humanly initiated burns?

Lake George, near Canberra, has a pollen and charcoal record stretching back to the Brunhes–Matuyama magnetic reversal almost 800,000 years ago, alternating between wooded interglacial periods and treeless glacial maxima from MIS 19 onward. After minor peaks in charcoal in interglacial periods MIS9 and MIS7, the last interglacial period (MIS5) around 120,000 years ago shows a charcoal peak several degrees of magnitude greater, as well as a decline in previously dominant casuarinas relative to a sharp increase in eucalypts (Singh, Kershaw and Clark 1981; Singh and Geissler 1985; Kershaw *et al*. 2002). Similarly, offshore from Queensland (Kershaw 1994; Kershaw *et al*. 2002), Bore 820 shows a sharp increase in charcoal in the same interglacial period (MIS5), followed by a maintenance of high charcoal levels and a dramatic decline in rainforest taxa. Does the sudden peak in charcoal represent the advent of people and their fires, or fuel build-up followed by catastrophic lightning-lit fire? The increase in charcoal record is maintained more continuously but with lesser peaks (i.e., less intense but more frequent fires) from then on, supporting the first possibility.

Bore 820 and Lake George have equally provoked controversy. For Lake George, Richard Wright (1986) accepted the interpretation, but rejected the date. For Bore 820, Peter White (1994) accepted the date, but rejected the interpretation.

Wright (1986) assumed that the ratio of age to depth remained constant throughout the record at Lake George, and therefore rejected Gudrup Singh's equation of Zone E with MIS5. However, a straight depth/age relationship would put the early climatic alternations at only half the age of their equivalents in the Bore 820 and marine records and would be inconsistent with the well-established date for the transition between palaeomagnetic stages at the base of the sequence (Kershaw 1994). For Offshore Bore 820, Peter Kershaw and Peter Hiscock (Hiscock and Kershaw 1992; Kershaw 1994) initially suggested that the sharp increase in charcoal in the last interglacial period 'adds substantially to the case for Aboriginal burning and an early date for human arrival in Australia', but this interpretation is now generally rejected. The Lake George and the Bore 820 findings are parallel, mutually reinforcing each other.

Peter Hiscock now (2008 and in a 2013 lecture) argues that such claims rest on ethnographic analogy and imply Aborigines must *always* have practised the 'firestick farming' encountered at European advent, whereas widespread burning may not have begun until the demise of the megafauna (Flannery 1990, 1994). It is not ethnographic analogy, but the long prehistory of anthropogenic fire across the globe that tells us that colonists, however early or late, must have entered the continent knowing how to wield fire.

Hiscock now rejects all such early claims, as do Jim O'Connell and Jim Allen (2004, 2012). A last interglacial date would shake accepted dogmas by implying human tenure of the continent is at least twice as long as most archaeologists now believe probable, and would be appallingly inconsistent with the currently accepted global scenario. But, in fact, available data are still too sparse to tell us with any significant statistical probability that people were absent before 50,000 or 60,000 years ago. The number of dates from 40,000 years ago or more is not adequate to ensure it includes the earliest millennia of colonisation: 'absence of evidence is not evidence of absence'. Given the early dates for hominin presence on the east end of the Indonesia island chain (Morwood *et al.* 1998) and knowing they must have used watercraft, it might be wiser to consider the possibility that limited numbers of people reached our continent much earlier. After the shock of the 'Hobbit' (Morwood *et al.* 2007) and the DNA evidence that archaic varieties of *sapiens* ("Denisovans") had some share in the ancestry of original Australians (Gibbons 2012), it would be rash to dismiss as 'archaeologically impossible' an earlier foray into the continent. Neither is there sufficient evidence to confirm or deny the accepted scenario of a late spread of modern *sapiens* along the south Asian seaboard as the sole source of Australian colonisation. Interpretations of charcoal peaks before 50,000 years ago remain equivocal.

In contrast to Bore 820, which records a wide region from which winds carried pollen and carbon offshore, Lynch's Crater is a volcanic lake in southern Queensland that record its immediate catchment. An unusually long pollen and charcoal sequence runs back through several glacial and interglacial phases (Kershaw 1986; Kershaw *et al.* 2002; Rule *et al.* 2012), showing two early, but minor peaks in successive dry phases. Dating from around 48,000 years ago, a peak that was a degree of magnitude higher has been taken to mark the human penetration of Queensland rainforests. At each previous minor peak, dry sclerophyll taxa, eucalypts and casuarinas, had gained ground at the expense of rainforest taxa. Eventually, with human impact from 40,000 years ago onward, rainforest yielded to sclerophyll. The previous setbacks to rainforest are attributed to climatic rather than anthropogenic factors, but, as rainfall is assessed from vegetation (Kershaw 1993), this can be a somewhat circular argument. The advent of humans was unlikely to have been synchronous or to impact equally in all ecological niches.

The Continental Diaspora

Rock shelters in the 'top end' of Australia show human presence from 50,000 years ago onwards, as charcoal-rich sands eroded from the plateau above and began to fill valleys and rock shelters at the foot of the plateau (Hope, Hughes and Russell-Smith 1985). Even when today's Arnhem Land lay deep inland from the Carpentarian plain as part of Greater Australia, the impact of people was sufficient to lead to devegetation and sand blows. As in New Guinea, settlers were using stone axes and fire to penetrate rain forests during the Pleistocene (Hiscock and Kershaw 1992; Hiscock 2008).

From what is now northern Australia, settlers rapidly penetrated into and through the one-time land of lakes, the savannah zone (Horton 1981) surrounding the then less arid centre, and also along the wetland studded coastal plains, wider and more continuous before the rise of sea level (Hallam 1987). They had penetrated the most southerly temperate rainforest zones by around 50,000 years ago, as evidenced by the early dates for Devils Lair, a limestone cave in the southwest (Turney *et al.* 2001).

Yet earlier human presence has been suggested in Mammoth Cave (Archer, Crawford and Merrilees 1980). In the early twentieth century, large quantities of fossil bones were recovered from around 30 cubic metres of sandy deposit under flowstone, and the taxonomy described by Ludwig Glauert of the Western Australian Museum included megafauna now extinct. Charcoal from overlying red sands was beyond the range of 1960s carbon dating ('greater than 37,000 years BP'), but the fauna indicate a climate drier than the present climate, probably correlating with a cool stadial around 70,000 years ago, suggested Duncan Merrilees. Mike Archer argues that a notch in a *Sthenurus* tibia has been cut by a sharp stone, rather than gnawed by a predator, in contrast to other bones that have been chewed, punctured or crushed. Patterns of femur breakage suggest they had been deliberately smashed open to get the marrow. Some bone fragments, including a *Zygomaturus* ulna, were charred, in ways that suggest cooking on a hearth, with only parts of bones protruding. The authors envisaged Aboriginal hunting parties bringing megafauna into the cave to be cooked and eaten well before 50,000 years ago, thus signifying an overlap between Aborigines, fires and megafauna. Such possibilities have gained little credence.

I have suggested that the deposition of the deep deposits along the Murchison and Greenough Rivers, and the 20-metre terrace of the Swan River, on which lies evidence of occupation dating from more than 40,000 years ago (Pearce and Barbetti 1981), may reflect the geomorphic impact of first settlers, burning through the inland and the valleys of the Darling Plateau to the east (Hallam 1989). Later lower terraces (Schwede 1983) may correspond to later surges in burning. Similarly, on the other side of the continent, Aboriginal firing and partial devegetation led to episodic erosion, valley fills and accumulation in rock shelters, all very late in geological terms (Hughes and Sullivan 1981). In the east, the main impact is Holocene, whereas the Swan, Murchison and Greenough Rivers may record late Pleistocene impact in the west. The lack of synchroneity is not surprising.

In Queensland, rainforests expanded again during the moister Holocene (the last 10,000 years), but were increasingly impacted by burning as populations rose. Penetration of the 'forested crescents' of the southeast and southwest also increased as population increased (Dodson, Fullager and Head 1992). In Western Australia's southern swamps, charcoal peaks from around 8,000 to 7,000 years ago onwards show that effective Aboriginal impact on the tall forests of the extreme southwest was very late (Churchill 1968; Christensen and Annell 1985; Hassell and Dodson 2003). The overall trend shown in pollen and charcoal records ranges from rare intense fires to smaller fires at lesser intervals.

Human spread, numbers and population density may have reached effective thresholds, sufficient for their burns to be discernable in the pollen record, at different times in different ecological zones, not simultaneously throughout the continent. The impact may have been felt very early along coastal plains and over the once moist interior, but later within large blocks of sub-tropical rainforest, and latest of all in the moist forested crescents at the southeast and southwest extremities of the continent. But over thousands of years people established a dynamic equilibrium with the vegetated landscape, a balance that constantly shifted as coasts and climate fluctuated and populations rose and adjusted to maintain local variety, patterning and accessibility of resources. The coming of Europeans disrupted those patterns, in ways that have been most closely investigated by David Ward (see above; also Pyne 1991, 2001, 2003, 2006).

David Bowman and twenty-one of his colleagues (Bowman *et al.* 2009) place the Australian story in a global space and deep time frame, concluding that historical meteorological data show the primacy of climate in driving large regional fires and that fires are among the drivers of global warming. Since indigenous burning patterns have given way to European regimes worldwide, large uncontrolled fires have swept across both hemispheres, reducing biodiversity.

Similarly, attempts have been made, through studying many long, continuous records of fine charcoal particles carried great distances by the wind, to quantify *regional* trends over time (Mooney *et al.* 2012), rather than to study local changes seen in pollen and charcoal records from lakes and swamps. The very few really long records are interpreted as showing the primacy of climate. As Australia became drier through the Cenozoic, fire activity increased, and over the last interglacial period, a strong relationship between climate and fire continued. Most records, however, span only parts of the last 10,000 years. Some low fire activity was evident around 7,000 to 5,000 years ago, increasing everywhere except in wet forests after 5,000 years ago, and again around 2,000 years ago. The Holocene rise in burning corresponds with similar trends in numbers of archaeological sites and presumably in numbers of people. Maximum fire activity occurred when Europeans first arrived and began large-scale agricultural clearance, and has been succeeded more recently by the lowest ever levels of burning – the prelude, as in the past, to huge catastrophic fires.

The complexity of the people/climate/landscape relationship renders all one-factor interpretations improbable. The interactions are all mutual and multiple.

Aboriginal and European Burning

There is no formula to relate past landscape management to present optimal procedures. When the first Australians stepped into uninhabited terrain, conditions and outcomes for firing were totally different from what they are today, different again when tens of millennia of indigenous toil had moulded biota to productive regimes and spatial patterns, and again as those patterns were disrupted by European intrusion. In contrast to all pre-European conditions, many more people and installations now need protection from fierce fire. A specific regimen of burning will have different effects in a landscape where Europeans have fragmented each habitat with roads, fields and built-up areas; introduced exotic species, including plants that prefer disturbed habitats; spread dieback; cleared for agriculture. Felling timber opened up the forest canopy, encouraging dense secondary regrowth and leaving debris as fuel, thus encouraging yet fiercer fires, that further open the canopy to spiralling flammability.

The objectives of burning are also different. Aboriginal objectives included catching and cooking small animals; 'cooking' rocks to 'soften' them and make them easier to knap (Akerman 1979); driving large game; attracting fish at night; signalling others; illuminating ceremonial dance; providing social focus and lighting; provisioning and hosting ritual gatherings and multi-group drives; and validating ownership of territory (Hallam 1975, 1985, 2003; Gammage 2011). The overriding concern, however, was long-term patterning of landscapes – producing yards, corridors, mosaics (Lewis 1985, Lewis and Ferguson 1988), forest margins for tuber crops, accessible patchworks of feed and shelter and open woodland.

Of these landscapes Europeans became heirs. The newcomers could take cattle-drawn carts through the forest from Perth to York in a few days, with little aid from axes (Moore 1831 in Cameron 2006: 43). Settlers could plough open land with only scattered trees. And into the twentieth century the Muir family drove their cattle through southwest forest to spend the summer on coastal pastures kept open by burns lit by Aboriginal stockmen (Muir and Muir, 1979, map and p. 3; personal communication).

There were no vast stretches of landscape blanketed by one fire regime decade after decade. No single regime is optimal for all elements of the biota (Burrows and Abbott 2003). A particular frequency of burns might be deleterious to some plant and animal communities if rigidly applied, but the irregularity, small scale and unevenness of indigenous burns guarded against this. Frequent low intensity fires left unburnt refugia and were self-limiting, stopping when they met ground fired last year or a predictable change in wind direction. In central Australia, air photographs show a small-scale mosaic of 370 burnt patches in 1953, subsumed within one huge wildfire by 1988, when indigenous burning had ceased and vast tracts had remained unburnt for thirty years (Burrows and Christensen 1990; Burrows, Burbridge and Fuller 2000). The diversity within the fine-grain patchwork that the Aborigines achieved contrasts with the monotony of large-scale burns ignited by lightning over huge neglected stretches (Bird and Parker 2004; Bird and Bird 2008).

Aboriginal burns provided protection of assets. Yam tubers or coppices of spearwood would be guarded by a firebreak and swamps would be protected from late summer peat fires, as were, no doubt, flammable installations such as wooden fish weirs. Huts would be built in areas already cleared by fire (Hallam 1975: 17–19). New growth in burnt areas would ensure the presence of large game on unfenced kangaroo pastures (Lewis's 'yards'). Throughout the continent, Europeans encountered a patchwork of woodland and park-like pasture, forest and clearing, crafted by the earlier Australians. The landscape itself, the estate, was the major asset maintained with immense labour and skill.

Burning also addressed aesthetic, religious and ritual desiderata. Fire in Aboriginal mythology was life giving, nurtured in the female womb. Traditional principles of caution and collaboration, incumbent among indigenous people in dealing with other species and their habitats, are an integral part of Aboriginal cosmology, which stresses close kin links between people and other creatures. Senior ceremonial managers have the responsibility of managing burns and firing regimes, drives and ceremonies (Nicholson 1981; Langton 1998). Religious and secular activities are inseparable. Landscape care is a sacred obligation.

Confronted by dense growth after years of absence, Aborigines would remark on the untidiness, the *wrongness* of the landscape and their imperative responsibility to begin 'cleansing', however undesirable the immediate effects of burning might be. Burning was a responsibility of the community, reinforcing close attachment to managed terrain, a sense of ownership, pride in skill and local knowledge and community tradition. After her people re-fired neglected country, Dinah Marrngawi reminisced rapturously, 'Look north, look east, look west… This is how it was when the old people were alive, look this country is burning, it has been lifted up, we have embraced it again' (Bradley in Rose 1995).

Twentieth-century foresters focussed for decades on one resource: timber. They sought uniformity rather than diversity, homogeneity rather than heterogeneity and closeness rather than openness, in their pursuit of taller timber. We now care more for Aboriginal desiderata – heterogeneity and 'biodiversity'; openness and access; control and predictability; and aesthetic appeal. But these aims are now more difficult to achieve. Access through open landscapes was lost as secondary regrowth choked the forests and bush reclaimed coastal pastures. We have to protect a far greater density of people, facilities and installations – roads and railways;

pastures and plantations; crops and fences; barns and bridges; farmhouses and outbuildings; industries and urban settlements; and people, people and more people.

Aboriginal communities knew their own terrain intimately and engaged in ritual and ecological maintenance unceasingly. Farmers and foresters once had something approaching this intimacy, but mechanisation and large-scale operations have eliminated the tree-by-tree knowledge of earlier generations. Control burns are now the function of specialised agencies with limited manpower resources, rather than the responsibility of a whole society. Few present day communities know, own and bear responsibility for their own patch as deeply as their Aboriginal forebears did – as though their lives depended on it. Nor can any community match the proportion of time, labour and resources once given by indigenous groups.

Deep local knowledge resulted in a combination of control and freedom. Although 'fires of choice replaced fires of chance' (Pyne 2006: 25; see also Pyne 2001), there were, nonetheless, random elements. Aboriginal procedures were diverse, ranging from minute and careful burns around assets to small-scale fires to diversify resources and random late burns allowed to creep away through 'rubbish country'. But 'once your burning system has stopped, it is one hell of a job getting it back again' (Latz 1995). Thus, 'reinstating fire...demands considerable work... It is costly, laborious, controversial and dangerous' (Pyne 2003). Other choices have also proved dangerous.

Prehistorians have always assumed that pre-farming peoples *adapted to* environments, whilst only farmers *changed* environments. But we now know that farmers sowed and pastured over landscapes whose vegetation, fauna and climate had already been moulded by people over millennia, largely through the agency of fire. Throughout their past, hominin societies have impacted the environment with global effects, incremental over time. Each generation operated in a milieu shaped by its forebears, and those forebears operated in terrain *their* predecessors had moulded. Indigenous Australians, in turn, tamed and maintained landscapes, using knowledge, authority, skill and sheer hard work. More people, and more technology, now ineluctably exert more impact, and present more problems.

References to the Afterword

Abbott, Ian, 'Aboriginal fire regimes in south-west Western Australia: evidence from historical documents', *Fire in South-Western Ecosystems: Impacts and Management*, edited by Ian Abbott & Neil Burrows (Leiden, Backhuys, 2003), pp.119–146.

Abbott, Ian & Neil Burrows (editors), *Fire in South-Western Ecosystems: Impacts and Management* (Leiden, Backhuys, 2003).

Adams, Mark & Peter Attiwill, *Burning Issues: sustainability and management of Australia's southern forests* (Melbourne, CSIRO, 2011).

Akerman, Kim, 'Heat and lithic technology in the Kimberleys', *Archaeology and Anthropology in Oceania,* vol.14 (1979), pp.144–151.

Anderson, Atholl, Ian Lilley, & Sue O'Connor (editors), *Histories of Old Ages; essays in honour of Rhys Jones* (Canberra, Pandanus Books, 2001).

Archer, Michael, Ian M Crawford, & Duncan Merrilees, 'Incisions, breakages and charring, some probably man-made, in fossil bones from Mammoth Cave, Western Australia', *Alcheringa: an Australasian Journal of Palaeontology*, vol.4:2(1980), pp.115–131.

Armstrong, Patrick, 'The Aboriginal practice of firing the bush; evidence of early newspapers', *Proceedings of the Royal Western Australian Historical Society*, vol.8, part 2 (1978), pp.31–34.

Armstrong, Patrick, *Charles Darwin in Western Australia; A Young Scientist's Perception of an environment* (Nedlands, University of Western Australia Press, 1985).

Balter, Michel, 'Earliest signs of human-controlled fire uncovered in Israel', *Science*, vol.304 (2004), pp.664–665.

Barbetti, Mike, 'Traces of fire in the archaeological record, before one million years ago', *Journal of Human Evolution,* vol.15 (1986), pp.771–781.

Barker, Graeme, 'The archaeology of foraging and farming at Niah Cave, Sarawak', *Asian Perspectives*, vol. 44 (2005), pp.90–106.

Barker, Graeme & 19 others, 'Prehistoric foragers and farmers in South-east Asia: renewed investigations at Niah Cave, Sarawak', *Proceedings of the Prehistoric Society*, vol 68 (2002), pp.147–164.

Barker, Graeme & 26 others, 'The "human revolution" in lowland tropical Southeast Asia: the antiquity and behavior of anatomically modern humans at Niah Cave (Sarawak, Borneo)', *Journal of Human Evolution*, vol.52 (2007), pp.243–261.

Baudin, Nicolas, 1800-1803, *Journal of Post Captain Nicolas Baudin, Commander-in-Chief of the Corvettes Geographe and Naturaliste assigned by order of the government to a voyage of discovery*, translated from the French by Christine Cornell (Adelaide, Libraries Board of South Australia, 1974).

Beaufort, L & 4 others, 'Biomass burning and Oceanic primary production estimates in the Sula Sea area over the last 380kyr and East Asian monsoon dynamics', *Marine Geology*, vol.201 (2003), pp.53–65.

Beaumont, Peter, 'The edge: more on fire-making by about 1.7 million years ago at Wonderwerk Cave in South Africa', *Current Anthropology*, vol.52 (2011), pp.585–595.

Bellomo, R V, 'A methodological approach for identifying archaeological evidence of fire resulting from human activities', *Journal of Archaeological Science*, vol.20 (1993), pp.525–553.

Bellomo, R V, 'Methods of determining early hominid behavioural activities associated with the controlled use of fire at FxJj 20 Main, Koobi Fora, Kenya', *Journal of Human Evolution*, vol.27 (1994), pp.173–179.

Berna, Francesca, P Goldberg, L K Horwitz, J Brink, S Holt, M Bamford, & M Chazon, 'Microstratigraphic evidence of in situ fire in the Acheulian strata of Wonderwerk Cave, Northern Cape province, South Africa', *Proceedings of the National Academy of the Sciences USA*, vol.109 (2012), pp.E1215–E1220.

Binford, Lewis, and C K Ho, 'Taphonomy at a distance, "the Cave Home of Beijing Man"?' *Current Anthropology*, vol.26 (1985), pp.453–475.

Binford, Lewis, & L M Stone, 'Zhoukoudian: a closer look', *Current Anthropology*, vol.27 (1986), pp.413–412.

Bird, D W & R B, C H Parker, 'Women who hunt with fire; Aboriginal resource use and fire regimes in Australia's Western Desert, *Australian Aboriginal Studies*, 2004, part 1, pp.90–96.

Bird, R B, D W Bird, B F Codding, C H Parker, & J H Jones, '"The fire stick farming" hypothesis: Australian Aboriginal foraging strategies, and anthropogenic fire mosaics', *Proceedings of the National Academy of the Sciences* (USA), vol.105 (2008), pp.14796–14801.

Blake, S & D M Welch, *Making Fire* (Virginia, NT, D M Welch, Aboriginal Culture Series, No.2), (2006).

Boaz, N T, & R L Ciochon, *Dragon Bone Hill: an Ice-age saga of Homo erectus* (Oxford University Press, 2004).

Bowdler, Sandra, 'Rainforest: colonised or coloniser?, *Australian Archaeology*, vol.17 (1983), pp.59–66.

Bowman, David M J S, 'The impact of Aboriginal landscape burning on the Australian biota', *New Phytologist*, vol.140 (1998), pp.385–410.

Bowman, David M J S, *Australian Rainforests: islands of green in a land of fire* (Cambridge University Press, 2000).

Bowman, David M J S, 'The Australian summer monsoon: a biogeographical perspective', *Australian Geographical Studies*, vol.40, part 3 (2002), pp.261–277.

Bowman, David M J S, 'Australian landscape burning: a continental and evolutionary perspective', *Fire in South-Western Ecosystems: Impacts and Management*, edited by Ian Abbott & Neil Burrows (Leiden, Backhuys, 2003), pp.107–118.

Bowman, David, M Garde & A Saulwick, 'Kunj-ken makka man-wurrk – "Fire is for kangaroos": interpreting Aboriginal accounts of landscape burning', *Histories of Old Ages: Essays in honour of Rhys Jones*, edited by A Anderson, I Lilley, & S O'Connor (Canberra, Pandanus Books, 2001), pp.61–78.

Bowman, David M J S, & 21 others, 'Fire in the earth system', *Science*, vol. 324 (2009), pp.481–484.

Bowman, David M J S, B P Murphy, G E Burrows, & M D Crisp, 'Fire regimes and the evolution of the Australian biota', *Flammable Australia: Fire Regimes, Biodiversity and Ecosystems in a Changing World*, edited by R A Bradstock, A M Gill, & R J Williams (Melbourne, CSIRO, 2012), pp.27–47.

Bradley, John, 'Fire, emotion and politics: a Yanyuwa case study, *Country in Flames*, edited by D B Rose (Darwin & Canberra, Biodiversity Unit, Dept of the Environment, North Australian Research Unit; and Australian National University, 1995), pp.25–31.

Bradstock, R A, J E Williams, & A M Gill, editors, *Flammable Australia: the Fire Regimes and Biodiversity of a Continent* (Cambridge University Press, 2002).

Bradstock, R A, A M Gill, & R J Williams, editors, *Flammable Australia: Fire Regimes, Biodiversity and Ecosystems in a Changing World* (Melbourne, CSIRO, 2012).

Brain, C K, & A Sillen, 'Evidence from the Swartkrans cave for the earliest use of fire', *Nature* vol. 336 (1988), pp.464–466.

Brown, Robert, *Nature's Investigator: the Diary of Robert Brown in Australia, 1801-1805*, compiled by T G Vallence, D T Moore, & E W Groves (Canberra, Australian Biological Resources Study, Dept of the Environment, 2001).

Bunbury, Lieut-Col W St Pierre, & W P Morrell, editors, *Early Days in Western Australia. Being the Letters and Journals of Lieut H W Bunbury* (Oxford University Press, 1930).

Burrows, Neil & Ian Abbott, editors, 'Fire in southwestern Australia; a synthesis of current knowledge, management implications and new research directions', *Fire in South-Western Ecosystems: Impacts and Management* (Leiden, Backhuys, 2003).

Burrows, N D, A A Burbage, & P J Fuller, 'Nyaruninpa: Pintupi burning in the Australian Western Desert', Paper presented to *International Symposium on Native Solutions, Indigenous Knowledge and Today's Fire Management* (Hobart, 2000).

Burrows, N D, & P E S Christenson, 'A survey of Aboriginal fire patterns in the Western Desert of Australia', *Fire in the Environment: ecological and cultural perspectives*, edited by S C Nodvin & T A Waldrop (Knoxville, 1990), pp.297–305.

CALM, *Fire in South-Western Ecosystems: Impacts and Management, Volume 2 – Community Perspectives about Fire. Proceedings of April 2002 Symposium* organised by the Dept of Conservation and Land Management. (Bentley WA, Dept of Conservation and Land Management, 2003).

Cameron, J M R, *The Millendon Memoirs: George Fletcher Moore's Western Australian Diaries and Letters, 1830–1841*, edited with an Introduction by J M R Cameron (Perth, Hesperian Press, 2006).

Christensen, P, & A Annels, 'Fire in southern tall forests', *Fire Ecology and Management in Western Australian Ecosystems*, edited by Julian Ford (Bentley, West Australian Institute of Technology, 1985) pp.67–90.

Churchill, David M, 'The distribution and prehistory of *Eucalyptus diversicolor* F Muell., *E. marginata* Donn ex Sm, and *E. calophylla* R Br. in relation to rainfall', *Australian Journal of Botany*, vol.16 (1968), pp.125–151.

Clark, Peter & Mike Barbetti, 'Fires, hearths and palaeomagnetism', *Archaeometry: an Australasian Perspective*, edited by W Ambrose & P Duerden (Canberra, Research School of Pacific Studies, ANU, 1982), pp.144–150.

Clark, J D & J W K Harris, 'Fire and its role in early hominid lifeways', *The African Archaeological Review*, vol.3 (1985), pp.3–27.

Clint, Raphael, 'Journal of an Excursion to the Mountain Range to the Northward and Eastward of Porrong-u-rup, Decr 20th 1831, by Raphael Clint (Asst Surveyor)', *Western Australian Exploration, Volume 1, 1826–1835*, edited by J Schoobert (Hesperian Press, 2005), pp.292–296.

Colhoun, E A, & G van de Geer, 'Darwin Crater, the King and Linda valleys', *Cainozoic Vegetation of Tasmania*. International Palynological Congress. (University of Newcastle, NSW, Dept of Geography, 1988), pp.30–71.

Collie, Doctor Alexander, 'Account of four Excursions in the vicinity of King George's Sound between 27th April and 15th June 1831, by Alexander Collie, Surgeon', *Journals of Several Expeditions made in Western Australia during the years 1829, 1830, 1831, and 1832*, edited by J Cross (London, Cross, 1833), pp.152–154; reprinted in *Western Australian Exploration, Volume 1, 1826–1835*, edited by Joanne Schoobert (Perth, Hesperian Press, 2005), pp.242–252.

Collie, Doctor Alexander, 'Account of an Explorative Excursion to the NW of King Georges Sound in 1832 by A. Collie, Surgeon, R.N.', *Western Australian Exploration, Volume 1, 1826–1835*, edited by Joanne Schoobert (Perth, Hesperian Press, 2005), pp.307–315.

Cowan, Peter, *Faithful Picture: the letters of Eliza and Thomas Brown of York in the Swan River Colony 1841–1852* (Fremantle Arts Centre Press, 1977)

Cowan, Peter, *A Colonial Experience: Swan River 1839–1888. From the diary and reports of Walkinshaw Cowan* (Perth, privately printed, no date).

Cribb, Roger, 'Shell mounds, domiculture and ecosystem manipulation on Western Cape York Peninsula', *Archaeology of Northern Australia*, edited by Peter Veth and Peter Hiscock, *Tempus*, vol.4 (Anthropology Museum, The University of Queensland, 1996), pp.150–173.

Dart, Raymond, 'The Makapansgat proto-human *Australopithecus prometheus*', *American Journal of Physical Anthropology*, vol. 6 (1948), pp.259–283.

Darwin, Charles, *The Descent of Man* (first edition 1874; John Murray 1901).

Darwin, Charles, *Journal of Researches into the natural history and geology of the countries visited during the voyage round the world of H.M.S. 'Beagle' under command of Captain Fitz Roy, R.N.* (second edition 1845; John Murray 1902).

Dennell, Robin, *The Palaeolithic Settlement of Asia* (Cambridge University Press, 2009).

Derbishire, Mr, 'Report from Mr Derbishire on the second expedition to the Northward in search of the Mercury', *Perth Gazette*, 6 December 1834, reprinted in *Western Australian Exploration, Volume 1, 1826–1835*, edited by Joanne Schoobert (Perth, Hesperian Press, 2005), pp.386–387.

Dodson, John, R Fullager & L Head, 'Dynamics of environment and people in the forested crescents of temperate Australia', *The Naïve Lands*, edited by John Dodson (Longman-Cheshire, 1992), pp.115–159.

Duyker, E & M, (translators and editors), *Bruny d'Entrecasteaux. Voyage to Australia and the Pacific, 1791 – 1793* (Melbourne: University Press, 2001).

Falk, Dean, *The Fossil Chronicles; how two controversial discoveries changed our view of human evolution* (Berkeley, University of California Press, 2011).

Flannery, Tim, 'Pleistocene faunal loss: implications of the aftershock for Australia's past and future', *Archaeology in Oceania*, vol.25 (1990), pp.45–67.

Flannery, Tim, *The Future Eaters: an ecological history of the Australasian lands and peoples* (Sydney, Read Books, 1994).

Ford, Julian (editor), *Fire Ecology and Management in Western Australian Ecosystems* (Bentley, West Australian Institute of Technology [now Curtin University], 1985).

Fremantle, Captain C H, 'Diary of Captain C H Fremantle Exploration of the Swan River, May 1829', *Western Australian Exploration, Volume 1, 1826–1835*, edited by Joanne Schoobert (Perth, Hesperian Press, 2005), pp.68–70.

Friend, Mary Ann, 'The diary of Mary Ann Friend', *Western Australian Historical Society Journal and Proceedings*, vol.1, part 10 (1931), pp.1–11.

Gammage, Bill, *The Biggest Estate on Earth. How Aborigines made Australia* (Sydney, Allen and Unwin, 2011).

Gibbons, Ann, 'A crystal-clear view of an extinct girl's genome', *Science*, vol.337, pp.1028–1029.

Gill, A M, R H Groves, & I R Noble, editors, *Fire and the Australian Biota* (Canberra, Australian Academy of Science, 1981).

Goren-Inbar, N, N Alperson, M E Kislev, O Simchoni, Y Melamed, A Ben-Nun, E Werker, 'Evidence of hominin control of fire at Gesher Benot Ya'aqov, Israel', *Science* vol 304 (2004), pp.725–727.

Goudsblom, Johan, *Fire and Civilisation* (London, Allen Lane, 1992).

Gowlett, J A J, W H K Harris, D Walton, & B A Wood, 'Early archaeological sites, hominid remains and traces of fire from Chesowanja, Kenya', *Nature*, vol.294 (1981), pp.125–129.

Gowlett, J A J, & 4 others, 'Beeches Pit: archaeology, assemblage dunamics and early fire history of a Middle Pleistocene site in East Anglia, UK', *Eurasian Prehistory*, vol.3 (2) (2005), pp.3–38.

Groube, Les, 'The taming of the rain forests: a model for Late Pleistocene forest exploitation in New Guinea', *Foraging and Farming: the Evolution of Plant Exploitation*, edited D R Harris & G C Hillman (London, Unwin Hyman, 1989), pp.292–304.

Groube, Les, J Chappell, J Muke, and D Price, 'A 40,000 year-old human occupation site at Huon Peninsula, Papua New Guines', *Nature*, vol.324 (1986), pp.453–5.

Haberle, S G, G S Hope, & S van der Kaar, 'Biomass burning in Indonesia and Papua New Guinea: natural and humanly induced fire events in the fossil record', *Palaeogeography, Palaeoclimatology, Palaeoecology*, vol.171 (2001), pp.259–268.

Hallam, Sylvia J, *Fire and Hearth; a study of Aboriginal usage and European usurpation in south-western Australia* (Canberra, Australian Institute of Aboriginal Studies, 1975).

Hallam, Sylvia J, 'A view from the other side of the western frontier; or "I met a man who wasn't there ..."', *Aboriginal History*, vol.7 (1983), pp.134–156.

Hallam, Sylvia J, 'The history of Aboriginal firing', *Fire Ecology and Management in Western Australian Ecosystems*, edited by Julian Ford (Bentley, West Australian Institute of Technology [now Curtin University], 1985), pp.7–20.

Hallam, Sylvia J, 'Coastal does not equal littoral', *Australian Archaeology*, vol.25 (1987), pp.10–19.

Hallam, Sylvia J, 'Plant usage and management in Southwest Australian Aboriginal societies', *Foraging and Farming: the evolution of plant exploitation*, edited by D R Harris & G C Hillman (London, Unwin Hyman, 1989), pp.136–151.

Hallam, Sylvia J, ' Peopled landscapes in the early 1800s: Aboriginal burning-off in the light of Western Australian historical documents', *Early Days. Journal of the Royal Western Australian Historical Society*, vol.12, part 2 (2002), pp.177–191.

Harris, Doctor Joseph, 'Journal of Dr Joseph Harris ... on an expedition to the Hotham River', *Perth Gazette*, 14, 21, 28 February and 7 March 1835; reprinted in *Western Australian Exploration, Volume 1, 1826–1835*, edited by J Schoobert (Perth, Hesperian Press, 2005), pp.396–409.

Hassell, C W, & John Dodson, 'The fire history of south-west Western Australia prior to European settlement in 1826–1829', *Fire in Ecosystems of South-west Western Australia: Impacts and Management*, edited by Ian Abbott & Neil Burrows (Leiden, Backhuys, 2003), pp.71–85.

Haynes, C D, 'The pattern and ecology of *munwag*: traditional Aboriginal fire regimes in north - central Arnhemland', *Proceedings of the Ecological Society of Australia*, vol.13 (1983), pp.203–214.

Higham, T F G & 5 others, 'Radiocarbon dating of charcoal from tropical sequences: results from Niah Great Cave, Sarawak, and their broader implications', *Journal of Quaternary Science*, vol.24(2) (2009), pp.189–197.

Hillman, Alfred, 'Mr Alfred Hillman's field book of an expedition from Albany to Nornalup in July 1833', *Western Australian Exploration, Volume 1, 1826–1835*, edited by J Schoobert (Perth, Hesperian Press, 2005), pp.330–334.

Hiscock, Peter, *Archaeology of Ancient Australia* (Oxford, Routledge, 2008)

Hiscock, Peter & A P Kershaw, 'Palaeoenvironments and prehistory of Australia's tropical Top End', *The Naïve Lands,* edited by John Dodson (1992), pp.43–75.

Hope, David, & Jack Golson, 'Late Quaternary change in the mountains of New Guinea', *Antiquity*, vol. 69 (1995), pp.818–830.

Hope, G, P J Hughes & J Russell-Smith, 'Geomorphological fieldwork and the landscape of Kakadu National Park', *Archaeological Research in Kakadu National Park*, edited by Rhys Jones (Australian National Parks and Wildlife Service, 1985).

Horton, David, 'Water and woodland: the peopling of Australia, *Australian Institute of Aboriginal Studies Newsletter*, vol. 16 (1981), pp.21–26.

Horton, David, 'The burning question: Aborigines, fire and Australian ecosystems', *Mankind*, vol.13 (1982), pp.237–257.

Horton, David, *The Pure state of Nature: Sacred cows, destructive myths and the environment* (Sydney, Allen and Unwin, 2000).

Horton, David, 'Fire and Australian Society', *Fire in South-Western Ecosystems: Impacts and Management, Volume 2 – Community Perspectives about Fire. Proceedings of April 2002 Symposium organised by the Dept of Conservation and Land Management* (Bentley WA, Dept of Conservation and Land Management, 2003), pp.6–11.

Hughes, P J, & M E Sullivan, 'Aboriginal burning and Late Holocene geomorphic events in eastern New South Wales', *Search*, vol. 12 (1981), pp.277–278.

James, S R, 'Hominid use of fire in the Lower and Middle Pleistocene', *Current Anthropology*, vol.30 (1989), pp.1–26.

Jay, William Taylor, 'Excursion to the Swan River Colony', *Western Australian Exploration, Volume 1, 1826–1835*, edited by J Schoobert (Perth, Hesperian Press, 2005), pp.128–140.

Jones, Rhys, 'The geographical background to the arrival of man in Australia and Tasmania', *Archaeology and Physical Anthropology in Oceania*, vol.3, no.3 (1968), pp.186–215.

Jones, Rhys, 'Fire-stick farming', *Australian Natural History*, vol.16, no.7 (1969), pp.224–228.

Jones, Rhys, 'The Neolithic Palaeolithic and hunting gardeners', *Quaternary Studies*, edited by R. P. Suggate & M. M. Cresswell (The Royal Society of New Zealand, 1973), pp.21–34.

Karkanas, P, R Shahack-Gross, A Ayalon, M Bar-Matthews, R Barkai, A Frumkin, A Gopher, M C Stiner, 'Evidence for the habitual use of fire at the end of the Lower Palaeolithic: Site-formation processes at Qesem Cave, Israel,' *Journal of Human Evolution*, vol. 53 (2007), pp.197–212.

Kelly, Gene, '*Karla wongi*: fire talk. A Nyungar perspective on forest burning', *Landscope*, vol.14, part 2 (1999), pp.49–30; reprinted in *Fire: the Force of Life*, (*Landscope*, special Fire edition, 2000) pp.9–14.

Kendrick, G W, K-H Wyrwoll, & B J Szabo, 'Plio-Pleistocene coastal events and history along the western margin of Australia', *Quaternary Science Reviews*, vol.10 (1991), pp.419–439.

Kershaw, A P, 'Climatic change and Aboriginal burning in north-east Australia during the last two glacial/interglacial cycles', *Nature*, vol.322 (1986), pp.47–49.

Kershaw, A P, 'Quantitative palaeoclimatic estimates from bioclimatic analyses of taxa recorded in pollen diagrams', *Quaternary Australia*, vol.11 (1993), pp.61–64.

Kershaw, A P, 'Site 820 and the evidence for early occupation in Australia – a response', *Quaternary Australia*, vol.12, part 2 (1994), pp.24–29.

Kershaw, A P, J S Clark, A M Gill & D M de Costa, 'A history of fire in Australia", *Flammable Australia: the Fire Regimes and Biodiversity of a Continent*, edited by R A Bradstock, J E Williams, & M A Gill (Cambridge University Press, 2002), pp.3–25.

Lamont, B B, D J Ward, et al, 'Believing the balga: a new method for gauging the fire history of vegetation using grasstrees', *Fire in Ecosystems of Southwest Western Australia: Impacts and Management*, edited by Ian Abbott & Neil Burrows (Leiden, Backhuys, 2003), pp.147–169.

Langton, Marcia, *Burning Questions: emerging environmental issues for indigenous people in Northern Australia* (Darwin, Centre for Indigenous Natural and Cultural Resource Management, Northern Territory University, 1998).

Latz, Peter, 'Fire in the desert', *Country in Flames*, edited by D B Rose (Darwin & Canberra, Biodiversity Unit, Dept of the Environment, North Australian Research Unit; and Australian National University, 1995), pp.77–83.

Lee, Ida, *Early Explorers in Australia. From the Log Books and Journals, including the Diary of Alan Cunningham, Botanist, from March1, 1817 to November 19, 1818* (London, Methuen 1925)

Lewis, H T, 'Burning the "Top End": kangaroos and cattle', *Fire Ecology and Management in Western Australian Ecosystems*, edited by Julian Ford (Bentley, West Australian Institute of Technology [now Curtin University], 1985), pp.21–31.

Lewis, H T & H A Ferguson 'Yards, corridors and mosaics: how to burn a boreal forest', *Human Ecology,* vol.16 (1988), pp.5–77.

Lindenmayer, David & J F Franklin, editors, *Towards Forest Sustainability* (Melbourne, CSIRO, 2003).

Lockyer, Major Edmund, 'Journal, Sydney to King George Sound, 8th November 1826 to 21st January 1827', *Western Australian Exploration, Volume 1, 1826–1835*, edited by J Schoobert (Perth, Hesperian Press, 2005), pp.3–13.

Mackay, Brendan, David Lindenmayer, M Gill, M McCarthy, & J Lindesay, editors, *Fire and Future Climate: a forest ecosystem analysis* (Melbourne, CSIRO, 2002).

McCaw, W L, N D Burrows, G R Friend & A M Gill, editors, *Landscape Fires '93, CALM Science, Western Australian Journal of Land Management, Supplement 4* (Bentley, Department of Conservation and Land Management, Western Australia, 1995).

McGlone, M, 'The hunters did it', *Science*, vol.335 (2012), pp.1452–3.

Mellars, Paul, 'Fire ecology, animal populations, and man: a study of some ecological relationships in prehistory', *Proceedings of the Prehistoric Society*, vol.42 (1976), pp.15–45.

Miller, G H & 5 others, "Ecosystem collapse in Pleistocene Australia and a human role in Pleistocene extinction', *Science*, vol.309 (2005), pp.287–290.

Mooney, S D, S P Harrison, P J Bartlein, & J Stevenson, 'The prehistory of fire in Australasia', *Flammable Australia: Fire Regimes, Biodiversity and Ecosystems in a Changing World,* edited by R A Bradstock, A M Gill, & R J Williams (Melbourne, CSIRO, 2012), pp.3–25.

Moore, George Fletcher, *Diary of Ten Years in the eventful life of an Early Settler in Western Australia; and also a Descriptive Vocabulary of the Language of the Aborigines* [separately paginated] (London: Wallbrook, 1884; Facsimile Edition, with an introduction by C T Stannage, Perth, University of Western Australia Press, 1978).

Morwood, M J, P B O'Sullivan, F Aziz & A Raza, 'Fission-track ages of stone tools and fossils on the east Indonesian island of Flores', *Nature*, vol. 392 (1998), pp.173–176.

Morwood, M J, R P Soejono, R G Roberts, *et al.*, 'Archaeology and age of a new hominin from Flores in eastern Indonesia', *Nature*, vol 431 (2004), pp.1087–1091.

Muir, Alison and Jim, *Muir Family. Pioneers of the South-West and Eucla, Western Australia* (Perth, privately printed, 1979).

Mulvaney, John, and Neville Green, *Commandant of Solitude: The Journals of Captain Collett Barker, 1838–1831* (Melbourne, University Press, 1992).

Nicholson, P H, 'Fire and the Australian Aborigine – an enigma', *Burning Issues*, edited by Gill, Groves & Noble (Canberra, Australian Academy of Science, 1981), pp.55–76.

Notaro, Michael, Karl-Heinz Wyrwoll & Guanshan Cheng, 'Did Aboriginal vegetation burning impact on the Australian summer monsoon?' *Geophysical Research Letters*, vol.38, L11704 (2011), pp.1–5.

Oakley, K P, 'The earliest fire-makers', *Antiquity*, vol.30 (1956), pp.102–107.

O'Connell, J F & J Allen, 'Dating the colonisation of Sahul (Pleistocene Australia – New Guinea): a review of recent research', *Journal of Archaeological Science*, vol. 31 (2004), pp.835–853.

O'Connell, J F & J Allen, 'The restaurant at the end of the universe: modelling the colonisation of Sahul', *Australian Archaeology*, vol. 74 (2012), pp.5–31.

Oldfield, Augustus, 'On the Aborigines of Australia', *Transactions of the Ethnological Society*, vol.3 (1864), pp.215–298; reprinted as *On the Aborigines of Australia*, with an Introduction by Helen Henderson (Perth, Hesperian Press, 2005).

Pavlides, Christina & C Gosden, '35,000-year-old sites in the rainforests of West New Britain, Papua New Guinea', *Antiquity*, vol.68 (1994), pp.604–610.

Pearce, R H, & M Barbetti, 'A 38,000 year old site at Upper Swan, Western Australia, *Archaeology in Oceania*, vol.16 (1981), pp.173–178.

Pettitt, Paul, and Mark White, *The British Palaeolithic: Hominin Societies at the Edge of the Pleistocene World* (Oxford, Routledge, 2012).

Potts, Mike and Mark Roberts, *Fairweather Eden: life in Britain half a million years ago as revealed by the excavations at Boxgrove* (London, Random House, 1997).

Preston, Lieutenant William, 'Observations on the coast &c from Cockburn sound to Geographe Bay, between 17 and 30 of Novr 1829 by Mr Collie and Lieut. Preston', Pyne, Stephen, *Burning Bush: a fire history of Australia* (New York, Holt, 1991)

Pyne, Stephen, *Fire, a brief history* (London, British Museum Press, 2001).

Pyne, Stephen J, 'Fire's lucky country', *Fire in Ecosystems of South-west Western Australia: Impacts and Management*, edited by Ian Abbott & Neil Burrows (Leiden, Backhuys Publishers, 2003), pp.1–8.

Pyne, Stephen J, *The Still Burning Bush* (Melbourne, Scribe Short Books, 2006).

Robert, Willem, *The Explorations, 1696–1697, of Australia, by Willem de Vlamingh*, edited by Willem Robert (Amsterdam, Philo Press, 1972).

Roberts, R G & M I Bird, '*Homo* "incendius"', *Nature*, vol. 285 (2012), pp.586–7.

Richardson, Henry, *A Pleasant Passage: The Journals of Henry Richardson, Surgeon Superintendent aboard the convict ship Sultana* (Fremantle Arts Centre Press 1990).

Roe, John Septimus, 'Journal of an expedition by J.S.Roe, Surveyor General, to Moorilup, the Hay and the Sleeman Rivers, &c, February 1835', *Western Australian Exploration, Volume 1, 1826–1835*, edited by J Schoobert (Perth, Hesperian Press, 2005), pp.410–418.

Roe, John Septimus, 'Journal of an Expedition from Swan River overland to King George's Sound, by J.S.Roe, Esquire, Surveyor General, 19 October to 21 November, 1835', *Western Australian Exploration, Volume 1, 1826–1835*, edited by J Schoobert (Perth, Hesperian Press, 2005), pp.457–497.

Roebroeks, Wil, & Paola Villa, 'On the earliest evidence for habitual use of fire in Europe', *Proceedings of the National Academy of Sciences*, vol.108 (2011), pp.5209–5214.

Rose, D B (editor), *Country in Flames. Proceedings of the 1994 symposium on biodiversity and fire in North Australia. Biodiversity Series Paper No.3* (Darwin & Canberra, Biodiversity Unit, Dept of the Environment, North Australian Research Unit; and Australian National University, 1995)

Rowlett, R M, 'Comments' [on Wrangham 1999], *Current Anthropology*, vol.40 (1999), pp.584–5.

Rule, S, B W Brook, S G Haberle, C S M Turney, A P Kershaw & C N Johnson, 'The aftermath of megafaunal extinction: ecosystem transformation in Pleistocene Australia, *Science*, vol.335 (2012), pp.1483–6.

Schilder, Gunter, *Voyage to the Great South Land. Willem de Vlamingh 1696–1697* (Sydney, Royal Australian Historical Society, 1985).

Schoobert, Joanne, editor, *Western Australian Exploration, Volume 1, 1826–1835* (Perth, Hesperian Press, 2005).

Schwede, Madge, 'Super-trench – Phase 2: a report of excavation results', *Archaeology at ANZAAS 1983,* edited by Moya Smith (Perth, Western Australian Museum, 1983), pp.53–62.

Singh, G & E A Geissler, 'Late Cainozoic history of vegetation, fire, lake levels and climate at Lake George, New South Wales', *Philosophical Transactions of the Royal Society of London*, Series B, vol.311 (1985), pp.379–447.

Singh, G, A P Kershaw & R Clark, 'Quaternary Vegetation and fire history in Australia', *Fire and the Australian Biota*, edited by A M Gill, R H Groves & I R Noble (Canberra, Australian Academy of Science, 1981), pp.25–54.

Stanton, Peter, 'A tropical Queensland perspective', *Country in Flames*, edited by D B Rose (Darwin & Canberra, Biodiversity Unit, Dept of the Environment, North Australian Research Unit; and Australian National University, 1995), pp.80–83.

Stokes, J L, *Discoveries in Australia; with an account of the coasts and rivers explored and surveyed during the voyage of H. M. S. Beagle in the years 1837 – 38 – 39 – 40 – 41 – 42 – 43.* (London, T & W Boone, 1846).

Storemon, EJ, editor and translator, *The Salvado Memoirs. Historical Memoirs of Australia and particularly of the Benedictine Mission of New Norcia and of the Habits and Customs of the Australian Native* (Perth, University of Western Australia Press, 1977

Stringer, Chris, The *Origin of Our Species,* (Penguin Books 2012).

Summerhayes, G R, M Leavesley, A Fairbairn, H Mandui, J Field, A Ford & R Fullager, 'Human adaptation and plant use in Highland New Guinea 49,000 to 44,000 years ago', *Science*, vol.330 (2010), pp.78–81.

Turner, Thomas, 'Mr Thomas Turner's Report of an Expedition to trace the Blackwood River to its source – 21st to 29th September 1834', *Western Australian Exploration, Volume 1, 1826–1835*, edited by J Schoobert (Perth, Hesperian Press, 2005), pp.368–374.

Turney, C S M & 10 others, 'Early human occupation at Devil's Lair, southwestern Australia, fifty thousand years ago', *Quaternary Research*, vol.55 (2001), pp.3–13.

Ward, David J, 'The past and future of fire in John Forrest National Park, Perth, Western Australia' (Report to the Western Australian Department of Conservation and Land Management, 2001).

Ward, David J, 'Bushfire history from grasstrees at Eneabba, Western Australia', *Journal of the Royal Society of Western Australia*, vol.92 (2009), pp.261–268.

Ward, David J, *People, Fire, Forest and Water in Wungong: The Landscape Ecology of a West Australian Water Catchment*, (PhD Thesis, Curtin University of Technology, Bentley, Western Australia, 2010).

Ward, David & S Sneewjagt, 'Believing the balga', *Landscope* (Autumn 1999)

Ward, David & Roger Underwood, 'Fire, flogging, measles and grass: the influence of early York settlers on fire policy in Western Australia", *Barladong: the York Society History and Heritage Journal*, vol.4 (2003), pp.16–27.

Weiner, Steve, Qinqi Xu, Paul Goldberg, Jinyi Liu, Ofer Bar-Yosef, 'Evidence for the use of fire at Zhoukoudian, China', *Science*, vol.281 (1998), pp.251–253.

Whelan, R J, *The Ecology of Fire* (Cambridge Studies in Ecology, Cambridge University Press, 1995).

White, N G, 'In search of Aboriginal diet – then and now', *Histories of Old Ages: Essays in honour of Rhys Jones*, edited by A Anderson, I Lilley, & S O'Connor (Canberra, Pandanus Books, 2001), pp.343–359.

White, Peter, 'Site 820 and the evidence for early occupation in Australia', *Quaternary Australasia*, vol.12, part 2 (1994), pp.21–23.

White, Peter J, K A W Crook, & B P Ruxton, 'Kosipe, a late Pleistocene site in the Papuan Highlands', *Proceedings of the Prehistoric Society*, vol.36 (1971), pp.152–170.

Wrangham, Richard, 'The raw and the stolen: cooking and the ecology of human origins', *Current Anthropology*, vol.40 (1999), pp.567–594.

Wrangham, Richard, *Catching Fire: How Cooking made us Human London* (London, Profile Books, 2009).

Wrangham, Richard & Rachel Carmody, 'Human adaptation to the control of fire', *Evolutionary Anthropology*, vol.19 (2010), pp.187–199.

Wright, Richard, 'How old is Zone F at Lake George? *Archaeology in Oceania*, vol.21 (1986), pp.138–139.

www.ingramcontent.com/pod-product-compliance
Lightning Source LLC
Chambersburg PA
CBHW020756160426
43192CB00006B/349